BEYOND DEDUCTION

BEYOND DEDUCTION

Ampliative Aspects of Philosophical Reflection

FREDERICK L. WILL

ROUTLEDGE

NEW YORK AND LONDON

First published in 1988 by
Routledge, Chapman & Hall, Inc.
29 West 35th Street, New York, NY 10001

Published in the UK by
Routledge
11 New Fetter Lane, London EC4P 4EE

Set in 10½/12 point Sabon
by Witwell Ltd, Liverpool
and printed in Great Britain
by Richard Clay Ltd
Bungay, Suffolk

Library of Congress Cataloging in Publication Data
Will, Frederick L.
Beyond deduction.
Includes index.
1. Logic.   2. Ethics.   3. Philosophy–History.
I. Title.
BC71.W53   1988   160   87–23535

British Library CIP Data also available
ISBN 0–415 00177 3

To my children Katherine and George

Mir hilft der Geist!
Auf einmal seh' ich Rat
Und schreibe getrost:
Im Anfang war die Tat!

Goethe, *Faust*, Part I

Contents

Preface

The traditional Problem of Induction, like other similar apparent intellectual enigmas, exemplifies in its generation some deep faults in the intellectual orientation of modern Western philosophy.

In an earlier book, *Induction and Justification* (1974), I explored generally the faults exemplified in this Problem and emphasized their sources in the influential Cartesian, justification, or foundation theory of knowledge.

Though at first view this Problem seems like a straightforward intellectual puzzle, it is not so. Its puzzle aspect is a deceptive form taken by a genuine philosophical concern under the powerful distorting influence of justification or foundation theory. The concern is for the development of a coherent, effective program of critical scrutiny and tendance – referred to in the present book collectively as 'governance' – of very broad and deep norms of thought and action. Since the ruling model of reflective governance in justification theory has been that of application of extant accessible norms, adherents of the theory devoted great effort to the identification and certification of certain ultimate norms that could serve as foundational in the applicative governing process because their own certification requires the application of no other norms. In the empiricist philosophies like those of Hume and Mill the supposition was that the proper identification and certification of these basal norms could be effected in a procedure in which they are elicited directly from certain patent uniformities in experience. This procedure came to be termed 'induction,' and the apparent impossibility of achieving a successful result, so persuasively argued by Hume, set for later adherents to this program the Problem bearing that familiar name.

The reverses suffered at this point by the empiricist versions of the deductivist program were matched by similar reverses in the rationalist versions: this in spite of the impressive preventative measures in this regard taken by Kant. Since both varieties of the program, as they were developed, were essentially analytic, applicative ones, they both required some resource capable of relieving the limitations inherent in such procedures when the norms available for application in them are exclusively prior accepted ones. Given the commitment to such procedures, strengthening the program seems to require expansion of the supply of applicable norms. This was conceived to be possible through the uncovering and introduction of certain accessible broad and deep original norms capable of serving as secure foundations for the extended philosophical process. Such was the preferred way of conceiving the certification that philosophical reflection could give to results that are novel or ampliative with respect to accepted norms, that is, not derivable by means of the secure, unproblematic application of these norms.

The intractable difficulties encountered by the deductivist programs of governance at their base levels are but a portion of the reasons for recasting our conception of the ways in which legitimate ampliative effects in the philosophical governance of norms are produced. It is to such recasting that the present book is directed. Several points of contrast between the ampliative aspects of governance as conceived in the book and as conceived in deductivist, foundational theory may at once be brought to the reader's attention. First, the primary determinant of the notion of ampliative processes that was developed as a supplement to the deductivist, applicative theory was that theory itself. Ampliative aspects of governance were conceived to be what they needed to be if that theory was to maintain plausibility. By contrast the primary determinative influence in the notion advanced here is the actual character of ampliative governance as it may be discerned both in historical experience and in present practice. Secondly, the ampliative phases of governance are not here conceived as segregated ones, logically separable and preparatory to deductive, applicative phases. Rather they are conceived as intimately, indeed logically connected with these phases and hence dispersed throughout the wide areas of life and thought in which norms are employed in the guidance of thought and action.

Finally, the ampliative phases of governance that are being explored here as complementary to the deductive, applicative ones are *not* extensions of these same phases at some special level and are fundamentally distorted by philosophical programs that strive to represent them as such. There is no good reason for, and much reason against supposing that for every need in the governance of norms there are extant accessible norms, resort to and application of which will fill the need. At some places deductive, applicative techniques, however ingenious and elaborate, are insufficient in principle. What is needed to supplement the application of extant, accessible norms is ampliative effects wrought upon the body of norms, not further applications of components of that body, not the development of further applicative techniques, perhaps in some organon of these. Those looking to find in this study of ampliative processes the elaboration of such techniques, or the prospectus of such an organon, will be disappointed. There are, however, other ways, as the book tries to illustrate, in which much enlightenment is to be derived from the careful investigation of the ampliative phases of our employment of norms and the functions these phases perform in the governance of norms both within and without philosophical reflection.

I am glad to have this opportunity to express publicly my appreciation of assistance from various sources in the production of this book.

The first of several drafts of the book was written with the support of a Fellowship of the National Endowment of the Humanities in 1976. During the following years I had the opportunity to use successive drafts as a basis for discussion with members of seminars in theory of knowledge twice at the University of Illinois at Urbana-Champaign and once at the University of California at Irvine. Recently preparation of the final version of the work was assisted by the careful editorial scrutiny given the preliminary version by Marcus G. Singer of the University of Wisconsin at Madison.

Portions of Chapter 5 were drawn from an article 'Rules and Subsumption' published in the April, 1985 issue of the *American Philosophical Quarterly* and appear here with the permission of that journal. Similarly portions of Chapters 1 and 3 drawn from an article 'Pragmatic Rationality' published in the April, 1985 issue of *Philosophical Investigations* appear with the permission of Basil Blackwell Ltd of Oxford.

Frederick L. Will
Urbana, Illinois
June, 1987

Introduction

1 The central aim of this book is to focus attention upon and illuminate the character of a certain phase of philosophical reflection: namely, that in which we engage primarily and directly in the governance of certain broad and deep norms of thought and action. More particularly, the primary object of study is not reflective philosophical governance in general, but that species of it that in ways that will be specified immediately may be called 'ampliative' rather than 'deductive.' Several terms employed here need to be explained: 'norms,' and 'governance,' as well as 'ampliative' and 'deductive.'

2 *Norms* and *governance*. As employed here the term 'norm' covers a vast variety of patterns of procedure that serve as guides or standards of thought and action in various fields. These fields include those of various forms of knowledge exemplified in the sciences and other cognitive disciplines. They include also morals, law, and politics; various practical arts and technologies; and everyday life. Norms may be, at one extreme, rules of refined calculation, and, at another, approved modes of practical action. They may be regulative principles of scientific observation or theory construction. Or they may be principles of moral, political, or legal procedure. Peirce and Dewey often used the term 'habit' to cover the patterns that are here called 'norms.' Peirce, both early and late in his writings, extended this usage to particular beliefs ('belief is a rule for action' (1878); 'a genuine belief, or opinion, is something on which a man is prepared to act, and is therefore, in a general sense, a habit' (1902)). An outstanding example of similar usage of the term 'habit' in application to moral practice is Dewey's treatment of habit (including custom) in *Human Nature and Conduct* (1922)

3 To an extent that is hard to exaggerate, custom is, as Hume proclaimed, the great guide of life. But few philosophical minds are content to stop there. We do constantly engage in the philosophical

1

criticism, correction, etc., of accepted norms. To cover all such activities the term 'governance' is employed here. It includes these activities both when they are carried on in philosophical reflection and when the reflection is non-philosophical; it includes them also when they are carried on outside the medium of reflection, since not all governance of norms is reflective governance. Applied to philosophical governance particularly the term embraces the two main phases of governing activity: (1) The more specifically critical and appraising functions that philosophical reflection performs, and (2) also the more positive, revising, generative, reconstructive ones.

4 Not every norm is of equal importance for philosophical reflection. That reflection, for many obvious reasons, is particularly concerned with norms that in one way or other affect widely and deeply our thought and action. It is somewhat misleading to refer to the norms that affect us in these ways as if they were simple single entities, since what does so affect us are huge, interconnected, more or less coherent complexes of patterns of thought and action. They are the kind of complexes that in the domain of scientific thought and action T. S. Kuhn called 'paradigms.' The division between Ptolemy and Copernicus in the sixteenth and seventeenth centuries, for example, was by no means just a division over the position of certain bodies in the geometry of the solar system. It was also a division over the mission of the institution of astronomy in the intellectual economy of the time, over the relation of this institution to other institutions, including the natural philosophy that we now call 'physics,' and, of course, the complexes of beliefs and practices of the Christian religion. Similarly the controversies over the application of causal categories to human action that pervaded philosophical thought during the past few centuries are no mere semantic ones that might possibly be resolved by agreement among the disputants about the usage of the word 'cause' and other cognate and closely related terms. Involved is such a broad and deep division over norms of thought and action with respect to ourselves, our place in the world, and our relations with our fellows, that one must sympathize with Kant's judgment that implicated in it is a division between two utterly different organons of 'reason.' Similar, finally, are the issues in the present highly divisive dispute over the practice of abortion. On the one side, some partisans of 'life' distort and unknowingly depreciate the significance of the issues by supposing that they could be resolved by some 'objective,' scientific determination of the moment in human reproduction at which there is something that

could be properly described as beginning human life. On the other hand, some partisans of 'choice' similarly distort and depreciate the issues by reducing them to questions about the rights of a woman to control her own body and to determine in the case of need whether a human fetus, like a troubling but non-essential organ, might be cast off. Viewing the issues in these ways obscures large issues of thought and action precipitated by changes in medicine, economic life, sexual practices, and other areas of individual and communal life. The issues extend to and deeply concern the traditional conception of the vocation of motherhood, the relation of this vocation to those of women, particularly those of the professional classes deeply engaged in work outside the home, and the effects of such engagement on a large scale upon the functions traditionally performed by the family as a basic organ of human culture.

5 Opinion has long been divided concerning the extent to which basal norms of thought and action are subject to control by philosophical reflection. Of more immediate concern than the question whether all, or nearly all norms, are in principle subject to such control, is the question of how that control proceeds when it is possible. Specifically, granted that reflective philosophical governance is often possible, does the authority of any result in it derive solely from accepted norms present in or adduced to the situation and employed in a purely applicative or deductive way? Except in possibly extreme cases, in which the governing norms and the resultant governed ones coincide, is it a necessary feature of acceptable governance that in it the warrant of governing norms is transmitted to the governed ones by a procedure in which the governed are logically assimilated to the governing ones as applications of them; so that the warrant of the resultant norms, whatever its degree, is none other than that antecedently resident in those governing it? Does a realistic examination of our practice support so restrictive a view? Or does it not reveal, rather, that when we think carefully and responsibly upon philosophical matters we often necessarily and legitimately achieve results that cannot be derived in this way? The latter view is part of what is conveyed by the title *Beyond Deduction*, and by the reference in the sub-title to ampliative aspects of philosophical reflection.[1]

[1] Peirce was addressing roughly equivalent questions when in his early essays in the *Journal of Speculative Philosophy* (1868) he formulated as one of the four distinguishing characteristics of modern Cartesian philosophy that in it, 'The multiform argumentation of the middle ages is replaced by a single thread of inference depending often upon

6 *Deductive and ampliative*. There is no philosophical category ready to mark neatly the phase of governance that is the principal object of investigation here. Of the supply of more or less apt terms, 'ampliative' has been taken from Peirce (with some apologies to his shade, after the strictures on the ethics of terminology that the career of 'pragmatism' aroused in him).

The main contrast for which Peirce employed the term 'ampliative' is that between kinds of argument (inference, reasoning). Those arguments he termed 'deductive' in which conclusions are restricted to explicating their premises and in which therefore the conclusions follow necessarily from these. Ampliative arguments, by contrast, are not so restricted. In them the relations of the conclusions to premises transcends the explicatory, analytic, necessary ones. (This attractively simple contrast required some adaptation by Peirce to accommodate forms of argument that in some respects resemble deductive ones although their conclusions are not related apodictically to their premises. These he recognizes under the title of 'probable deductions.' This anomaly and the intellectual epicycles Peirce introduced to deal with it may be neglected here.)

Writing on the syllogism in 1878 Peirce wrote of the familiar form *Barbara* that in it, 'The conclusion applies the rule to the case and states the result: *Enoch is mortal*. All deduction is of this character; it is merely the application of general rules to particular cases' (*CP*, 2.620).

(Here again Peirce's own stipulation concerning deduction requires some adaptation to fit apparent deviant cases in which conclusions are deduced from premises in ways that do not fit the 'application of general rules to particular cases' formula. From the premises that Achilles was a child of Thetis and that Thetis was a goddess we easily deduce that Achilles was a child of a goddess. There are a variety of ways in which anomalies like this can be made more or less plausibly to conform to Peirce's stipulation, but exploration of them is not necessary here, since the focus of examination in the general topic 'application of general rules' is not how much may be usefully included under the name 'general rule,' but how much under the term 'application.' Governing processes being stipulated to be ones in which,

inconspicuous premises.' In opposition to this methodological prepossession Peirce urged that philosophy should proceed only from 'tangible premises' that can be subjected to careful scrutiny, and should 'trust rather to the multitude and variety of its arguments than to the conclusiveness of any one.'

employing some norms – 'rules,' to use Peirce's word – we effect governance of others, the question about the character and limits of deductive governance becomes a question of the character and limits in that governance of the applicative use of norms.)

7 Departing somewhat from Peirce's usage, his terms 'deductive' and 'ampliative' seem better than available alternatives (e.g., 'analytic' and 'synthetic') for drawing a contrast between two ways in which effects upon norms are produced in governance. One way is that of deriving effects as end products of a succession of steps each of which represents the application of prior accepted norms. This method is distinguished here as 'deductive.' In some cases employment of this procedure involves very concrete application of the norms used in the derivation. Applying concretely prior norms of plant pathology, one may, for example, develop specific norms for the detection of beetle damage in birch trees, or, using prior accepted norms of mechanical engineering, develop norms for the detection of malfunction of the timing chain in certain kinds of internal combustion engine. In a much more abstract way, exploiting prior norms defining the employment of such broad terms as 'change' and 'cause,' Aquinas set out to prove the existence of God, just as in a somewhat analogous procedure Descartes endeavored to show that among our human components the mind is more easily known than the body, while Hume endeavored to show that the existence of either of these, as they were conceived in his time, must be judged extremely dubitable.

8 Complementary to the deductive phase of the employment of norms, and here termed 'ampliative,' is a phase in which effects are wrought upon norms themselves in conjunction with their applicative use.[2] These effects may be great, small, or sometimes negligible, but they are genuinely governing ones. Two points need to be emphasized about these two phases. First, they are closely related, are ordinarily separated from each other only by abstraction. Secondly, they are phases of processes that are by no means restricted to what would ordinarily be referred to as argument, reasoning, or inference. Indeed, as the book attempts to show, these phases cannot be well understood,

---

[2] Peirce used the term 'ampliative' to cover all non-deductive arguments. These he subdivided into two species, induction and abduction, the latter being also referred to as presumption, hypothesis, and retroduction. 'Retroduction,' by its prefix, might serve better to mark off the reactive phase of the employment of norms than the less etymologically suggestive 'ampliative,' but at present it remains too much of a neologism for ease in extended employment.

separately or jointly, unless they are seen as instances of much wider processes than those of philosophical reflection. They are phases of processes much wider than those of reflection in general, but in all of which we not only follow norms but also, in following, exercise governance over them. In some of our activities, one of these phases, the applicative, deductive one may dominate. The primary use of the norm may be to guide thought or action. In other activities, sometimes closely conjoined with the applicative phase, the other, ampliative use may be prominent, even dominant. The primary objects of determination are then, not particular instances of thought or action following the norms, but norms themselves as possible objects of maintenance, mutation, or even elimination.

Peirce's term 'ampliative,' though helpful, is not without defect, since it suggests, as Peirce wished it to, a kind of *argument* that is similar to deductive ones in extracting conclusions from premises, but yet not limited by the familiar requirement that the conclusions be logically entailed by the premises.

Ampliative conclusions (better: results, or effects) are not conclusions of arguments. It is a serious mistake to think of them so, to think that parallel to deductive arguments, with their premises and conclusions, there are ampliative ones that have the capacity to lead to results that are like the results of deductions except that they are not limited by the traditional requirements of logical entailment. Then one is led to look, as Peirce did, for the source of this mysterious capacity, for this curious validity that is not quite logical. And then, like Peirce again, one may suppose that this validity, this 'justifying' character in some of these argument forms can be located in a quasi-formal, self-correcting character of guaranteeing to yield closer and closer approximations to true conclusions if continued in some indefinitely extended long run.

The repeated exposure of the hollowness of such justifications as this for inductive procedure, probable judgment, and the rest, is but one sign that, however valuable the argument model is for illuminating some processes of governance, it is extremely obscuring for others. This obscuring effect can be avoided, and the whole panorama of deductive and ampliative processes more illuminatingly encompassed and mapped for intellectual exploration if, giving up the exclusive claims of this model to provide intellectual sanction, one assimilates the deductive phases of governance to which this model applies into the wider, more general body of governing processes.

9 *Deductivism.* Corresponding to the usage of 'deductive' and 'ampliative' here followed, 'deductivism' is employed to designate the view that dictates the extrusion of ampliative processes from the repertory of philosophical reflection. This view is revealed under scrutiny to embrace among its components particular views about how norms are employed in the guidance of thought and action, about what effects upon thought and action and upon the norms themselves may be attributed to this employment, and about the bearing of these effects upon the general process of governing norms. The general view is propagated much more by exemplification in practice than by explicit doctrine. A good portion of recent and contemporary puzzlement and distress over the philosophical governance of norms may be traced to the exclusive preoccupation of many philosophical writers with this one phase of the employment of norms, to their presumption that only processes exemplifying this phase qualify as legitimate components of philosophical governance. Legitimate critical judgment of accepted norms of thought and action is taken to be always and only a procedure of testing and reforming these by means of already extant norms used in an exclusively applicative way. No impugnment of the value of deductive employment of norms in philosophy, as elsewhere, is entailed by the judgment that exclusive preoccupation with this aspect of our employment has seriously obscured the full sources of authority of philosophical thought and correspondingly impeded philosophical practice.

10 One readily accessible concrete example of such a view of governance is the now pretty much discounted view that proper juridical legal reasoning is confined to a formal, scientific (often called 'syllogistic') elaboration of law, legal rules, and principles. The radical movement of legal realism in American jurisprudence in the fourth decade of this century was in part a response to a recognition that juridical governance confined in this way is incapable of performing its politically required function of legal elaboration. By the fifth decade E. H. Levi, noting that such a view of juridical reasoning had long been under attack, and referring to Jerome Frank's legal-realistic book *Law and the Modern Mind*, characterized as a 'pretense' the view that the law is 'a system of known rules applied by a judge.' Rather, Levi wrote, 'the kind of reasoning involved in the legal process is one in which the classification changes as the classification is made. The rules change as the rules are applied.'[3]

---

[3] *An Introduction to Legal Reasoning* (1948), pp. 1–4.

11 In similar though broader ways the insufficiences of deductivist programs have been exhibited at various points by the reverses encountered by the analytic strains of recent and contemporary Anglo-American philosophy. The broad analogue of strict legal interpretation in this philosophical tradition has been strict analysis of concepts or conceptual schemes. By and large the practitioners of analytic philosophy, both in its Oxbridge forms and in the counterpart positivism imported from central Europe, agreed on the manner in which philosophical reflection performs its governing role with respect to norms. Beneath a division of opinion in detail about how philosophical analysis should be carried out – whether by careful attention to aspects of 'natural,' everyday languages and conceptions (e.g., Moore, Austin), or by the construction of parallel highly disciplined artificial symbolic systems (e.g., early Wittgenstein, Carnap) – beneath the division about how the task should be carried out was a deep agreement about the deductive character of the procedure. But exclusive reliance upon the applicative use of norms requires that for the purpose of governance in any field there be accessible some body of extant norms (1) competent in application to determine governantial results and (2) deriving their character and governing authority from sources other than and independent of these results. The location and definition of norms suitable for the purpose, and the wide discrepancy between the results of their application and the recognized desiderata of philosophical governance, have been the two major sources of difficulty of deductivist programs throughout modern philosophy. Examples of such supposed archetypes appealed to in early modern philosophy of science were, on the rationalist side, innate ideas, and, on the empiricist side, immediately accessible natural regularities of the sort that Hume referred to under the collective term of 'the relation of cause and effect.'

12 One of the most influential recent demonstrations of the inadequacy of the deductivist position was that of Kuhn in his now famous monograph on scientific revolutions. Kuhn called attention to the limitations of a philosophy of science modeled upon periods of scientific development in which the tasks of research are primarily those of elaborating grand paradigms of scientific achievement. In such periods the tasks, in their relation to the grand complex of practices and ideas within which scientists work, are primarily applicative. Scientific development is primarily by accumulation. A view of science limited to faithfully reproducing this phase of scientific development is, Kuhn argued, in principle incapable of representing and illuminating those

very different phases of development in which the major task faced in a discipline is not the accumulation of further results of an accepted paradigm, but the devising and establishing of a new one. Translated into the language of norms and governance, and of deductive and ampliative processes, Kuhn's thesis becomes one that a theory of governance restricted to the deductive, applicative use of norms is adequate only for the intra-paradigmatic phases of scientific development, in contrast to the inter-paradigmatic ones.

13 Deeply embedded in the deductivist philosophy here exemplified, so deep that it is little attended, is a broad logical view of what norms of thought and action are like, and, closely related to this, of what it is like to follow them, what adherence to them entails. On this view norms are kind of archetypes or models of instances of thought or action that serve us as templates for the guidance of performance in these media. These templates are variously thought to reside in individual minds, in symbolic systems, in some special realm of platonic forms or even in external nature. Correspondingly, on this view, what we do when we follow a norm is reproduce it, produce a replica of it in some particular context of thought or action. Following a norm requires just this, is strictly limited to this, and is logically violated if in employing the norm alterations are produced in it. The grip of some such Idol as this is an effective obstacle to understanding well how governance of norms in general, and philosophical governance of them in particular, takes place. Proceeding upon this basic misconception we are naturally led to separate in a radical way the processes of *following* norms from those of *governing* them. Thinking of the employment of norms on the model of pure replication, we are led on logical grounds, in inquiring about the governance of them, to exclude from consideration the governing effects that are the constant natural accompaniments of their employment. We are led to identify juridical interpretation with a conceived kind of strict interpretation *à outrance*, and like Kuhn to view the events of paradigm shifts as necessarily effected primarily by extra-paradigmatic revolutions. Like Quentin Skinner we find ourselves confronted by a great quandary of 'How can we possibly hope, by using (as we are bound to) our own local assumptions and canons of evidence, to construct a theory which is then employed to criticize those precise assumptions and canons of evidence?[4] How, in short, can we, through the legitimate employment

---

[4] Review of Richard J. Bernstein's *The Restructuring of Social and Political Theory*, *The New York Review of Books*, 15 June, 1978, p. 28.

of norms, develop further norms that, since they can be used to criticize the originals, must also transcend and sometimes negate them?

14 A key step toward answering this last question is breaking out of the confines of deductivism and developing an appreciation of the resources of governance that reside in the ampliative effects upon norms of their own employment. What is disputed by the deductivist position is not the prevalence of these effects, but their incorporation in philosophical procedure. Common as these effects are in the employment of norms of thought and action, and closely associated as they are with common forms of deductive process, they have been rigorously excluded from the highly abstract forms of deduction that have been installed as canonical in governance. Together with the restoration to governance of the ampliative aspects of the employment of norms, a more adequate view will include a reassessment of the effects of this restoration upon our conception of deductive processes themselves.

For certain purposes, in certain contexts, it is desirable to neglect ampliative effects. Misunderstanding of the reasons and conditions of this neglect has contributed to the mistaken view that universally they may be neglected, may be regarded as psychological side-effects negligible for philosophical purposes. These effects include:

1   Effects upon norms of their own direct application to specific instances of thought and action.
2   Effects produced in them by their interrelations, both reinforcing and conflicting, with other norms in the various bodies of which they are constituents.
3   The general effect of wider existential conditions that is transmitted to norms through their interrelations with others.

Appreciation of these various effects leads one to recognize that governance of norms is not a process altogether separable from their use in guiding thought and action, not something that must be imported to norms from supervening sources. So pervasive are these effects, and so integral to the character of norms, that one may soberly say of norms, concretely considered, though not of course of the abstract symbolic surrogates that are sometimes misidentified with them, that an uncriticized, ungoverned norm is contradiction in terms.

15 Though not all governance is philosophical, and not all is reflective, the inclusion of ampliative processes among the processes of reflective governance entails some considerable reassessment of the position of reflective processes in the wide area of governing activities. When reflective philosophical governance is restricted to its deductive phases, it is easy to think of it as a very refined intellectual specialty requiring in its paradigmatic forms the cultivation of experts specially gifted or trained in the art of discerning fundamental archetypal norms of human thought and action and devising general directions for their application.

One effect of the incorporation of ampliative processes in reflective philosophical governance is the exposure of the important family relations of this form of governance with non-reflective forms. Appreciation of these relations leads to alterations in our conception of what we are doing when we engage in reflective governance. One alteration is an expansion of the notion of philosophical governance to include aspects of the evolution of ideas, of norms, of forms of life, as well as the more studied deliberative forms that are carried on in individual reflection. In consequence one begins to look upon an individual engaging in the reflective governance of norms, both in its deductive and its ampliative phases, as participating in a process that includes but extends far beyond the processes and the effects of this individual engagement. There are ways in which a community unreflectively, largely unknowingly, effects governance of the constitutional commitments under which it lives, just as there are also ways in which communities do reflectively and knowingly engage in these activities. It is the same with the broad communal philosophical commitments embodied in accepted norms of thought and action.

16 It was an attraction of the deductivist theory and program that in its elaboration of the replicavist model of deduction it appeared to offer a general explanatory theory of governantial method, together with a persuasive account of the authority that attaches to the results of its application. From the time of Hume the withdrawal of these benefits, as they had been tendered by a repeatedly failing deductivism, has been frequently commented upon with concern and regret. Whether the concern and regret are justified, whether these apparent benefits are as genuine as at first glance they may appear, is nevertheless debatable. A strong case can now be made, and is briefly outlined in the book, that the exclusion of ampliative phases of our employment of norms by the deductivist position interferes in a subtle yet serious way with its

11

capacity to give a satisfactory account of certain aspects of the deductive phases of governing themselves, the phases that it favors and that are its primary concern. It appears that the autonomy of deductive phases of governance striven for by the extrusion of the ampliative phases is but specious. For the understanding of certain aspects of deductive governance, the independence of such governance from its ampliative counterpart, installed as an aid, eventually proves an obstacle.

17 The conception of reflective philosophical governance as one particular species of a wide array of social processes helps to regularize and make understandable the employment of widely varied and context-relevant considerations in the actual practice of assessing, confirming, revising, and reconstructing norms of thought and action. Reflective philosophical governance appears widely and in a variety of forms in all those domains of human activity – science, law, morals, and the rest – in which those engaged in the activities, and particularly those leaders who naturally play strong roles in their guidance, are, as a necessary part of their participation in these activities, engaged in the critical scrutiny and governance of implicated norms.

18 Readers whose ambitions in governance were inspired and shaped by deductivist philosophy may expect from a study of ampliative processes the development and display of models, decision procedures, and paradigm patterns of research for these phases of our philosophical activities. If the portrayal by the book of ampliative phases of governance is essentially sound, such an expectation is bound to be disappointed. It is of course a gross mistake to construe emphasis upon the ampliative character of certain phases of reflection as implying a general blanket philosophical certification of all results generated in these phases. It is likewise a mistake, though by no means so obvious a one, to expect ampliative governance to yield formulae and techniques comparable to those developed in and for deductive governance. The primary source of this mistake seems to be a rejection at some level of consciousness of ampliative processes themselves. Like some unruly impulses in Freudean psychology these processes are repressed by strict deductivist super-egos unless and until they are able to take on deductive disguises. The program to develop a coherent, critical understanding of the intellectual, social, and metaphysical pre-suppositions and values represented in a certain discipline, say, astronomy or psychology, may be radically transformed into that of devising abstract semantic master norms that will enable one to discriminate in advance of concrete inquiry the more from the less

projectible predicates. The impulse to achieve broad understanding of the practices of constitutional legal interpretation may be translated into a program of rationalizing these practices by viewing them as exemplifying the aims and principles of utilitarian calculation. After two hundred years of intermittent exposure and criticism, the attachment of philosophers in the Anglo-American tradition to deductivism remains strong. In ways that we are hardly aware of we are influenced in various steps we take in governance by the deep-seated preconception that to whatever extent issues of governance transcend the competence of deductive, applicative processes, they transcend the competence of philosophical governance altogether.

19 *The book.* The program of the book for increasing understanding of the significance for philosophical reflection of ampliative processes is, first, to present a more concrete and, for the purposes, a more adequate view of norms than that favored by the deductivist philosophy. This is a first, indispensable step in a movement to close the breach installed by that philosophy between the deductive and ampliative phases of the employment of norms. After expanding upon these more general, theoretical topics, the book proceeds to deal in detail, and with numerous examples, with aspects of the ampliative governance of norms in general, and, in particular with that species of this governance that is exemplified in reflective, philosophical thought.

Before commencing the positive account, however, some attention must be paid to the deductivist position from which much of the present perplexity and controversy over governance derives. To this topic the first of the three parts of the book is devoted. Chapter 1 explains in detail the difference between ampliative and deductive processes. Chapter 2 outlines some of the main intellectual sources of the deductivist view. Chapter 3 considers examples of the philosophical untoward consequences of deductivism in three different fields: philosophy of science, philosophy of law, and moral philosophy.

Part 2 is devoted to the topic of norms. Chapter 4 urges the restoration to norms of some of the concrete aspects of them that have been purposely extruded from the presently regnant ways of conceiving them. Such restoration entails a different way of looking at the logical processes of subsuming instances under a rule. One dividend accruing from this more concrete view is the light it sheds upon a topic of much recent and current interest in the philosophy of logic, namely, what it is like to follow a rule. These logical topics are treated in Chapter 5.

Chapter 6 concludes this portion of the book with a discussion of two basic metaphysical topics implicated in the revised view of norms: (1) universals, and (2) the determination of human conduct. The chapter concludes with a brief notice of the bearing of these two topics upon the conditions of the apt employment of the techniques of atomistic, monadic logic.

The specific character of ampliative philosophical governance is the central topic of Part 3. This character is expanded upon generally in Chapters 7 and 8, and illustrated concretely in Chapter 8 in connection with an extended critical analysis of certain analogous views advanced by Michael Oakeshott and strongly criticized by Julian Franklin. These are views of political reasoning in general, and of reasoning about the legal status of women in particular. Chapter 9 gives a critical evaluation of one objection made to ampliative philosophical governance as it is portrayed here, namely, that it is in principle weighted in favor of conservative results. Chapter 10 gives a brief account of certain key episodes in the development of modern physical science, as they are seen and illuminated from the point of view of ampliative philosophical governance. Readers familiar with current philosophical literature may be assisted in comprehending this point of view by the concluding contrast drawn between it and the comparable but somewhat more negative views on the conduct of philosophy advanced by Richard Rorty in his widely read *Philosophy and the Mirror of Nature*.

Part 1
DEDUCTIVISM

1

Ampliative and Deductive Processes

Topical Outline

17

determinants of these.

1 Much work in philosophy in the United States in the past two decades has been in reaction to a challenge fundamentally similar to that of Hume's demonstrations two centuries ago of the various fundamental incapacities of the 'human understanding.' A major vector of the latter-day challenge was T. S. Kuhn's monograph on scientific revolutions.[1] The effect of this influential work was to reinforce in a dramatic and very stimulating way the destructive impact of a variety of criticism that had long been advanced against a general view and program in the theory of knowledge of which logical positivism was at the time a foremost example. The view is commonly referred to now as a foundational one. At the heart of the view is a conception of what genuine, philosophically defensible knowledge is, and how, therefore, philosophical criticism of putative items of knowledge should proceed. The two main items in the view and program are (1) the location of secure 'foundations' from which proper claims of knowledge could and must begin, and (2) the 'building' of further claims upon these foundations by strictly deductive methods. Expanded from science to metaphysics, morals, and other domains, the view proposed as a method of discriminating the valid from the invalid, the acceptable from the unacceptable, among already accepted and proposed items of knowledge, a procedure of conducting a regress to these secure foundations, followed by progress from them by means of a sequence of transitively competent validating steps.

As was observed in the Introduction, the element of most significance in the characterization of the building procedure as deductive is not the degree of certainty that can be attributed to its results in some cases, but the manner in which in any case cogency, validity, or legitimacy is

[1] *The Structure of Scientific Revolutions* (1962).

conferred upon results. It is not just that the foundational components are necessary to the sanction of the derivative ones, but also that they are sufficient: sufficient in the sense that no derivative item has any sanction other than that already resident in the foundations from which it derives. Proper, philosophically defensible development in knowledge consists in exploiting the foundations in such a way that the sanction of any derived item is extracted exclusively from its foundations. Foundations lead to further sanctioned items of knowledge, not by stimulating the discovery of new sanctions for these items, but by disclosing that for these items the sanctions of the foundation items suffice. All sanction is foundational sanction, which is transmitted to derivative items by logical conduits. All proper development based upon foundations is, in its relation to its foundations, accumulative: this, not because such is the way cognitive activities are carried on by and large in everyday life, science, and elsewhere, but because it follows from the essential nature of intellectual sanctions that this is the way it *must* be.

2 Such in outline is the deductivist view of and program for the philosophical criticism and development of the corpus of human knowledge. Grounds for rejecting the deductivist view and program had long been available, not only in the negative criticisms of Hume, but also in the positive alternative offered by the tradition of critical philosophy that stemmed largely from the revision of the original Kantian philosophy made by Hegel. But cogent as were both these kinds of grounds, they were much more abstract and much less effective than the concrete demonstration offered by Kuhn of the incapacity of the deductivist philosophy of science to provide an adequate account of some of the crucial episodes in the development of modern physical science. These episodes illustrated in a very striking way what more abstract and general reflection had long suggested, namely, that sometimes the development of knowledge is not by accumulation but by transformation. Sometimes when previously attained positions in knowledge are employed as grounds for further attainments, the effect is not to provide increments to a body of wholly unaffected intellectual capital that serves as grounds for these attainments, but rather to alter in important ways the character of the grounds themselves. Put in the not altogether apt idiom favored by many philosophers, the process is one in which the 'premises' employed to establish 'conclusions' undergo change themselves in the process of delivering the conclusions, and undergo this change, not through blunder or inattention, but as a

AMPLIATIVE AND DEDUCTIVE PROCESSES

necessary condition of establishing the conclusions in question. This kind of process resisted assimilation to the deductivist view of knowledge.

3 The mere presence of these processes, even their widespread presence in human thought and action, is not controversial. What is controversial is their indispensability for philosophical purposes. However widespread such processes are in the various fields which are the objects of philosophical criticism and reconstruction, a tenet of the foundational view has been that in the operations of criticism and reconstruction themselves these processes have no place. They are not themselves proper philosophical procedures. Classic exemplars of this attitude were both Descartes and Hume: Descartes with his insistence that knowledge 'is obtainable in no other way' than intuition and deduction; Hume in his judgment that while all of what he called 'inferences from experience' are the effects of custom, and custom therefore is the great guide of life, all these processes must be sharply distinguished from genuine reasoning.[2] Hume's denigration of these processes as 'custom' was matched by the general features of Kuhn's philosophical categories that dictated the conclusion that the processes capable of effecting 'proof' in scientific activity are exclusively those of 'logic and experiment' operating along general lines defined by some influential paradigm of scientific achievement.[3] Both Hume and Kuhn, though committed to deductivist standards, were led to conclusions concerning the exclusive philosophical competence of processes that strictly adhere to these standards. Hume's 'custom' and Kuhn's 'revolutionary science' represented for each writer a large and crucially important domain of cognitive practice which resisted explication in terms of accredited procedures belonging to a favored canon of proof. By means of the standards of this canon, practices in these domains could not be rationalized, and in consequence their intellectual legitimacy and all the important phases of cognitive practice that depended upon them, when challenged in the court of philosophical criticism, were seriously compromised. This is not to say that the canons of 'proof' were conceived by these two philosophers, or for that matter also by Descartes, to be exactly the same.

[2] Descartes, *Rules for the Direction of the Mind*, III; Hume, *Enquiry Concerning Human Understanding*, Section V, Part I.

[3] *Structure*, pp. 93, 149.

4   The thesis of deductivism under examination here is not restricted to questions about knowledge, but extends widely to philosophical thought wherever it is engaged in the philosophical governance of norms of thought and action. Leaving aside, for the moment, further explication of both 'norms of thought and action' and 'deduction,' we may think of 'governance' as a broad term covering both the critical and the constructive activities in which we are engaged with the character, establishment and maintenance of norms, as well as with their disestablishment and elimination: their development, criticism, refinement, reconstruction, reinforcement, weakening, and elimination. Of these activities – or even more broadly – processes that as individuals and groups we participate in in a great variety of ways, only a small portion could be called philosophical. Philosophical thought is one particular species of this vast genus of process. It is distinguished from others basically but not exclusively by its objects. These are very broad, deep, and often deeply entrenched norms, norms that in analogy with the law we may call 'constitutional' in relation to the domains of thought and action to which they pertain.

It is part of the view presented here that philosophical species of governance cannot be well understood in isolation from other species. Philosophical governance, to adapt that useful formula of Clausewitz, is a continuation of governance by special means. Paradigmatically these are reflective means: of deliberate criticism, construction and the rest, engaged with broad and deep norms of thought and action. These processes carried on at the level of consciousness are closely related with others that occur constantly and widely at much less conscious levels.

Thus what distinguishes philosophical governance as a species is not so much its agency, as its objects, and the mutations effected upon the process by adaptation to those objects. Philosophical thought is by no means the special preserve of some special class of mandarins, academic or otherwise. It is engaged in invarious areas of life when constitutional principles call for attention. For example, in mathematics when there is dispute concerning certain methods of proof; in physics when it begins to appear that certain elements of the traditional concept of objectivity are brought into challenge by situations in which, in principle, it is not possible to make a strict and absolute distinction between the observer and the observed; in politics when one tries to understand how broad principles of majority rule, or self-determination, apply to religious divisions in Northern Ireland, or ethnic and religious ones in the Israeli-occupied territory of the West Bank of the Jordan. Such incapacity in an extreme degree both Hume and Kuhn urged that they had discovered in basic accepted norms followed in the pursuit of knowledge. The norms in question, in the case of Hume, were those that he held to be basic in all 'reasonings concerning matters of fact' founded upon 'experience.' In the case of Kuhn the norms were, less generally, those represented by the paradigms of investigation accepted in certain eras of modern science, and the incapacity was the incompetence of these norms to serve as guides for thought and action in those periods of scientific development in which the progress of research required not intra-paradigmatic but trans-paradigmatic development, 'revolutionary' instead of 'normal' science.

5 A very imporant stimulus to philosophical thought directed to the governance of norms is the occurrence of what, in the language of the law may be referred to as 'hard cases.' These are ones that call for decision but for which accepted norms do not provide unequivocal answers.

The saying in law is that hard cases make bad law. Whether bad or not, law is certainly in some sense 'made', or, less controversially, determined. The term 'juridical' is sometimes employed, in preference to the broader term 'judicial,' to mark off those aspects of judicial decisions, opinions, reasoning, and arguments that are specifically concerned with determinations of *law* rather than of *fact*. Obviously there is a special possibility of misjudgment in juridical decisions in hard cases. There is also a greater possibility of the kind of contribution that can be made in juridical decision and reasoning, so that, though hard cases may indeed in many instances make bad law, without hard cases carefully attended to, the contribution of juridical investigation of the law would be greatly altered and reduced. It is similar generally with hard cases in the philosophical governance of norms. In them the greater possibility of misgovernance accompanies the greater possibility of governance, and with that the greater possibility of making the kind of contribution that reflection can make to the norms of thought or action that are revealed to be in need of some kind of determination.

Philosophical reflection, discussion, and the rest – philosophical inquiry in its various forms, like a stormy petrel of the intellect, has as its natural habitat the conditions of disquiet, puzzlement, and controversy that surround the hard cases, in which the appeal to accepted patterns of thought and action provides no definite clear answers to questions of what the disposition of the cases shall be. It is ironic that repeatedly through the centuries this characteristic of philosophical inquiry, which is rather a favorable sign that its practitioners are attending to their business, has been urged as a sign that they are not tending it well. The celebrated urge, tracing back to Leibniz and beyond, to replace the indecision, lack of decision procedures, and turbulence of philosophical investigation with calculation, with logical algorithms, is not an invitation to progress, but to defeat. We do not complain that there seems to be a concentration of hard constitutional cases on the docket of the Supreme Court, any more than we complain of the concentration of nurses in the intensive care units of the local hospital. Conditions of serious illness are the natural habitat of the surgeon. He may, like the rest of us, sometimes falter, sometimes do more harm than good. He, like his medicines, may have harmful side effects. But it is a strange judgment that because most of his patients are seriously ill, the illness must be produced by the treatment. It is surely the rule, despite exceptions, that they are in the surgery because they are ill, rather than ill because they are in the surgery.

A concern with governance in hard cases is integrally related with a concern with it in the easier ones. Similarly, a concern with philosophical governance is integrally related with a concern with non-philosophical governance, and a concern with reflective governance so related with non-reflective forms. These integral relations will be elaborated upon in the book in the process of developing a broad view of philosophically governing processes. It may be of value here to observe in a preliminary way that as hard cases, or, more accurately degrees of hardness of this particular kind, reflect the insufficiency of deductive processes to effect their disposition, so deductivism, the view of philosophical governance centered exclusively on deductive processes, represents an extreme, and what might be thought of as a limiting view of the role of such cases in governance. One aim of that view is to disclose that the repertory of acceptable governing processes can be completed exclusively with deductive ones. As this is a manifestly impossible aim so long as one takes as one's initial premises some small sub-set of accepted norms, a plausible version of the view requires an appeal to some special set of norms, the foundational ones, the deductive capacities of which will suffice for the needs of this methodologically reductionist program.

6 Partial truths are notoriously dangerous ones. While Hume, and latterly Kuhn, performed a great service in calling attention to an

important distinction; and while it was perhaps necessary for pedagogical purposes that the distinction be set forth with a maximum degree of sharpness and dramatic contrast, the result is a distinction that is invidious. Unquestionably there is a difference here, and one of enormous significance. It is a difference that can be referred to summarily, though not very finely, as that between *deductive* or *analytic* processes, on the one hand, and *inductive* or *ampliative* ones, on the other, or (to emphasize the close interdependence of these, in the sciences and elsewhere), as the deductive and ampliative phases of certain forms of human conduct, forms that Hume referred to under the broad term of 'custom,' and which later the classic American pragmatists, Peirce, James, and Dewey, treated under the title of 'habit.' The term 'deductive' (or equivalently 'analytic') distinguishes different ways in which conduct is determined by learned patterns that may be conveniently embraced under the wide term 'norms.'

This term is used here in a way comparable to that of 'mores' in sociology and anthropology, except that its application to conduct, like that of the term 'conduct' itself, is conceived much more broadly. Norms are accepted precepts and practices, modes of proceeding, modes of action in the wide sense of action that includes not only overt forms, but forms of thought itself, and with it such elements of the famous Cartesian complex as understanding, believing and doubting, affirming and denying. Norms are learned patterns of conduct rather than unlearned or instinctive ones, not in the extreme sense that everything about them can be fully explained as due to some post-gametic learning, but in the sense that whatever basis their development may have in the original constitution of the individuals embodying them, they would not be developed and embodied as they are, would be undeveloped or substantially different without the effect of some learning. They are approved ways of proceeding in thought and action, ways of thinking and acting followed by individuals and groups in all the various fields in which there are such more or less settled proprieties. In the second half of this century the term 'forms of life,' favored by Wittgenstein, has frequently been employed by some writers to refer to norms of very wide and fundamental application in major fields of knowledge. In the philosophical tradition that sprang from Hegel's *Phenomenology of Spirit* whole constellations of these were embraced under the title of 'forms of consciousness.'

7 Included among norms are – in addition to all kinds of commonsense

habits, practices, customs, beliefs, opinions, judgments, assumptions, etc. – the corresponding items in the more refined and technical disciplines, in the sciences and the humanities, for example, in physics, mathematics, history, law, morals, and religion. It is not necessary, or helpful, always to think of physical laws or mathematical theorems as norms of procedure. Nevertheless, they do so serve. We may find it important sometimes to concentrate instead upon what would commonly be thought of as their descriptive aspect, to think of them, in their capacity to convey true information about their objects. But they are also, because they are capable of being true of their objects, capable of providing us with norms for reasonably dealing with them either in thought or in action. It is not reasonable procedure to try to divide a set of seventeen objects into four equal sets, because the number seventeen is not divisible by four. Similarly the reason why it is not reasonable for one to expect to lift an object weighing one hundred pounds with another object weighing a hundred pounds by means of a simple pulley lies in principles which would be more commonly thought of as truths of mechanics than as norms of procedure. Because they have been ascertained to provide us with sound information about their objects, we confidently employ them as guides to what is reasonable procedure in such relevant contexts as these.

What is being treated here as the same, for the purpose of investigating ampliative philosophical processes, is a very diverse collection of items. Some of them are as different from each other as are the Ten Commandments from the laws of motion or the axioms of set theory; as different as are the latter from the information in a handbook of chemical engineering or a repair manual for a particular make and model of motor car; and as different as these in turn are from the large body of lore that is gradually assimilated by a scientist, lawyer, physician, carpenter or plumber in the achieving of progressive mastery of his profession or occupation. Included in it, along with items exemplifying the mode commonly discriminated as propositional knowledge, are also, though no doubt not so obviously, those of non-propositional knowledge, knowledge of 'how' as well as knowledge 'that.' Though for some items in the corpus the terms 'rule,' 'custom,' 'habit,' 'practice,' or the plural 'mores,' seem more fitting in ordinary speech, the term 'norm,' though not altogether appropriate, seems to stretch more elastically to cover both portions of the corpus that are formulated in symbolic expressions and those which are not. The former of these are exemplified, not only in propositions, statements, judgments, assumptions, but also in rules, precepts, maxims, injunctions, imperatives, and so on. The latter include all the ways of proceeding in which we are inculcated, and which we absorb in becoming culturated in the various kinds of communities to which we all belong as lay citizens or as professionals: political communities, religious communities, scientific communities, business communities, and the rest. The dimension of the norms of this kind, of which we are all for a time the legatees and trustees, and then the transmitters and donors, is vast, including as it does so very much that we learn that is not, so to speak, 'book learning,' namely, something that can be communicated without a significant remainder by verbal instruction. A recognition of this aspect of learning is one of the primary reasons why no philosophy of science, no theory of knowledge, no philosophy of morals, or no theory of reasoning, can be remotely realistic which takes as its sole or almost exclusive subject matter the discourse employed in these several spheres of human activity. A person is no more capable of being made a scientist by being informed of and brought to give assent to a central body of propositions extracted from the science in question, than one is capable of being made a religious believer by successful assimilation of the tenets of faith set forth in a catechism. What instruction restricted to these aspects of science or religion neglects is the rich nature of the sciences and the various forms of religion as social institutions in which human beings are formed to become the living bearers and cultivators of a complex body of practices, of a way of proceeding in dealing in thought and action with some more or less definite domain of subject matter.

8 The terms traditionally employed in philosophy in place of 'norms' and similar ones to designate such items of our cultural equipment have been 'idea' (e.g., Descartes) and 'concept' (e.g., Kant). In recent and contemporary philosophy the latter term has been dominant. It is mostly in terms of conceptual systems and conceptual development that issues about rationality have been broached and debated in recent years in the philosophy of science. A paradigm instance of this has been the ongoing work of Stephen Toulmin on *Human Understanding*. The first and now published part of this work has the title *The Collective Use and Development of Concepts* (1976); the second and third projected parts are correspondingly advertised as dealing respectively with the individual grasp and development of concepts, and the rational adequacy and appraisal of concepts.

The discussion in Part I of that work exhibits clearly some of the serious disadvantages of treating rationality within the restrictions of a theory of concepts. The term 'concept,' as it has been employed in philosophical studies, has been a very deceptive and troublesome one. In view of its checkered career it has to be regarded as a very unreliable performer, to be put into service sparingly, circumspectly, and only in circumstances in which some less risky terminology will not suffice. It suggests mental entities, instances of some independent mental substance, capable of having careers of their own in an 'internal' world quite independently from bodies, objects, living things, etc., in an 'external' world. It also suggests, when one has become sensitized to the close relation between thought and language, a kind of entity which can be satisfactorily treated in the rubrics of language and linguistic usage; suggests, to put the matter much too narrowly but wide enough to indicate the point, that concepts can be understood by treating man as the source and recipient of verbal signals, as *homo loquens et audiens*.

It is clear that Toulmin intends neither of these suggestions, that what he has in mind under the title of 'conceptual evolution' is something very wide indeed. One of the suppositions that he is reacting against, a supposition more often exemplified in practice than explicitly avowed, is that to the effect that rationality can be identified with 'logicality,' the ordering of 'concepts and beliefs in tidy formal structures . . . 'the inner articulation of conceptual systems whose basic concepts are not currently in doubt.' At the center of rationality, Toulmin urges, is opposition to 'fixed ideas, stereotyped procedures . . . [and] immutable concepts.' Thus, 'A man demonstrates his rationality . . . by the manner in which, and the occasions on which, he changes . . . [his] ideas, procedures, and concepts.'[4]

9 Even in these brief passages, it should be noted, Toulmin speaks of fixed procedures and changes of *procedure*, as well as of fixity and change in ideas and concepts. Here and for the most part in the book he shows himself to be well aware that the story of the development of knowledge in science and in other areas cannot be told without including an account of the development of procedures and practices. Scientists, for example, do much more; much more is involved in the conduct of scientific inquiry and in effectng scientific development than collecting 'empirical data,' on the one hand, and inventing and polishing substantive expressions, on the other. Taking the word 'transmit' as a term to refer to 'the set of concepts representative of a historically developing discipline,' Toulmin strongly emphasizes the

[4] Pp. vii, 84, x.

breadth and complexity of this legacy which each generation of master scientists is engaged in developing and passing on to junior apprentices. The core of this transmit which in a process of culturation is passed on, with or without modification, is a 'repertory of intellectual techniques, procedures, skills, and methods of representation, which are employed in "giving explanations" of events and phenomena within the scope of the science concerned.' The set of rule-governed modes of explanatory behavior in a branch of science that forms 'the collective transmit through which a set of scientific concepts finds its professional expression ... is itself "institutionalized" in ways that make conceptual learning in a science comparable to initiation in a social institution.'[5]

It is readily apparent that in order to make the terms 'concept' or 'system or set of concepts' cover all this, these terms will have to be employed in a very broad, extended way. They will have to be construed in such a way that included in a concept, in addition to (1) its linguistic aspect, are (2) the representational techniques associated with the linguistic term and (3) the appropriate application procedures. In Toulmin's words, 'for philosophical purposes ... we must keep all three groups of elements in view, and discuss scientific "concepts" not in abstract linguistic terms alone, but in a more concrete procedural idiom.' One might indeed, as he says, with only the slightest exaggeration, compress the message concerning the breadth and complexity of concept-use in science into the epigram, 'Every concept is an intellectual micro-institution.'[6]

10 Toulmin has much more to say that is valuable concerning the collective, social, procedural, and behavioral aspects of science that concepts must be construed to cover if the story of large-scale scientific change is to be written in terms of conceptual change. This much has been abstracted from the whole for the purpose of explaining a bit further the choice made here to discuss ampliative philosophical processes in terms of the development and criticism of norms rather

[5] Pp. 158, 159, 166.

[6] Pp. 161, 162, 166. This usage of the word 'institution' is less exaggerated than extended, and properly so. As Ernest Gellner said in a talk on 'Concepts and Society' at the Conference of the Society for the Philosophy of Science held at Oxford in 1958, 'Concepts and beliefs are themselves, in a sense, institutions, amongst others; for they provide a kind of fairly permanent frame, as do other institutions, independent of any one individual, within which individual conduct takes place.' The paper which developed from this talk is reprinted in B. R. Wilson, ed., *Rationality* (1970), pp. 18–49.

than of concepts. Either of these ways involves some considerable expansion of the accepted usage of the key term chosen. 'Concept' for example, involves the kind of expansion which Toulmin has given it; it involves one embracing so much of our scientific and other cognitive institutions under this term that it is hard to see what remains to be contrasted with it. Yet 'concept' in common philosophical usage is, though not exactly a polar term, one which does strongly suggest a contrast with such items as statements, propositions, theories: items differentiated from concepts in conveying full assertions, claims that are capable of being true or false. Like the similar distinction between theory and observation, this concept-proposition distinction is one of those divisions which are obvious and valuable at a certain level of analysis. But its value as well as its sharpness can be and is greatly overestimated; and, further, when, as commonly, it is treated as the manifestation of some kind of epistemological axiom, endowed with the kind of immunity from criticism claimed by some for theological dogmas, it can be and is in some cases, rather than a source of illumination, an obstacle to understanding.

11 The effectiveness of this long-standing prejudicial distinction helps to explain why, having extended the definition of concept in what is in relation to accepted usage a radical way, Toulmin does not apparently appreciate the full effect of this redefinition and at some important places actually writes of concepts in a way that his redefinition has made inappropriate. Apparently so intent is he upon the point that concepts change as against the platonists in this matter, and that therefore rationality with respect to concepts cannot be identified with 'logicality,' i.e., the installation of certain ordering relations among the concepts in being at any one time, that he does not appreciate that in the argument for change he has marshalled strong grounds for the conclusion that what, under the name of 'concept,' does change is something of a very different kind from what is conceived under this name by those who do identify rationality with logicality. If concepts are the complexes of linguistic, representation, and pragmatic features which Toulmin holds them to be; if it is sensible and helpful (and it is) to treat them as micro-institutions, then it is not sensible, but positively harmful, to speak of the inner articulation of conceptual systems as something that could be striven for and achieved independently of the representation and applicational features which, together with the linguistic ones, are essential aspects of concepts as richly conceived.

There are now a variety of well-established disciplines of conceptual analysis, of the formal and informal articulation of conceptual systems. It is a question of some importance whether it is judicious philosophical usage to combine under the one term, 'concept,' both the abstract, linguistic objects of these investigations, and the extremely concrete, pragmatic objects of the investigation of the norms of thought and action, and the processes by which these are criticized, changed, and controlled. Innovation and stasis, radicalism and conservatism, extend, though in greatly unequal degrees, to all the domains, scientific, moral, legal and so on, of which norms are major features. The traditional language of concepts, of conceptual analysis, of conceptual systems and of possible alternative conceptual schemes, without doubt tends to divert attention from the aspects of change and development among these norms. In this manner it tends to promote effects in the non-linguistic, the more institutional aspects of our intellectual equipment in a way that is more indirect, less conscious, and consequently less critical than it otherwise might be.

There is, as Peirce observed long ago, an 'ethics of terminology.' There is also a prudence of terminology. It has been for broad important reasons of philosophical prudence, to avoid the kind of untoward consequences just outlined, and to keep in the forefront of attention the broad communal, social, pragmatic, and institutional aspects of our ways of thinking and acting that the term 'norm' has been chosen to refer to these, rather than the more traditional 'concept.'

12 A stronger competitor to 'norms' as a way of referring to patterns of thinking and acting is the roughly equivalent term 'practices.' On occasion in the ensuing discussion this alternative will be employed. These two terms differ somewhat in their reference to approved ways of proceeding, in their relative emphasis upon the aspect of prescription and that of the actual conformity of actions with the prescription. In both terms there is a latent ambiguity that the context commonly dispels: between what is approved and what as a matter of course is actually done. The term 'norms' bears on the surface the aspect of approval, emphasizing that among possible ways of proceeding, the indicated way is a fitting or right one. 'Practice' emphasizes more strongly the conformity of actual conduct with the indicated mode of procedure. Deep and complex topics may here be circumvented concerning the closeness of these two aspects of norms or practices: that of acceptance and that of conformity in action. For to some extent even conscious, sincere acceptance is rendered hollow by lack of conforming

action, just as conforming action, unaccompanied by conscious commitment, may in some circumstances nevertheless count as genuine acceptance. Important as these topics are for some purposes, definition and commitment upon them is not required for the exploration of the feature of ampliative processes at hand.

13 Philosophical theories, like theories generally, are developed for various purposes and cannot be judged as adequate or inadequate without some reference to these purposes, without some reference to the kinds of question they were devised to answer, what their objects are, and what features of these objects they were meant to illuminate. The choice of the term 'norms' (or, alternatively, 'practices') here represents a very basic philosophical judgment, contrary to what has become the prevailing one in the past hundred years to the effect that *since* controversies over broad patterns of thought and action are carried on in philosophy in terms of linguistic and other symbolic representations of these patterns, *therefore* these controversies are essentially ones concerning these symbolic representations and the internal mental processes of which these are taken to be expressions.

The contrary judgment here is that in the past hundred years the deficiencies of philosophical thought due to a neglect of the close relations between symbols and patterns of thought and action have been responded to with an overemphasis upon these symbolic representations to the neglect of the patterns themselves. Without question the relation between those symbolic forms and the patterns is close, indeed integral. In particular, the patterns would not be what they are apart from these forms; apart from them they are not conceivable as they are. But, at least for certain purposes, it is necessary to distinguish these two kinds of items, and not be misled into supposing that the patterns can be reduced without a remainder to the forms.

A first and indispensable step in the understanding of the ampliative processes through which norms of thought and action are criticized and controlled by conscious reflection is a grasp of the ampliative processes exhibited in these norms in general: the processes of their generation and degeneration, their maintenance, revision, and reconstruction. And what applies here to norms generally applies and needs to be attended to faithfully when the norms in question are the very broad and often deeply entrenched ones that are the particular concern of philosophic thought. It is difficult to overestimate the extent of the misdirecting effect in the philosophical thought of the past hundred years of the misidentification of the symbolic representations of patterns of thought and action with these patterns themselves. When philosophy became identified with the criticism of language, when *logos* as reason became restricted to *logos* as word, and reasoning came to be more or less unthinkingly restricted to these processes that are tractable to linguistic theory construction, deep categorical presuppositions were formed that obscured the omnipresent effects of ampliative processes upon norms of thought and action, relegating these effects to the domain of metalinguistic determinations and choices of logical frameworks, symbolic or conceptual schemes.

14 The most important item in the contrast between deductive and ampliative processes is that indicated by Kuhn in connection with the processes of scientific research by the word 'proof.' Deductive or analytic processes are forensic or *probative*: not in the sense that they are necessarily directed to achieving certainty, but rather that they are directed to producing conviction or assent. In the sense that is commonly used in much contemporary philosophy, the processes are justificatory or establishing ones. Implicit in them is the presumption that there are available in certain circumstances proper norms, containing in their prescriptions definite answers to various questions about how we should think or act in such circumstances.

A second important feature of these processes, intimately related to their probative aim, is that with respect to accepted norms they are essentially *applicative* or subsumptive, rather than generative or defining. The results achieved in them are ones for which the available procedures are themselves sufficient; and deviation in following these procedures counts as violation. If it can be shown that achieving a certain result requires substantial deviation, the result, as arrived at in this process, is invalidated, just as a result in ordinary arithmetic would be invalidated if it required for its production a violation of the rules of multiplication. This applicative employment of accepted means is exhibited strikingly in the kinds of scientific research to which Kuhn gave the name of 'puzzle-solving,' that is, research carried on in periods in which what he called 'paradigms' of theory and practice are deeply entrenched.[7] As in a puzzle, the pieces out of which the solution of the problem is to be formed are already given. What counts as a piece in the puzzle or a proper step in the solution is not contingent upon what solution is reached. The solution is validated by the pieces and the steps;

[7] *Structure*, Chapter IV.

its validity flows from them, not *vice versa*. The term 'puzzle-solving' is not to be taken as minimizing the difficulty that may be encountered in producing a solution from the given materials. In many cases the task may be very difficult. Great effort and ingenuity may be required to devise a solution from the materials, just as, in a limited way, these are sometimes required to solve the harder problems at the end of the chapter in a textbook of mathematics or physics.

A third and fourth closely related feature characterize the central paradigm of deductive processes. The activity in question is conceived paradigmatically to be one *engaged in by individuals*, in their capacity as individuals, and also as one that is *conscious* and intentional. The capacity to engage in this activity, whether largely a native endowment, as the rationalists conceived it, or an exclusively acquired character, as the more extreme empiricists maintained, is regarded as a feature that is developed in and manifested by individuals in commerce with other individuals and with themselves. It is primarily individuals who engage in argument, set out to achieve conviction or settle disputed issues, just as it is primarily individuals who inform, teach, advise, praise and blame themselves and each other. And again, the fully developed, model examples of these are activities carried on between individuals knowingly engaged in them, just as it is knowing individuals who make and receive promises, make contracts, put questions, receive answers, make calculations, and so on.

15 *Ampliative* processes contrast with deductive processes on each of the four features just noticed. These contrasting features emerge more and more clearly as one concentrates attention upon concrete human norms or practices, as they are realized in human thought and action where they are generated and through which from time to time they are in various degrees modified. It is typical of norms to be embodied in action plurally rather than singly, and for the form of their embodiment to be affected by their complex relations with each other. In conformity with this they are plastic in various degrees, variable in their disposition to alter in response to different configurations of practices with which they come to be embodied. This is a most important clue to understanding the distinctive character of the processes by which norms are modified, processes that, rather than primarily probative and, in consequence, applicative, are *testive* or critical with respect to norms, and, in their effects upon them, *generative* (molding and defining).

In keeping with their generative and defining functions, these processes employ norms in such a way as not only to derive certain results through their application, but also, in deriving results, to mold and accredit the norms, and, of course, sometimes to *dis*credit them. Here these processes diverge widely from the puzzle-solving, deductive ones. Not all the pieces of *this* 'puzzle' are given antecedent to the process. Rather it is only when this kind of puzzle is solved, and as a consequence of the solution, that what constitutes the pieces, and the nature of the pieces, are for this particular puzzle finally determined.

The processes by which both the habits of individuals and the customs of groups are modified are of course *by no means always, nor even paradigmatically, conscious*, deliberate, or knowing ones. These processes are constantly ongoing, and though sometimes the changes are effected under careful scrutiny and direction, sometimes they occur at or beyond the penumbra of consciousness. Both individuals and groups may be taken by surprise at ways, sometimes considerable ways, in which their modes of proceeding have altered without their notice. With some shock a man who was once a model of scrupulous personal grooming may be led to discover that he now pays much less attention to such concerns than he recently did and had continued to suppose that he did. Similarly, a religious congregation once adamant concerning points of dogmatic theology may be surprised by a recognition that in a relatively uneventful and inconspicuous way the position of these traditional goods in its order of values has been substantially altered. Furthermore, as the above comments already indicate, these processes of modification, especially those that occur outside the reaches of consciousness, are in many cases *social* ones, that is, ones that occur primarily in groups, and occur in individuals primarily because and in so far as they are members of communities sharing these practices and the effects of communal change in them. Because the practices followed by individuals vary widely in their social character, the processes by which practices are modified likewise vary widely in this respect. The social character of these processes is especially prominent in the cognitive norms that are constitutive of modern science and modern scientific technology, and also in the domains of moral, political, and legal thought and action, as well as the sub-domains of religious belief and practice that are commonly referred to as 'organized religion.'

However ill-designed are the methods with which a variety of post-Humean philosophers have tried to deal with them, it is these processes that they have had to deal with in that part of their philosophies commonly referred to as dealing with 'induction.' Similarly it is the processes fitting the forensic model, 'argument,' that during this same period have commonly been referred to under the title of 'deduction.' By this time, however, centuries of usage under empiricist presumptions have so strongly marked the term 'induction' as to render it unsuitable as a general name for the processes in question. Over the years since Bacon, through Hume and Mill, a particular way of conceiving the generative, definitive processes has come to displace the more general ones in the connotation of this term. The idea of a process by which 'universals' could be made grow by some intellectual *tour de force* where none whatever grew before, generated out of pure particulars, has been a typical feature of modern empiricism, especially since the basic Cartesian philosophy underwent its mutation under the influence of the empiricist theory of ideas. This development was considered by the present writer in more detail in Chapter 2, 'The Shaping of the Problem', of *Induction and Justification* (1974). Analogous reactions in politics and law are interestingly dealt with in Alexander M. Bickel's discussion of contractarianism in *The Morality of Consent* (1975), and in Paul Freund's discussion of legal libertarianism in 'Justice Robert H. Jackson – Impact on Civil Rights and Civil Liberties,' *University of Illinois Law Forum*, vol. 1977, pp. 551–76.

Philosophers in the empiricist tradition naturally took the task of understanding the processes by which we modify general norms to be, first, that of understanding how we can construct them entirely anew, and second, how we can do this by some kind of primal extrapolative inference. As the most likely source of means to manage this feat seemed to be that of the mathematical theory of probability, as it is applied to statistical methods, the project of explicating the generative processes become transformed into that of devising some kind of pristine generalizing process out of theorems borrowed from the calculus of probability. In by-passing this project, and in an effort to escape the confining and distorting presuppositions which the now well-worn term 'inductive' seems so easily to insinuate, the alternative term 'ampliative' serves better to designate the processes that are being compared and contrasted here with the deductive or analytic ones.

16 Grasp of the social character of the broad norms of thought and action that are central objects of philosophical concern, and an appreciation of the consequences of this character in what may seem at first very remote quarters, have been among the sorest needs in modern philosophy. For the natural tendency of a modern philosophical mind and personality is individualistic. The theory of knowledge, for example, in its dominant strain in modern philosophy, has been

devoted to telling a story of how knowledge is achieved by human beings exploiting together, though in varying degrees, two great resources available to them as individuals, namely, the input of experience and the reflective capacities of what were often called 'understanding.' Between the philosophical schools of rationalists and empiricists, and between these and Kant, there were of course the well-known divisions of opinion concerning the exact nature of these ingredients, their relative importance in the mix, and the consequent character of the mix itself. Though in many respects revolutionary, in its bearing upon this topic Kant's theory of knowledge represented a refinement and theoretical reorganization of preceding thought rather than a radical break. In a fabulously systematic and detailed way, supporting himself step by step with strong and ingenious arguments, Kant developed an impressive and what seemed for a time definitive account of how such scientific knowledge of the world as is possible for us is a kind of joint product of two components: the native integrative informing powers with which we are all individually endowed, and certain materials available to us individually through the senses.

One of the most impressive parts of Kant's theoretical philosophy, the deductions of the categories, was designed to show the validity and fix the character of these informing elements of the understanding. Corresponding arguments were to perform the same functions for the discriminated forms of intuition, space and time. These informing features were transcendental features of our knowledge, not subject to alteration due to differences of time, place, or social culture. For example, those identified with the operation of the understanding, the categories, were determined to be what they are by the transcendental unity of apperception. The philosophical account, showing that this is the way it is, was the answer provided by the theory to any question which might be raised concerning the ground and stability of these features of our scientific empirical knowledge.

17 Anthony Collins, a free-thinking English deist of the early eighteenth century, was so struck with the incapacity of the means employed by the Boyle lecturers of his time to demonstrate the existence of God that he commented sarcastically that the effect of these performances was often to raise a question about this matter which otherwise few would have entertained. Similarly, with many people the thought that alternate forms of consciousness or knowledge are conceivable was more convincing than the attempted Kantian proofs that one specified member of this possible plurality is the correct one,

constitutes an absolute standard, conformity with which is a necessary general condition of correct ways of proceeding in scientific empirical inquiry. Throughout the nineteenth and continuing into the twentieth century there have been a variety of influences leading to what might be called 'the naturalization of the transcendental unity of apperception,' that is to say, in less arcane language, the removal of the forms of consciousness from the domain of the transcendental to that of the historical and the social. The philosopher whose teaching and writing were most influential in effecting this transfer was Hegel. In his writing and teaching Hegel was not of one mind in this matter, the transcendental side of Kant remaining alive and well (if such really *is* intellectual health) in the deductions of his greater and lesser *Logics*. The portion of his thought in which the forms of consciousness are conceived, with now and then some wishful looking back at the would-be abstract deductions of the *Logics*, are those dealing with the phenomenology of the spirit, with history, with topics in social and political philosophy, ethics, and religion. In recent times much that Hegel seems to have been seeing darkly and expressing even more darkly about the social character of the forms of reason and consciousness have been discerned and expressed in a less Delphic way in a variety of historical and social disciplines, in many of which there was indeed some Hegelian influence, including social psychology and cultural anthropology.

The introduction of some contemporary philosophers to a general view of thought which emphasized the influence of social custom, though not social evolution, was in the later philosophy of Wittgenstein, particularly those portions which emphasize the basis of language, thought and logic in our social forms of life. Another important influence had been the writings of Kuhn. If in place of the community at large and its forms of thought and consciousness, one substitutes a scientific community and its forms of thought and action, and if one subtracts, or discounts some of the broad skeptical conclusions which Kuhn intimates and sometimes draws, one will find in *The Structure of Scientific Revolutions* a view of the development of scientific consciousness which, though clearly not in inspiration, is in its import strongly Hegelian. The notion of paradigms of scientific thought emphasized in that work is a specialized one, and the influence of these paradigms is treated in relation to only one special class of community, namely, scientific ones. But the basic teaching concerning the influence of paradigms upon the development of thought in such a community is Hegelian in its insistence upon the social determinants of what are the broad presuppositions of such a community concerning proper scientific procedure.

The further teaching concerning the necessity of intellectual revolutions for effecting changes in paradigms is, in its emphasis upon the abruptness of these changes, and the consequent discontinuities in the procession of procedures considered rational from time to time, more in agreement with the Marxian revision than with the original Hegelian doctrine. Those critics of Kuhn who have maintained that he greatly exaggerates the degrees of discontinuity and incommensurability among contending views in certain episodes of rapid scientific change were expressing a view more in agreement at this particular point with the general Hegelian conception of the course of social, intellectual, and religious development. Furthermore, in his emphasis upon the basically non-rational character of the processes by which great changes in scientific thought are effected, Kuhn diverges sharply from the historical rationalism of both Hegel and Marx. A doctrine to the effect that fundamental changes in the procedures of thought and action are effected basically by non-rational means is quite opposed to the doctrine of the historical dialectic. That is to say, a doctrine that the processes by which these fundamental changes are produced are in principle and hence necessarily deviant from those that a sober philosophy can assimilate as acceptable, reasonable, legitimating ones – such a doctrine is contrary to one according to which it is only by reference to the processes and results of actual change, historical and in individuals, that the character of acceptable, reasonable, legitimating procedures can be philosophically identified.

18 The emphasis here upon the social character of the norms of thought and action is not intended to imply any discount of other determinants of these, be they physical, biological, or psychological. That there are such determinants is undeniable. To what extent that they determine the norms that human beings collectively and individually develop remains a confused and controversial question. It is certainly the case that, to whatever extent Descartes or Kant was right in supposing that our norms of thought, for example, have a basis in our original nature, the story of their development from this basis is in good part one of the complex, integrative interaction of this nature with many external stimuli, suppressants, informing and molding influences. The doctrine that these norms are social does not imply,

then, in the term 'social,' that there are no limitations upon the effect of custom, that the power of nurture and culture is without limitation in the non-social, individual nature of men in its capacity to develop norms of any character whatever. Granted that there are and indeed must be such limitations, and granted that a priori theories of knowledge have generally greatly underestimated the extent of the possibilities of development left open by these limitations, it is with these possibilities that the present investigation is concerned.

19 In use, norms from time to time, for a variety of reasons, and in various degrees, falter and fail, providing stimuli and grounds for change. Bodies of norms enduringly – sometimes more and sometimes less – suffer from two contrasting deficiencies, namely, those of incompleteness and of inconsistency. At any given time there are in our repertory of norms serious lacunae. Occasions for decision, conviction, fixation of opinion and action arise for which there is no ready decision procedure. The question or issue falls through the interstices in the texture of the body of norms. Similarly, inconsistency appears at various places in the repertory where contrary procedures seem to apply, yielding indecision which can be resolved only if some revision of the body of norms can be effected so as to reduce the debilitating opposition. Further, as a result of the corporate character of these bodies, changes generated or coming to be generated in one set have impacts upon others, including sometimes responsive changes and sometimes defensive dispositions to resist change. Sets of norms have to be accommodated to each other. Stress, abrasion, and confusion generated among them provide motives for this accommodation, the kind of motive which Hegel referred to as the 'tremendous power [*ungeheure Macht*] of the negative.'[8] What may appear in its local environment as merely faltering, failure, or confusion in certain readily formalizable procedures, in a larger context may be revealed to play a most important positive role. The faltering, failing, and confusion may provide not only motivation for revision of these procedures, but also indications of the general location where revision is called for and the general direction the revision should take.[9]

20 A realistic view comprehending both deductive and ampliative processes must reflect prominently that there is no sharp line dividing these. Normally they occur together. Normally ampliative modification of norms occurs in conjuction with their employment in broadly

[8] *Phenomenology of Spirit* (A. V. Miller, trans., 1977), Preface, 38.

deductive ways, in consequence of results derived in this employment. Ampliative processes may be thought of as ones through which the broad organon of deductive practice alters itself. Yet, since an essential part of the process by which ampliative modifications are produced lies in the generation through them, under deductive exploitation, of certain results, it may likewise be said that deductive processes are ones through which ampliative modifications are produced. Thus the ampliative modifying, constructive effects produced by deductive activity upon deductive norms themselves must be recognized, and similarly the probative, conviction-bringing uses of processes that are generally primarily exploratory and constructive in design. Rather than quite independent kinds of process, these two contrasting ones are in actual thought and action closely intertwined in many complex as well as simple ways. They ordinarily represent two aspects of what we are doing, as we live, think, and act according to accepted practices, rather than two ways of altogether different doing. Though not altogether separable, these aspects are distinguishable, and it is of first importance philosophically to recognize the role that each plays in the determination of thought and action.

21 The processes by which norms are modified on a wide social and historical scale, processes extending far beyond and often embracing generations of those who employ these norms, are also replicated to

---

[9] Some of the perplexity in the debate that flourished briefly a short time ago on the question whether there is a logic of discovery was due to the fact that, on the affirmative side, there was an intuitive recognition that the activities in which new views in science and elsewhere are generated and formed abundantly exhibit responses to reasons or grounds so thorough, sensitive, and judicious that it is hard to see what more could be required in order for them to qualify as intelligent, knowing, or rational; yet, on the negative side, these activities cannot be made to fit into the mold which the term 'logic' suggests to many, namely, one constructed exclusively on the model of deductive processes. Of course there is no logic of discovery, if the term entails, for example, that the processes by which new theories are developed out of old ones in science must, in order to qualify as logical, be of this particular kind. The stifling and distorting effect here of a procrustean theory upon a genuine human practice repeats an effect that was realized in the philosophy of deductive processes themselves at the hands of John Stuart Mill. The empiricist theory of knowledge and semantics embedded in Mill's logical theory left him so incapable of accounting for the fact that the reasoning in a simple categorical syllogism could be valid and yet not circular, that he was forced to conclude that this time-honored and paradigmatic form of reasoning is in fact not reasoning at all. *A System of Logic* (eighth edition, 1887), Book II, Chapter III. For a modern try at the 'enigma' see M. Dummett's 'The Justification of Deduction' (1973), reprinted in *Truth and Other Enigmas* (1978).

some extent in miniature in the lives and activities of single individuals. There, *in fore interno*, individuals who are reflective may become intimately aware of the processes in which, out of the abrasion, conflict, and confusion of competing modes of activity – all of them settled features of one's character – modifications, adjustments, accommodations of these are effected, some of them enduringly successful and some much less so, and some of such magnitude as to amount to Gestalt-shifts in the characters in which they occur. A familiar example of such processes operating at an individual level is that by which in elementary mathematics we lead a student to recapitulate the evolution, accomplished by our ancestors with extreme travail, of the concept of number from that of whole numbers, to those supplemented by zero, then fractions, then roots, including the irrationals and the imaginary numbers, and so on. The term 'calculus,' derived from the Greek word for the pebbles used in reckoning with whole numbers, strikingly reminds us that it was by no means by operations that could be exemplified by the manipulation of pebbles that the enrichment of number theory in the above ways was achieved. Each of the large steps just referred to in the development of the theory was made in history and is recapitulated in the indoctrination of individuals by a procedure that entails some change in the basic concept of number itself and hence in basic premises employed in reasoning about numbers. At each stage in the historical development there were reasons both for and against these changes, though some obliviousness to the latter is a natural and normally serviceable consequence of custom to the deeply entrenched theory. Likewise in physics it was not by thinking restricted to employing mechanical models of the sort favoured and effectively used by Lord Kelvin that we have come or could have come to understand the partly particulate and partly undulatory behavior of what we discriminate as photons, protons, and electrons, in response to which, over time, there has been an alteration in the concept of a particle and in premises employing this term in reasoning in the sub-atomic domain. Similar examples of ampliative, reconstructive processes can be demonstrated at will in the learning processes by which pioneering scientists and their beneficiary students have achieved and do achieve knowledge of a variety of facets of the natural world. It is an especially prominent form of thought throughout science in that process, commonly called the 'development' of theory, in which a broad theory is altered by its use through the decades (think of the Darwinian theory of evolution by natural selection) in the discovery and explanation of, and adjustment to, a changing array of observational phenomena.

Closely similar processes are exemplified in various activities directed to the determination of the law in types of case in which significant indeterminancy at some point needs to be reduced. Examples would be the various processes of thought and action of individuals and other agencies through which a corporate body like that of a modern nation-state continually defines key provisions of its constitutional law, such as the provision of the United States Constitution that no state 'shall deny to any person within its jurisdiction the equal protection of the laws.' Does or does not this clause, as the courts of the United States have been called upon to determine during recent years, forbid racially discriminatory entrance qualifications at a medical college (University of California), tolerate similar qualifications for promotion among employees of a large industrial corporation (Kaiser Aluminum Corporation), and require racially determined assignment of pupils and teachers in the public schools of large cities like Boston, Chicago, and St Louis? Deductive elaboration of legal formulae is without question an important facet of the whole process of legal determination in such cases. But it is no more sufficient by itself in these than it is to determine whether birth control or abortion (even in cases of rape or incest) violates the Mosaic commandment 'Thou shalt not kill.' What can be soundly based on the key formula in these constitutional cases depends upon the significance of the formula in United States constitutional law. And this is itself something dependent upon, that reflects in its own character, complex social processes through which over time – sometimes slowly and sometimes rapidly, sometimes reflectively and sometimes with remarkably little conscious thought – the very conceptions of equal protection of the law, and of persons entitled to this protection, undergo revision.

22 As remarked earlier (§15) the processes whose general features have just been delineated are the deeper, more real ones underlying the apparent ones about ravens, swans, and similar objects of generalization which have received so much attention in Western philosophy since the time of Mill. During this time, indeed from the time of Hume's proclamation that custom (rather than reason) is the great guide of life, some important role has been assigned to these delineated processes in the actual conduct of life and thought. But though the processes have been recognized as having important effects, their manner of producing these effects has not been widely regarded as one needing to be

42

incorporated in reflective philosophical thought: this because the processes are not considered to be philosophically legitimating ones. However pervasive are the effects of the processes in the actual generation, criticism, refinements, reconstruction, maintenance, re-enforcement, and elimination of norms – in short, in the governance of them – these effects, when subjected to philosophical inspection, are taken as *mere* effects, *de facto* and not *de jure*, philosophically unauthenticated unless and until they can be reproduced by further 'justifying' processes which are themselves strictly probative and applicative, rather than generative and defining. Regularly, and indeed frequently in recent years, the discovery of the indispensability of ampliative process in the governance of norms in certain areas, the infeasibility in philosophical governing thought of replacing these processes altogether with deductive ones, has been taken to be a sign that at these points the limits of acceptable philosophical thought in the governance of norms have been reached, that the domains of life and thought affected have been revealed as to this extent inescapably determined by 'causes' rather than 'reasons,' permeated by influences that are not tractable in principle to acceptable philosophical procedure. And without question, a most important ground leading to this depreciating appraisal of these processes has been just their wide divergence in character from deductive ones, their relative intractability to the kinds of analysis that have achieved such great intellectual prestige through successful application to various widespread and fundamental forms of deductive activity.

Philosophers against whose vocation the tyranny of particular methods is a cardinal sin, have in this connection displayed an outstanding susceptibility to that very intellectual weakness, and to the narrowness in investigation which it promotes. Commenting upon this weakness in investigation in the philosophy of mathematics, I. Lakatos in 1963 drew a satirical analogy that can easily be applied more generally. Opposing the limitation of investigation in the philosophy of mathematics to what can be achieved by formal techniques carried on in mathematics, and objecting to the contention of A. Tarski that only those deductive systems which are strictly formalized are suitable as objects of scientific investigation, Lakatos wrote:

> Nobody will doubt that some problems about a mathematical
> theory can only be approached after it has been formalized, just as
> some problems about human beings (say concerning their anatomy)

can only be approached after their death. But few will infer from this that human beings are 'suitable for scientific investigation' only when they are 'presented in "dead" form,' and that biological investigations are confined in consequence to the discussion of dead human beings – although I should not be surprised if some enthusiastic pupil of Vesalius in those glorious days of early anatomy, when the powerful new method of dissection emerged, had identified biology with the analysis of dead bodies.[10]

23 So strong is the general deductivist predisposition in Western philosophy, particularly in its English and American branches, that little is accomplished by securing abstract, general assent on the part of those affected by it to the importance for philosophical thought of the understanding and cultivation of extra-deductive processes by which norms of thought and action are maintained and modified. Those who by teaching and long intellectual habit will countenance as acceptable only those philosophical processes having the general character of deduction (argument, ratiocination) naturally interpret their assent as indicating, not that the study of deductive forms must be supplemented by the study of forms that are essentially non-deductive, but that the non-deductive processes need to be legitimated by some kind of reconstruction that will transform them into exemplification of some yet to be recognized form of deduction. Deep preconceptions about method stand in the way of the comprehension and assimilation of ampliative processes in their own character. Thus, as the analogy of Lakatos suggests, a general abstract endorsement of the study of ampliative processes is quickly transformed into a study of processes that are not ampliative, but rather deductive surrogates of such: what they become when their essential testive and generative characters are replaced by probative and applicative ones.

The result of a commitment to the study of these processes by inapt means is repeatedly the abashed discovery that, judged by the criteria embodied in the means the ends of the study cannot be reached. The processes under study cannot be illuminated; sensitive appraisals of their efficacy cannot be made; a theory of these processes cannot be constructed that will serve as a helpful guide to activity exhibiting these processes. In preceding comments on Hume and Kuhn reference has

[10] 'Proofs and Refutations,' *British Jo. Phil. Sc.*, 14, (1963–4). Reprinted, Cambridge University Press (1976), p. 3, n. 3.

been made to general untoward results that attend a program of philosphical governance committed exclusively to deductive procedures. These comments need to be supplemented by more concrete examples of these results as they appear in the form of quandaries in programs of governance in science and similar areas of knowledge, as in Hume and Kuhn, also in law, in morals, and in politics. The primary lesson to be learned from these quandaries concerning the recognition of ampliative processes and adaptation to them in philosophical study will be more readily apparent, however, if first some attention is devoted to the philosophical roots and broad philosophical character of the widespread, enduring effort to assimilate ampliative processes to deductive ones.

2

The deductivist position

though what exactly was revealed in this way seemed
to him always open to doubt. Both these
philosophical positions exemplified the abstraction of
the applicative aspect of the employment of norms
from its ampliative complement and the neglect of the
latter aspect of the development of norms. Some
convergence of anti-replication, anti-deductivist
implications of Hume and Kuhn with ones in
Wittgenstein.

1 The name 'deductivism' has been chosen here to designate the view
that legitimate processes in the governance of norms are, in the sense
already defined (Intro., §§6–8), exclusively deductive and not
ampliative. It was pointed out both in the Introduction and in Chapter
1 that it is more accurate though stylistically less convenient to speak of
deductive and ampliative *phases* of governing processes, rather than of
different processes themselves.

The deductivist view, in singling out deductive processes and
separating them from their ampliative complements has produced a
distorted and impeding image of them. The chief distortion is in a
certain cast of the view, a certain deep way in which deductive processes
are looked upon that seems to be integral to taking them to be
completely separable from ampliative ones, to be capable of producing
governing results in a manner that is completely independent of
ampliative considerations.

The resultant deductivist view is related to deduction similarly to the
way in which scientistic philosophical views are related to science. To
its advocates, scientism, more commonly referred to as positivism,
seems to explicate, defend, generalize, and celebrate scientific methods,
the general scientific way of thinking. To its critics it may appear,
rather, to suffer from a one-sided and distorting emphasis upon one
aspect of scientific thinking, sometimes taken to be verifiability, or
falsifiability, experiment, or the utilization of mathematical methods.
The critics therefore wish to make clear that their objections are not to
science itself, but to a certain philosophical view of science and its
broad implications for life and thought that seriously misrepresent these
objects. Similarly it is important for a critic of deductivism to make
clear that his objections are not to deduction but to a certain
philosophical view about it. What is objected to in the view is both its
conception of deductive methods and the wide implications that this

misconception has for our understanding of how the governance of norms is carried out by philosophical reflection in such wide areas as metaphysics, philosophy of mind, theory of knowledge, logical theory, moral and legal philosophy, history, and elsewhere.

2 Central to the deductivist view is the model or metaphor of replication, so that a central component of the view may be called 'replication theory.' According to this theory what we are doing when we use norms in the guidance of thought and action is replicating them in the thought and action. Thought and action are informed by the norms, given character by the norms, just to the extent that we reproduce in thought or action the character that the norms display in their own specific mode or modes.

3 Three kinds of influence supporting this view are (1) metaphysical, (2) epistemological, and (3) logistic.

An important metaphysical source is the position toward fundamental, constitutional norms taken generally by Christian theism at the time that the early lines of modern philosophy were laid down. Fundamental norms, according to this position, are set for mankind by a higher authority. They are set *for* mankind, independently *of* mankind. They are not developed by human beings in thought and action dealing with the affairs of life. Or, more precisely, whether so developed or not, they do not derive their authority from this development. Their authority lies elsewhere.

So deeply embedded in Western mind is this relic of Christian theism that many who follow it in thought are oblivious of its influence. Modern philosophy, in the process of developing out of theology, retained this among other traits of its progenitor. After the model of divine commandment has waned, the commandment aspect remains and is given a new sanction, that of Reason, Experience, Nature, or even Instinct. Taken for granted is that criticizing, maintaining, controlling norms of thought and action require some kind of standards set for us, not by us, in the form of archetypes somehow, somewhere. In this respect we are not yet ready to walk alone, not ready to assimilate in philosophical thought, in the governance of broad and deep norms of thought and action the freedom that in other areas of life we never tire of extolling. Unthinkingly we shun this freedom in the philosophical governance of norms, not seeing that in our employment and scrutiny of very broad and deep norms of thought and action there must be provision for generation as well as conformity, for exploration and mutation as well as replication and conservation. Philosophical technicians playing our restricted roles in small corners of the intellectual establishment, we cannot see what the fierce genius of Nietzsche enabled him to see clearly a hundred years ago when he wrote,

> The greatest recent event – that 'God is dead,' – that the belief in the Christian god has become unbelievable – is already beginning to cast its first shadows over Europe.

And further,

> After Buddha was dead, his shadow was still shown for centuries in a cave – a tremendous, gruesome shadow. God is dead; but given the way of men, there may still be caves for thousands of years in which his shadow will be shown – And we – we still have to vanquish his shadow, too.[1]

4 The relations between these metaphysical roots of deductivism and other, epistemological ones are worth brief notice. Reliance upon strict application of certain master, archetypal norms in the authentication of the more common norms of thought and action – the treatment of the more common norms as unworthy of acceptance in rigorous philosophical reflection apart from their relation to the master norms – this is in important respects similar to certain doctrines about salvation and grace that were central to Christian theism in the early modern period, especially its Protestant branches. Matching the total depravity of all members of mankind, who can be redeemed by divine grace alone, is the total lack of authentication, apart from the supreme master norms, of accepted norms of thought and action, no matter how deeply entrenched in human life these norms may be and no matter how smoothly they perform as components of human life. Too striking to be altogether coincidental is the analogy between the global skepticism with respect to accepted norms of thought and action that in deductivist philosophy overwhelms the intellect in want of master governing norms, and the utter impotence to attain salvation that in these early theological views is the lot of any human soul deprived of the free gift of divine grace. Further, as in traditional Christian theology God's gifts to mankind includes reason, as an instrument to supplement revelation, so in this more secular analogue, deductive, applicative processes supplement the more general guidance provided by the master

[1] *The Gay Science* (2nd edn, 1897), Walter Kaufmann, trans., §§343, 108.

norms in the governance of accepted, detailed ones. These processes govern by applying the general norms concretely, and in that application determining what can and cannot be authenticated by their progressive detailed employment.

5 In recent philosophy the epistemological influences associated with the challenges of large-scale philosophical skepticism have been conspicuous. Widespread preoccupation with the task of meeting these challenges does much to explain similar widespread concentration upon forms of deductive process that are extreme in their intended abstraction from and presumed independence of ampliative ones. In the kind of situation in which those who accept these challenges conceive themselves, like Descartes in the *Meditations*, engaged in the project of overcoming their skeptical opponents in fair debate, what seems to be mandated is the employment of a kind of procedure that is exclusively probative and the interdiction of those that are ampliative, experimental and generative. Pure reason requires pure replication. For the task is altogether to convince, not discover; it is to use norms to produce conviction. To employ them otherwise, in an ampliative, testive, and generative way, to tolerate generative effects upon the probative means, would, as critics of such employment have repeatedly charged, entail reliance upon norms that already, in the admission of the skeptical challenges, have been foreclosed. In this way a concentration of epistemological effort upon skeptical challenges has tended to restrict the repertory of epistemological methods to ones that could plausibly be viewed as purely deductive; and the more these efforts have been stalled, the more intense the concentration has tended to become. In consequence much epistemological inquiry, rather than contributing to the understanding of ampliative, generative processes, and by that understanding to the reflective governance of them, has been diverted to the proving of skeptically challenged norms of principles: for example, to the effect that the profusion and course or sense-data are grounds for believing in the existence of material objects; that the behaviour of some of these objects is grounds for believing that there are other minds; that the future will be like the past; and so on.

It was over such epistemological tasks that the empiricists and rationalists contested from the time of Descartes and Locke. The program of governance in philosophical thought in the domains of science, religion, morals, and elsewhere became concentrated upon the project of somehow authenticating the first norms, the axioms of governance implicated in these apparent first epistemological steps.

This project proved to be an intellectual cuckoo's egg laid in the philosophical nest. Hatched, increasingly over the centuries it monopolized the intellectual energy that was available for philosophical purposes. The varieties and subtleties of the endeavors to resolve the difficulties posed by the program at this stage are a tribute to the ingenuity of the philosophical imagination, if not its achievement in illuminating the actual tasks of philosophical governance. The sources, character, frustrating career of this program were dealt with in detail by the present writer in the earlier *Induction and Justification*.

6 During the past century the increasingly influential logistic model of subsumption, of the employment of norms in the guidance of thought and action, has seemed to many to provide massive support for a replicative view of this guidance. The successful exploitation of this model for the development of deductive calculi encouraged some philosophical investigators to suppose that the model could serve adequately and exclusively as a paradigm for understanding governance in general and philosophical governance in particular. It encouraged them to suppose that in their efforts to understand this governance they could adequately conceive of norms themselves in abstraction from their contexts in life and action, as components of some isolated universe of discourse, some form of *universales ante res*. In consequence, understanding of what we are doing when we engage in philosophical criticism and advocate philosophically grounded modification of accepted norms (or practices) has suffered. Preoccupation with linguistic analogues of norms, and with syntactic analogues of their governance, has led to the abstraction in philosophical thought of these forms from their matrix in actual thought and action.

The general type of abstraction exemplified here by no means began with nor did it altogether depend upon this logistic influence. Rather, this influence colored, carried on, and reinforced a way of thinking that had earlier been advanced in psychic or more remote ontological terms. Whether the products of the abstraction are thought of in these terms, or the more familiar linguistic ones, is less important than the embracing presumption that for philosophical purposes the abstract objects that emerge from the process can be adequately understood as entities having a status so independent of the activities they inform that their role in governance can be exhaustively explored through these models.

The impetus given by logistic results to an already present inclination to restrict the philosophical study of governance to those forms that could be rationalized in a strictly replicative way is nevertheless noteworthy. Writing from a different point of view than that taken here, Hilary Putnam remarked upon the effect upon the philosophy of science of the revolution in logic that began approximately a hundred years ago with Frege's discovery of an algorithm for what is today standard second-order logic. This Putnam judged to be the most striking event in the generation of logical positivism. That the algorithm is complete for the elementary theory of deduction, sufficient for the proof of all the valid formulae of first-order logic, he wrote,

> inspired the hope that one might do the same for so called 'inductive logic – that the 'scientific method' might turn out to be an algorithm, and that these two algorithms – the algorithm for deductive logic (which, of course, turned out to be *incomplete* when extended to higher logic) and the algorithm-to-be-discovered for inductive logic – might exhaustively describe or 'rationally reconstruct' not just *scientific* rationality, but all rationality worthy of the name.

Though the expectation of these two complete and exhaustive algorithms has by now pretty well dissipated, the scientism of which this expectation was one expression remains, in Putnam's judgment, an obstacle in present-day philosophy. An excessive attachment to 'formalization,' to formal studies in logic, semantics and confirmation theory, though important, appear to him to be 'rather peripheral to philosophy' and to divert its practitioners from the task of 'giving a sane and human description of the scope of reason.'[2]

7 It needs to be emphasized that what is being criticized here is not abstraction in general, but abstraction in certain contexts and for certain purposes, where the goal of philosophical illumination requires consideration of aspects of procedures that the characteristic modes of abstraction purposely neglect. For example, from the time of Aristotle, and spectacularly in the past century, the great benefits of abstraction in the study of certain forms of logistic practice have been on display. The scientific exploration of these forms, and with it the formalization of vast domains of demonstrative and probable reasoning, have required and profited greatly from a mode of inquiry in which the abstraction has been rigorously maintained. But one side-effect of the concentration upon and successful extension of this mode of inquiry has been that

[2]*Reason, Truth and History* (1981), pp. 124–6.

52

certain philosophical questions concerning these forms have been deferred and, as a result of this deferral, cast in an unfortunate way.

The shift of attention from the body of forms of practice to more or less successful symbolic transcriptions of them was an indispensable step and remains a fruitful basis for the development of deductive calculi. It represented a division of labor that in its own way was comparable in productivity to the division of labor in modern manufacture. But division of labor does not entail separation in all respects and for all purposes. For some purposes the administration of the division requires the consideration of the larger operations to which the divided labor contributes: for example, in manufacture, the uses to which the products are put and the commercial conduits and transactions through which they find their ways to the consumer. Neglect of the wider considerations can lead to serious and sometimes economically fatal misunderstanding and mismanagement of the productive process. Similarly the conduct of philosophical criticism and philosophically grounded activity in the maintenance and reform of practices of thought and action may be and has often been seriously debilitated by a one-sided, almost exclusive concentration upon the symbolic replicas of practice that for good reasons in some circumstances are treated as surrogates of the practices themselves. Fixation upon these, and consequent neglect of other features of practices themselves, have led in the theory and practice of philosophical criticism to a variety of distorting effects. For one thing, the components of a calculus or other highly organized symbolic system have a kind of fixity both of individual character and of relation with each other that renders such a system a poor model for investigating certain questions about so loosely organized, untidy, and internally dynamic entity as a body of accepted practices. The components of such a symbolic system, by being organized in the way they are and having the kind of identity conferred upon them in this organization – in short, by being well designed for their primary purpose – are not well designed to represent the kind of modification that forms of activity undergo naturally in use. In particular, as models, they do not illuminate, but rather obscure, both the important *direct*, local effect in the control of the character of individual and closely related groups of practices that activity informed by these practices may have, and also the *indirect* effect that modifications produced in this way may have upon more remote components of the total body. Likewise such a model does not represent well the great variety in degrees of inertia and mobility that is one of the striking features of the components of a body of procedures. An effect of viewing systems of practice solely through the lenses of systems of linguistic and other symbolic entities is a strong reinforcement of a tendency among philosophical observers, springing from a variety of sources, to conceive of these as bound together in a highly totalitarian organization. And when, while viewing these systems in this fashion, one wishes to take account of the effect of practice in the determination of their character, one will naturally be led to conceive this effect in a similarly totalitarian manner.

The consequences of overemphasis upon the effects of use in producing *global* changes, and of neglect of the local but less dramatic ones, are pronounced in recent philosophy. Global modifications – changes of 'logical frameworks,' of whole 'conceptual schemes' or systems of categories, of 'scientific paradigms,' of whole systems of practice – viewed as single steps, or as massive alternatives confronting human choice, are, in an extreme way, whether in individuals or in groups, resistant to direct reflective, deliberate determination. Concentration upon these global modifications, and neglect of those of a more modest kind, has helped to *segregate* generally the processes by which procedures are determined by use, and to ascribe to them all generally, as thus segregated, the kind of unsusceptibility to reflective scrutiny and control that would be ascribable only if that scrutiny and control were attempted always and necessarily on some extremely massive scale, only if the processes were those effecting in single, giant, revolutionary steps the displacement of whole systematic codes of procedure.[3]

8 Replication theory, reflecting these important influences among

---

[3] Such was the effect of three influential recent writers whose exploration of the pragmatic aspects of knowledge came in connection with interest in and exploration of large-scale, abstract symbolic systems. C. I. Lewis, *Mind and the World Order* (1929); Rudolf Carnap, 'Empiricism, Semantics, and Ontology,' *Rev. Int. de Philosophie*, 4th year (1950), pp. 20–40; *The Continuum of Inductive Methods* (1952); 'Replies and Systematic Expositions,' in Paul A. Schilpp, ed., *The Philosophy of Rudolf Carnap* (1963), pp. 859–1013; W. V. Quine, *Word and Object* (1960), *Ontological Relativism* (1969).

In the book referred to in the preceding note Putnam agrees with these writers to the extent of accepting as a kind of global task the articulation and justification of a single grand conception of scientific rationality. Not unexpectedly, the kind of justification he finds it possible to offer for such a large-scale codification is similarly sweeping. It is that the kind of representation system that is incorporated in science is 'part of our idea of total human flourishing, of Eudaemonia' (p. 134).

others, has surely been a major source of the fixation of philosophers upon deductive, probative processes, the exclusive recognition of them by many as the kind of process that can be employed with good intellectual conscience in the philosophical criticism, defense, and revision of norms. Among the uses of that protean and usually honorific term 'rational' is a philosophical one in which, like the term 'good' in general use, it functions to express approval: in this case to signify that a certain procedure or process used in reaching or supporting some philosophical result is a legitimate or proper one. Following this usage, deductivism may be expressed as a thesis concerning the kind of processes that may be employed in the rational governance of the kind of norms or practices with which philosophers are particularly concerned.

9 Implicit in the deductivist view of what it is like to employ norms or rules of thought and action is a certain notion of what norms or rules themselves are like. It is that whatever else they are, they are entities of a sort that are grasped by us by becoming components of our minds, bodies, brains, nervous systems, or some similar loci of patterns of procedure. There they serve as models or templates of thought and action. To follow a norm in thought and action is thus to replicate such a template in these modes.

This notion of action, overt or in thought, following a norm excludes on principle whatever effects such action may entail in the norms themselves. What is action according to a norm is fixed exclusively by the norm in *statu quo ante*. The norm, so conceived, is the exclusive formal cause of the action in so far as the action is an instantiation of the norm. For various reasons individual examples of action may vary, but to the extent that they are actions in accordance with the norm they are invariate.

10 Without question this is one aspect of the use of norms. The deductivist view fixes attention exclusively upon this aspect and neglects the aspect in which the norms guiding action are themselves affected.

The replicative aspect of the employment of norms of thought and action is prominent in one variety of this employment, namely, the routine, as contrasted with the problematic. Deductivism as a view is concentrated on this variety, so that what emerges is a conception of a purely deductive, purely applicative and replicative use of norms.

11 Such a view has exerted a very great attraction in modern Western philosophy, in both its empiricist and rationalist versions. It

has seemed to offer a conception of the use of norms that could fit and illuminate their use in philosophical thought, including that phase of thought that performs a critical, governing function with respect to norms. The view sought to explicate this function by means of an extremely refined and strict version of the model of replication.

In consequence governance was taken to be exclusively a recursive process. The sound development of norms was one that could fit the general Cartesian model of philosophical reconstruction: the kind of process in which each stage developed from preceding ones derives its legitimacy from its character as a result of the strict replication of these. Sound governance was deductive governance. And since consequent norms were shown to be legitimate by being exhibited as the results of the replicative use of antecedent ones, the kind of development of norms that could be made in and accredited by philosophical thought was strictly incremental, not transformative.

12 A not inconsiderable portion of the attraction of this view of governance derived from the fact that the procedure represented seemed to be a kind that, as in its original Cartesian ancestor, could be engaged in by individual minds isolated from the influence of custom and tradition. The cultural roots of this extremely individualistic, asocial and atraditional emphasis are very broad and deep. One source, already touched upon, is the challenge of philosophical skepticism; another is the increasing emphasis, in the influential Protestant version of Christianity, upon the validating power of the individual mind, soul, or person as an entity capable of receiving divine salving grace independently of accepted religious, political, or scientific authorities. Thus Peirce identified three of the four planks of the 'spirit of Cartesianism – that which principally distinguishes ... modern philosophy from the scholasticism which it displaced' as (1) the teaching 'that philosophy must begin with universal doubt,' (2) the teaching 'that the ultimate test of certainty is to be found in the individual consciousness,' and (3) a reliance upon 'a single thread of inference depending often upon inconspicuous premises.'[4]

Thus one may describe the deductivist program for the governance of norms as a 'discover and apply' program, 'apply' being construed in a strictly replicative way.

13 In a variety of ways the general infeasibility of this program has been displayed in philosophical reflection over the years. This reading

[4]'Some Consequences of Four Incapacities' (1868), Collected Papers, 5.264–5.

of the skeptical conclusions of Hume and Kuhn was given in Chapter 1. In Hume the infeasibility of the program surfaced early, in his discussion of all reasonings concerning matters of fact, their 'foundation' on the relation of cause and effect, and the eventual conclusion that no putative conclusions from experience can be arrived at by reasoning alone. It is clear in the *Enquiry*, in which the discussion proceeds in the above terminology, that what Hume is searching for as a 'foundation of all conclusions from experience' are what might be called 'basic norms' of thought about material matters, such as that bread nourishes, and fire heats. It is clear that he is conceiving of knowledge of 'matter of fact beyond what is immediately present to the memory and senses' as being developed by the application of such norms, yielding such conclusions as 'nourishes' and 'heats' from the premises 'bread' and 'fire'. And what he is finding is that it is impossible to make the first steps in fleshing out this conception, for if all 'inferences' beyond the evidence of our senses require the application of some such 'material leading principles' (Peirce's term), the accounting of knowledge in accordance with this conception is going to require (Achilles-like) the completion of an inexhaustible sequence of inferences. Hence the conclusion that all such inferences are the effects of some ultimate principle in us that may be called 'custom' or 'habit,' or, transferred into the objective mode of speech, that the future will be like the past or, more generally (*Treatise*) 'that the course of nature continues always uniformly the same.' But such a principle can itself not be derived from any available evidence in experience; conclusions of such inferences can in no case be reached solely by 'reasoning,' 'argument,' or 'logic' (all Hume's terms); hence the general infeasibility of this form of the governance project.[5]

14 The infeasibility of the deductivist program of applying available norms to the evidence of experience appears in Kuhn most prominently in his emphasis upon the incapacity of the applicative use of such norms to account for certain striking 'revolutionary' episodes in the development of modern science. The vocabulary of that writer is different from that employed here in discussing governance, but the conclusion drawn that there is a radical difference between the ways in which the grand paradigms of thought and action are employed by scientific communities in normal, quiescent periods and the way they

---

[5] *Enquiry*, Section IV, Part II; Section V. *Treatise*, Book I, Part III; Sections VI, XIV–XV; Part IV, Section I.

are employed, contested, modified, or replaced in periods of rapid, fundamental change – this conclusion does bear upon the feasibility of the deductivist program. This clearly was a major reason why the philosophical community found Kuhn's persuasive presentation of his results so disturbing. Revolutionary science, as Kuhn presented it, is science as it is carried on and developed in periods in which fundamental norms of thought and action undergo change, in which the hitherto secure routine application of these norms in 'puzzle-solving' operations gives way to indecision about the norms themselves. The understanding of such periods, Kuhn indicated in the very first pages of his monograph, cannot be achieved on a model that treats scientific development universally as 'piecemeal' or 'incremental,' as 'development by accumulation.' At least in these periods, one could conclude, philosophical reflection on the path of scientific development was mistaken to the extent that it conceived the logic of this development exclusively on the model of recursive procedures.[6]

15 A deductivist view of the philosophical governing process is a component of the broad foundationist view that has been much discussed in recent theory of knowledge. Foundationism conceives reflective governance as fundamentally an ancestral or, to shift the metaphor radically, a construction procedure. Deductivism prescribes the character of the permissible construction procedure (deducing). Foundationism further prescribes that, inasmuch as the construction is conceived as deductive, legitimate governance requires the availability of given, unconstructed, and hence fixed, certain, incorrigible foundations (premises). This general deductivist-foundationist view, in its application to the philosophy of knowledge, was referred to in *Induction and Justification*, with some unavoidable unfairness to some components of Descartes's own philosophy, as 'Cartesian theory,' or equivalently, 'justification theory.' The use of the term 'justification theory' in this way represented a judgment at the time of writing that book that the Cartesian view of governance had become so dominant in modern philosophy that although there are surely, in some senses of this word, aspects or phases of 'justification' in the critical processes encompassed in the philosophy of knowledge, it was extremely difficult, if not impossible, to continue to use the word to refer to these aspects of phases without conveying some of the deductivist, foundationist presuppositions with which this term had become saturated.

[6] *Structure*, pp. 1–2, 91–109.

Some easing of the grip of foundationist preconceptions seems to have occurred in the intervening years, enabling one sometimes, speaking circumspectly, to refer to the justificatory aspects of governance without, by an unfortunate choice of words, entangling oneself in the complex of foundationist, and hence Gordian knots. In this present book, when the advantage in expression seems to outweigh the risk, the chance will be taken with this wayward philosophical term. Otherwise, when 'justification' is employed, coupled with 'theory,' the compound term will be used to refer, as before, with some slight difference of emphasis, to the general view of governance that in modern philosophy traces mainly back to Descartes, to a theory that places exclusive trust, as means of legitimate philosophical governance, in components of the kind just specified.

16 The interpretation of foundationism as a form of deductivism involves no disregard of those forms of this philosophical view in which the requirement of certainty in the constructive steps is loosened to permit steps of probability only. For the term 'deduction,' as it is used here, is by no means restricted to processes aimed at elaborating strictly necessary consequences of given rules, propositions, statements, and so on. In the preceding chapter (§14), in drawing the distinction between deductive and ampliative processes, and in characterizing deductive processes as ones directed to proof, 'proof' itself was construed as having the sense, not of entailing certainty, but of soliciting assent through the application of well-defined accepted rules, norms, procedures. Governing processes vary greatly in the degree in which they are deductive rather than ampliative, or ampliative rather than deductive. They are deductive to the extent that they are directed to achieving results through the application of agreed upon norms, rather than through any substantial extension, revision, generation, or reconstruction of norms themselves. Some precedent for a broadened use of the term 'deduction,' though not exactly the usage followed here, is available in a variety of philosophical thinkers and logical practitioners whose usages range from Peirce's 'probable deduction' to the even broader deductions with which Sherlock Holmes regularly amazed Dr Watson.

17 Understanding philosophical governance as it more fully is, rather than the truncated form of it that is identified as such in the deductivist view, requires that, circumventing as far as possible the distinctive presuppositions of this view, one achieve a fresh look at the object itself. It entails understanding primarily and in the first instance

the reflective activities that scholars, scientists, lawyers, politicians, religious leaders – professional and practical workers of all kinds – engage in that may be rightly said to have a governing effect. It means understanding also certain broader processes, not primarily of a philosophically reflective character, that are relevant to and need to be taken account of in understanding the philosophical and reflective processes. And it means finally, in accordance with the defining character of philosophical concern, giving special attention to these activities or processes as they exhibit themselves in their engagement with norms or practices of a very broad and deep kind.

18 Philosophical governance of norms embraces processes of critical appraisal that are by no means stimulated exclusively by or limited to questions about possible *change* of the norms appraised. The motive and result of critical appraisal may be the confirmation, the endorsement of some presently accepted norm, or norms, rather than a judgment for change. It is however helpful sometimes on simplifying and sharpening certain issues about governance, to concentrate upon those cases in which the major concern in the appraisal is with change. The concentration is helpful in examining one aspect of the philosophical issues posed by a deductivist view of governance, namely, that of the source and character of the grounds upon which, in general, critical judgment can be supported. Accordingly in the few remaining pages of this chapter grounds of change, rather than of both stasis and change, will be the focus of attention. The presumption is that what is said with reference to this one type of governing situation can easily be applied, with suitable accommodations, to questions of governing judgment in general.

19 What is the authority upon which under philosophical examination some broad and deep accepted norm, or body of norms, can be judged to be needing modification or replacement? More pointedly, what is the authority, when changes in the form of new or revised norms cannot be derived by deductive procedures, that is, by procedures in thought and action conforming to already accepted norms? The body of resource constituted by accepted norms is a very large and rich one, embracing as it does norms of logical, mathematical, scientific, technical, scholarly and practical procedure of many various kinds. Much at any given time may be achieved in the way of governance of norms by means of procedures that do not depart in any significant way from accepted modes of thinking and acting. In this

broad sense of 'deductive' the capacities of deductive governance are great. Yet again and again we transcend these by introducing into the broad canon of accepted norms components that, if challenged at their entry, cannot be validated exclusively by thought or action conforming to the already accepted norms, components that may in very significant ways constitute not merely additions to accepted procedures but contraventions of them.

20 Deductivist theory is committed to deny the possibility in proper philosophical governance of such anomalous phenomena. To be sure, at any time norms may emerge in governance that cannot be developed applicatively from others accepted at that time. But the resources of governance are not restricted to these. There are accessible to us basic templates of thought and action, norms of a sort that extend beyond these and which when attended and incorporated in our supply of accepted norms provide us with intellectual resources for the development of hitherto underivable ones. Here one is reminded of Descartes's warning to 'the learned' about the richness of the supply of truths accessible through intuition and deduction, namely, 'that there are many more such truths than they think.'

The rationalist and empiricist advocates of deductive governance of course emphasized different aspects of the supposed sources of norms accessible for this purpose. The norms had to be such that, though themselves not derivable deductively from already accepted ones and therefore requiring an altogether different authority, could nevertheless be applied to generate, modify, and even extrude others. The rationalists put wider and deeper trust in the norms embedded in our human nature and reflecting in this way the benevolence of our Creator toward our pursuit of truth. Hume identified the source principally with the course of nature as revealed in experience. But lacking Descartes's trust that our Creator would supply us with, in Locke's words, 'that portion and degree of knowledge ... suited to our station and concerns,' he developed irrepressible misgivings about lapses in the experienced uniformity.

What is far more important here than the details of these two deductivist philosophies is the way in which in each the deductivist view of the governance of cognitive norms led to the placing of the basis for trust in norms already accepted or in candidates for acceptance altogether outside their capacities to perform both in direct practice and in their relations with others in the guidance of thought and action. The treatment of the sources of new, anomalous components in the body of norms illustrates in its own way a key feature of the deductivist, applicative view of acceptability of norms, namely, its denial of the capacity of norms of any sort by their own performance to earn or maintain philosophical acceptability. With the sources of the acceptability of norms rigorously excluded from norms themselves in the performance of their functions, what more plausible candidates remained than the course of nature presented to us in experience or intellectual proclivities implanted within us?

21 It is thus not by accident, inadvertence, or oversight that those devoted to the deductivist program of governance neglected ampliative effects of the employment of norms. The exclusive preoccupation with the replicative aspects of the employment of them, the endeavor to treat these aspects in philosophical governance in abstraction from the ampliative ones was motivated by the replicative view of the function of norms that lay at the heart of the program, a replicative view that extended both to the authority of the results of the employment of norms and to the authority of the norms themselves. The result was an attitude toward philosophical governance that in other domains would be termed formalist or legalistic, but that in the ambience of uncertainty that surrounds much philosophical investigation was often prized for its intellectual rigor. But the central idea of replication that the theory sought to exploit in accounting for the authority of both its basic norms and others expected to be developed out of them, was exposed over the centuries as deficient in most serious ways. Of these philosophical reverses the ones emphasized here were by no means alone, though they were among the most influential. After Hume's conjuration of the demon of non-uniformity interposed between those 'instances, of which we have had experience' and those of which we have not, any trust that norms of a scientific character could be authorized in some simple, direct deliverances of experience had to be judged naive. Kuhn's elaboration of the indeterminacy of scientific observation when detached from an accompanying body of interpreting theory masterfully reinforced a point that had been much more laboriously taught by Kant and Hegel. The same point had to be learned, and in view of the powerful influence of Frege remains largely to be learned again concerning the derivation of norms from the inspection of the internal relations of our ideas. The historical trial of the claims of independent sense and thought to present us directly with archetypes which we need only reproduce to develop needed norms of thought and action was recently re-enacted in shortened form in the rise

and subsidence of logical positivism, and indeed in the life of one philosopher, namely, Wittgenstein. After having formulated in the *Tractatus* a constitution for logical positivism, in his later philosophy he advanced profound considerations against the claims of those two classical resources, sensory and rational intuition, to constitute sources for the governance of norms by providing us, in a way that was itself quite independent of such norms, with discernible replicas of such entities. His criticism of putative sense is illustrated in his discussion of a private language and of 'seeing as' in the *Philosophical Investigations*; his criticism of independent a priori thought, rational intuition, in his discussions of logical necessity in the same book and in the *Remarks on the Foundations of Mathematics*.

3
Consequences of Deductivism

Topical Outline

This blindness of theory dispelled by 'the first and most trivial event in life.' Hume's appeal to custom as guide. The independence of 'reason' (in relation to custom) purchased at the price of irrevelance to the affairs for which it was originally appealed to.

What skepticism discovered was not the incompetence of reflective processes to effect philosophical governance of norms, but the incapacity of foundation theory, and thus the incapacity of foundational deductive processes alone as instruments of reflection.

1 *Agnosticism in science.* The effects of the work of Hume and Kuhn already referred to are but two widely separated examples of the skeptical effect that has generally followed the philosophical segregation of deductive and ampliative processes and the consequent

neglect of the latter. In examining the processes by which knowledge may be developed both these writers emphasize the exclusive rationality of deductive, probative processes, and both report the severe limitations upon scientific knowledge to which such reservation leads. Looking at conclusions drawn from 'foundations' in 'the present testimony of our senses, or the records of our memory,' Hume challenges the reader to produce the processes – the 'reasoning,' 'the argument,' the 'logic' – by which they may be *inferred* from these foundations.[1] What is acceptable is that for which some 'proof' can be given.

Corresponding to Hume's thesis of the joint incapacity of reasoning and the testimony of our senses to deliver what we commonly accept as 'conclusions from experience' is Kuhn's thesis of the joint incapacity of basically these same resources to deliver kinds of important results that characterize periods of radical scientific change.[2] With 'logic and experiment' construed in the manner of the dominant mid-twentieth-century positivist philosophy of science, what the argument about normal and revolutionary science discloses is an incapacity in this philosophy, a philosophy dedicated exclusively to forms of inquiry operating according to antecedently agreed upon norms, which is to say, deductively. On principle such a philosophy excludes from its resources of rationalization all the many and various unruly processes by which the forms of thought and action, including broad categories of thought and paradigmatic scientific procedures, are themselves molded and modified through time, by individuals and groups, and under great variations of degrees of reflective consciousness.

When, in setting out to appraise the claims to acceptance of a pattern of scientific procedure, one excludes all these processes from consideration and seeks a form of rationalization that operates altogether independently of them, one has surely set for oneself another trap. From the confines of this trap one will eventually be obliged to report, like Hume, that rationalization is impossible, that 'custom' or some other component conceived as radically different from 'reason,' is the great guide of life. The more one succeeds in extruding ampliative processes from reason and experience, the more restricted is the capacity of these resources for the performance of broad philosophical governance. In relation to them linguistic practices will be, in principle, 'underdetermined,' and fundamental indeterminacy of 'logical

---

[1] *Enquiry*, Section IV, Part II.
[2] *Structure*, Ch. IV.

frameworks' and 'conceptual schemes' irreducible. More insidiously, within logical frameworks and conceptual schemes themselves, the links of logical necessity will be loosened in a disturbing way. Though we may have thought that it is by freeing logical forms from dependence upon broad social practices that pure, absolutely binding logical necessity in them may be discerned, we have now strong reasons, uncovered by Wittgenstein, to suppose that utter separation from these practices ensures not a strengthening and clarification of this necessity, but its dissipation.

Many years ago, in their general program of bringing Hegel to the masses, Marx and Engels called upon their readers to recognize the great extent to which our ideas are molded by the complex social processes through which our lives are lived. Although their own elaboration of this point was distorted by various influences, among them a reaction against some features of the original Hegelian philosophy, the central point remains a sound one. And one who has absorbed it will be aided greatly in understanding some of the philosophical quandaries concerning the irreducible indeterminacy of conceptual frameworks, conceptual schemes, linguistic systems, and cognitive paradigms that have proved so vexatious to many in contemporary philosophy of science and in the philosophy of knowledge generally. At the heart of these quandaries careful inspection reveals again an abstraction of intellectual forms from their roots in human life, and a correlated propensity to raise questions about the possible governance of modifications of these forms in isolation from, in a studied lack of consideration of, the ways in which they are actually generated in human practice and modified in use.

2 *Legal realism*. The largely unintended effects of agnostic philosophy in paving the way for fideism in religion, ethics, and metaphysics have been pointed out by various writers. Richard H. Popkin, for example, persuasively described the generation of this effect in the philosophy of religion by Hume's criticism of the competence of philosophical governance in science, morals, and metaphysics. Processes of governance that conform strictly to philosophically defensible principles of the 'understanding' or 'reason,' Hume contended, are by that very conformity rendered incompetent to perform their governing task in all these fields. Such a contention was welcomed by many interested in defending the role of faith in religious life, for the relief it seemed to offer from the commonly and often invidiously made distinction

66

between matters of faith and matters of knowledge.[3] It could not be regarded as a defect in some article of religious belief, they reasoned, if under challenge it could not be defended by philosopically acceptable means, since Hume had apparently demonstrated that the same incapacity lay concealed in every item, without exception, of what we ordinarily take to be knowledge.

There are many areas of life and thought in which agnosticism of this sort, levelling in one deflationary sweep whatever does not fit the deduction paradigm, has little practical effect. It is otherwise in some areas in which at some points the governance of norms of thought and action is itself pre-eminently philosophical. Thus philosophical doctrines that on principle exclude from the study of governing processes those by which ideas and procedures implementing these ideas are modified in practice have seriously affected both the study of juridical interpretation and the juridical decisions in which these interpretations are applied. Years ago, in the opening pages of his *Introduction to Legal Reasoning*, E. H. Levi briefly struggled with the quandary of how the processes of legal interpretation to which his monograph was directed and which deviate so markedly from deductive models, could be legitimately given the title of 'reasoning.' Putting aside 'the pretense . . . that the law is a system of known rules applied by a judge,' Levi argued that in legal interpretation the rules are not so much known and then applied, as coming to be known *as* they are applied. A most important kind of legal interpretation is one in which the rule that is interpreted is forged and hence modified in the interpretation, in which the classification system employed in the rule undergoes change as the interpretation proceeds. The prominence of this aspect of some forms of legal interpretation suggested the question whether they qualify as reasoning at all. A negative answer to this suggestion Levi reflectively rejected. 'Reasoning appears to be involved,' he wrote. 'The conclusion is arrived at through a process and was not immediately apparent. It seems better to say there is reasoning, but it is imperfect.'[4]

The major question is not whether 'there is reasoning' of some sort, somewhere in the juridical process in which laws are interpreted and applied to particular and sometimes very puzzling cases. Much more sharply defined than this, it is a question about the philosophical status of that phase of the juridical process in which conclusions are arrived at

[3] 'Hume and Kierkegaard,' *Journal of Religion*, vol. XXXI (1951), pp. 274–81.
[4] 1948, pp. 1–4, 8.

by a process of reflection that does not conform, and cannot plausibly be made to conform, to the deductive model of reasoning. Cases abound in which, in order to make a definite determination whether some putative instance does or does not fall under the rule, the rule has to be further defined in such a way as to undergo definite modification. The rule requiring that states provide equal protection to all persons in their jurisdictions is so defined as to forbid deeply entrenched racially segregating pupil-to-school assigning practices by public school authorities in the states. The rule forbidding Congress to make any laws respecting the establishment of religion is construed so as to exclude various non-denominational religious practices, such as officially permitted prayers, in the same schools. Capital punishment, legitimately practiced for nearly two centuries, is found almost unreservedly to be in conflict with an equally old constitutional provision against cruel and unusual punishment.

Of course, if the prescription of equal protection is taken in a certain way, if equality is measured in such a way that the 'separate' of segregation entails 'inequality,' then a valid deductive conclusion will be that the segregation in question violates the prescription. But this interpretation of equality could be and was contested on constitutional grounds just as it could be and was advocated on such grounds. The situation in constitutional law in the United States at mid-century was that either decision on the separate-entails-unequal issue would itself entail some alteration in the law, if for no other reason, because the law was seriously equivocal and contradictory on the matter. Reduction of the indeterminacy and contradiction in what may be called the law of equality embodied in the Fourteenth Amendment of the Constitution required a thorough consideration of the significance of the key provisions of this Amendment in American law, the function that these provisions had come to perform in the law of the country, and the grounds for this in American life, in morals and politics as well as in strictly legal practice. It is in the light of such considerations that the equal-protection clause had to be interpreted, and in the process of interpretation, defined, modified, adjusted to and correlated with facets of life with which this law of equality was integrally related.

As reflective activity of this kind, effecting modification and adjustment, does not fit the model of deduction, those exclusively preoccupied with this model do not find it acceptable. When deviations from the deductive model are seen to be deviations from the path of reason, reasoning, reasoned interpretation, and yet such deviations, in the form of responses to moral, political, and economic considerations, are seen to be inevitable, then the main components are available for a view that legal interpretation in such controverted cases is a process that necessarily and fundamentally contravenes philosophically acceptable procedures. Such a view of necessary direct action on the part of judges in their function of defining the law was widely propounded under the name of 'legal realism' in the fourth decade of this century and has remained an important strand of American jurisprudence to this day.

As the effect of deductivism in Hume was to erase the line between science and faith in matters of fact, so the effect in legal realism was to erase the line between legitimate and illegitimate practice in all those cases of juridical judgment in which the definition of the law was made on political, moral, economic and other wide social grounds. If any interpretation that is determined in any substantial degree by political or moral considerations *of any sort* has thereby forfeited its claims to be a reasoned interpretation, then scruples about such considerations may be forgotten. If the distinction between a wise, informed response to moral considerations, and the blindest subservience to personal, partisan, or class moral imperatives is thought to be dissolved on the basis of profound philsophical theory, dissolved also is the obligation and motivation in juridical practice to keep arduously to the former and resist the often great seduction of the latter. The record through the years of all too many juridical decisions traceable to political, economic, racial, and religious prejudice counsels caution in the acceptance of a philosophical view which has among others this effect upon its adherents: that the barriers against juridical prejudice, often enough difficult to discern, are rendered quite invisible.

3 In a recent comment upon the jurisprudence of W. O. Douglas, Ronald Dworkin dealt in a somewhat different way from that followed here with the narrow view of reason employed by the adherents of legal realism in deprecating the rational pretensions of juridical decisions.[5] A decision guided by reason, as the realists used this term, was, as Dworkin puts it, one 'logically compelled by prior legal doctrine whose content all reasonable men must recognize on pain of contradiction and which was, in that sense, there for reason to discover.' Quite rightly the realists insisted that 'few, if any, important judicial decisions could be

[5]'Dissent on Douglas,' *New York Review of Books*, 19 February 1981, pp. 3–8.

said to be entirely guided by reason in that sense.' Rather, important juridical decisions such as those in which the Supreme Court moves to interpret the broad and abstract provisions of the Bill of Rights, require for their justification appeals 'to some consideration of justice or fairness or policy which . . . [is] not a matter of logic and with which all competent lawyers would not in fact agree.' With 'based on reason' given so narrow a construal as to exclude such appeals, the legal realists, in the manner of Hume, assigned these appeals to categories that this exclusion seemed to require, namely, 'emotion' and 'inclination.' Even at the hands of so masterful a philosopher as Hume, dichotomies like this, between reason and emotion (Hume's term was 'the passions') turned out to be seriously misleading and, in the end, mischief-making. All the processes that in the preceding chapter were marked off and embraced under the title of 'ampliative' now appear under the curious banner of 'emotive.' 'Most rules of law,' Dworkin continues, 'are to some degree indeterminate in their application, and often require "interpretation" that . . . according to this inapt terminology depends upon emotion.' Incautious use of such terminology, with which it was most difficult to preserve caution, easily led to such disastrous results as the suggestion

> that no important distinctions needed to be drawn within the large class of reasons that judges might have for a judicial decision that clearly went beyond binding legal precedents. There was no important difference, for example, between the argument that a decision was right because it was required by some general theory about fundamental political rights that could be defended both in the abstract and as tested against hypothetical counterexamples, and the cruder argument that the decision was right because it seemed appealing to the community as a whole or to the judge in particular. The choice of such arguments was an 'emotional' one and not much more needed to be said.
>
> That refusal to countenance obvious distinctions suggested, in turn, a particularly deadening form of moral skepticism – dark, unexamined, but carried in the vocabulary of legal realism as that apparently enlightened philosophy spread through American law schools. It was, I am afraid, left behind there, in the walls, even when later generations of law teachers and students finally and decisively rejected the less dangerous because more patently absurd idea that law is a matter of what the judge had for breakfast.

The effects of such doctrine upon the jurisprudence embodied in the opinions of Justice Douglas were in Dworkin's judgment serious and debilitating. During his career on the Supreme Court Douglas came, as Dworkin portrays him, to believe with some intensity and act upon 'the idea of moral rights distinct from and often opposed to the will of the majority.' This commitment to moral rights presupposed that a certain degree of objectivity is attainable in moral and legal judgment that is incompatible with the view, central to legal realism, that such commitments in legal matters on the part of any judge have 'no more independent validity than his tastes in food and drink.' Maintaining a commitment to moral rights that could not be squared with his 'realist' philosophy, Douglas was rendered by the lingering effects of this philosophy incapable of providing a clear and coherent defense of the commitment in his legal opinions. Lacking a clear and coherent philosophical basis for the decisions that he was obliged by his office to make, he was reduced to the process 'of deciding first and finding reasons later, a process that exchanged philosophical skepticism for philosophical cynicism. He ... began to write opinions that he knew would be described by the profession as careless, hasty, and contemptuous of the whole process of legal reasoning.'

In a brief published comment upon this article, Warren Lehman of the University of Wisconsin Law School echoed and confirmed Dworkin's fears of the skepticism and cynicism about the juridical process that a philosophy of this kind generates. 'It would be hard, I suspect,' wrote Lehman, 'to get through an American law school today without getting the impression that the law is merely an excuse for policy. The law is how policy is mystified. That kind of cynicism is ... only the latest of the bad consequences of realism.'[6]

4 During its flourishing years of the late 1940s and 1950s this realism was accompanied by a view in moral philosophy that drew analogous skeptical conclusions about moral judgment. As with legal realism, the popular 'emotivism' of this period seemed to gain considerable illicit plausibility from an indiscriminate use of the category of *emotion* to cover whatever forms of judgment could not be assimilated to a narrow paradigm of what rational or 'cognitive' judgments must be. And, as with legal realism, a great part of this plausibility seemed to ebb when it became obvious to its twentieth-century advocates that the conflation of such extremely diverse elements

[6]*Ibid.*, 28 May 1981, p. 52.

under the title of 'emotion' would have to be supplemented with a recognition of the highly diverse character of the elements that were being referred to under the common title. Furthermore, when one had begun to make these discriminations one was more receptive to the question of how valuable the initial conflation was proving to be. By the seventh decade of this century, when moral advocacy in both the courts and the academy was in flood, a skeptical view of moral judgment, however titillating it had been to an earlier generation and however useful as an instrument of attack against features of established morals that present generations wished to oppose, quickly displayed its essential incapacity to serve as a platform upon which moral advocacy of any kind could be consistently, successfully rationalized.

5 *Moral intuitionism.* Throughout this century a somewhat less skeptical, but still uneasy view of moral judgment has been taken by various writers in whose moral philosophy intuition has come to play a role somewhat similar to that of emotion in legal realism. In two papers on intuitionism presented to the Aristotelian society a few years ago by D.D. Raphael and J.O. Urmson, these two noted and able British philosophers found themselves somewhat unhappily driven to accept the fundamental thesis of intuitionism concerning the considerable degree to which the irreducible plurality of moral principles generates moral conflict in practice.[7] The utilitarian philosophers among others attempted to treat this problem by dissolving it: that is, by urging that the conflicting principles can be replaced by a single, consistent one. This attempt, Raphael and Urmson agree, has not succeeded. The principle of promoting the greatest happiness for the greatest number does not provide a single standard for a morally right action. Neither does, Raphael adds, the famous Categorical Imperative of Kant. We are left with a plurality of moral principles, and the ever-present possibility of conflict among them. This possibility might still be met by the introduction of some meta-principle installing a fixed priority among moral principles in the manner proposed by John Rawls. But to do this violates the pluralistic character of the moral life, making certain moral claims absolute. Says

[7]D. D. Raphael, 'The Standard of Morals' and 'Appendix to S. of M.'; J. O. Urmson, 'A Defense of Intuitionism'; *Proc. Arist. Soc.*, LXXV (1975), pp. 1–12E, 111–19. Reference numbers on p. 73 are to these articles.

Raphael, 'Moral dilemmas are so difficult precisely because none of the conflicting claims are absolute' (12). And supporting this negative judgment, Urmson maintains that while it is 'theoretically possible to have a set of first principles, or primary reasons, with the decision-procedure which intuitionism lacks,' and while he would rejoice if such a procedure were discovered, he is inclined to believe that the discovery of such a procedure is effectively precluded by the recurring strain and disharmony which one must acknowledge among moral principles (116, 119). There is in moral decision-making an unavoidable need for an intuitive weighing and judgment of reasons for and against competing alternatives. Yet, far from anomalous is our situation in this respect. It is 'our ordinary predicament with regard to reasons in most fields,' readily exemplified in the normal procedures by which we weigh evidence in issues of rational belief, or appraise the relative prudence of alternative courses of practical action (119, 117). In view of this, Urmson finds the conclusion of the intuitionist moral philosophers that there is no substitute for the intuitive weighing up of reasons in situations of moral conflict to be 'neither surprising nor unduly distressing' (119).

6 In an appendix to a later published version of his paper Raphael returns to the topic of the rationale of decision in a conflict of obligations. It still seems to him, he reports, that the existentialists are right, as against views like that of the utilitarians and Rawls, that in many cases of deep moral conflict between two contending courses of action on the part of individuals or social groups, 'it cannot be correct to say that one policy is objectively right and the other objectively wrong' (12E). Nevertheless, contrary to the arbitrariness emphasized by the existentialists, there must be some rationale applicable to such decisions. For often in them there is an appeal to reasons; the decision is preceded by deliberation; and, it is possible sometimes, looking back upon former decisions of this kind to say that they were mistaken (12A–12B). These processes fit the categories of neither deduction nor induction; they 'cannot be fitted to a precise formula'; perhaps they should be classified as forms 'of "rhetorical" reasoning, such as goes on in debate, and notably in juridical debate ... since it is notorious that one cannot give a precise form to the alleged logic of rhetorical reasoning,' nor can one say of such debate and deliberation that they are 'altogether irrational or non-rational' (12D).

There is some coincidence between Raphael's insistence that certain processes sometimes pejoratively characterized as 'intuitive' are not thereby excluded from the scope of rationality, and the insistence in this book upon the inclusion in the investigation of processes relevant to rationality, not merely those exemplifying accepted practices, but also those less ruly ones by which these practices are modified. All the latter have been included here under the broad character of ampliative. There is likewise some coincidence with Urmson's insistence upon the recognition of situations of conflict in morals, as widely in other fields, for which there are no available more or less routine means of decision-making and which, if they are to be handled reflectively, require recourse to some kind of intuitive weighing up of reasons.

There is, nevertheless, a great difference between a defensive, grudging admission of the insufficiency of routine application of accepted practices to provide guidance for thought and action in certain situations, and a positive recognition of the distinctive functions in life and thought that alternative ampliative processes perform. The concession that these processes have some rationality about them, perhaps of a rhetorical kind such as is exemplified in debate, hence 'are not altogether irrational or non-rational' (Raphael), seems to testify by its meagerness to the strength of the deductivist model of rationality from which it represents a small divergence. And though Urmson's judgment that the intrusion of such processes into moral philosophy, if inevitable, should not be regarded as 'scandalous' or an 'irrational' anomaly, since this is 'our ordinary predicament with regard to reasons in most fields,' it still bespeaks loudly of an attachment to a model of rationality, when inevitable falling away from that model is termed a 'predicament,' and conforming discovery of a credible decision-procedure, though conceded to be unlikely, is pronounced to be an event that would lead that author to 'rejoice.' Thus, gratified at first by this much divergence from the general deductive model, one is struck upon reflection by the distance by which it falls short of a thoroughgoing recognition of the vital testing, controlling, modifying, and reconstructive functions performed generally in life and thought by indispensable non-deductive processes.

7 Attachment to a machine which fails to perform is not uncommon and can be traced to various sources. Some of the principal sources of the attachment of a large segment of the philosophical community to the machine of justification theory and its central generating component, deductivism, were briefly described in Chapter 2. What is most germane to the main topic here is not the causes of attachment,

but its effects. One effect of the attachment upon philosophical work in elucidating the character of rational governance is to divert this work to and entrap it with a task which presents itself as a preliminary one to the main one, but which, because of its Sisyphean character perennially postpones and thus displaces the main one. In effecting displacement in such a case nothing succeeds like failure. An aspect of the failure of the theory to enable its adherents to make a satisfactory response to the challenges of skepticism by discovering and discriminating degrees of acceptability among actual and possible norms, is its capacity to lead those who are firmly committed to the theory to deny the presence and differential realization of acceptability in the governance of these norms. To those not committed to the theory and repelled by what William James called, in connection with the empiricist versions of it, its 'sweeping negations,' this denial appears less a failure in the subject matter than a blindness engendered by a theory failing to articulate with that subject matter.

It is not strange that a theory of governance which at the macro-level of historical development excludes important processes at work in effecting great changes of life and thought should likewise in a most signal way fail to recognize similar processes in many more restricted episodes of thought and action. Generations of students fitted early and securely with intellectual blinders by their indoctrination in the theory, perennially display their incapacity to recognize governance when confronted with it as an object for analysis, and a consequent firm disposition to refuse the title of reasoned philosophical governance to anything but deductive processes and results. A consequence, of course, is that a vast expanse of instances of what to the fortunately less-tutored represent genuine and even sometimes paradigm examples of governance in such domains as science, law, politics, or morals, is disregarded. Instances in these pre-eminently important domains are by narrow principle prevented from making their contribution to the development of the theory of governance, and deprived of the contribution that a thus enriched theory could make to them in return. So great is the attachment of many to the narrow theory that they are profoundly puzzled by the phenomenon that many activities should be so commonly treated as governance of a reasoned philosophical kind, which so markedly do not fit the models which they have been prepared by authoritative instruction to follow. To this sense of puzzlement, in the more committed and aggressive, may be added a sense of outrage at what from their point of view must seem to be an inexhaustible supply of impostors, the elimination of which from philosophy warrants the kind of purging conflagration which Hume long ago recommended for philosophical books that violated what he came to regard as minimum standards of intellectual procedure.

8 But this is a blindness that, as Hume said about the clouds of skeptical doubts which his own investigations aroused in him, requires for its survival sequestration from the affairs of life, abstraction from the kind of situations in practical life in which we naturally make, because we must, the kinds of discrimination of which we find ourselves totally incapable on those occasions when we are fully faithful to philosophical principle. Our natural dispositions and 'the first and most trivial event in life,' Hume said, suffice to dispel such doubt and indecision on our part, 'Nature ... [being] always too strong for principle.'[8] Attachment to justification theory and the consequent general blindness to discriminations between the more or less reasonable which it entails, are luxuries that can be afforded by philosophical minds only in monastic intellectual retreat, and only at a cost paid both by themselves and by their society for this retreat. Though 'Nature' may be counted upon to terminate the brief interludes during which, in solitary chamber or insulated seminar, we nourish skeptical doubts and the renunciation of judgment which they imply, and though 'Nature' again, and 'Custom' through which she speaks, may for the most part provide immediate and sure clues for the making of the judgments she calls upon us to make, her voice in custom is not always audible, or clear, or even univocal. Hence the hard cases; hence the need for special efforts to determine what the voice of custom is, if there is such a voice, in those cases in which, in contrast to the easier ones, the voice cannot be heard speaking clearly and determinantly in settled modes of response. Given time and opportunity, custom may, unassisted, reveal all this, since there are many other ways besides reflection in which its voice finds expression. But there is no guarantee that it will so express itself, even in cases where expression through reflection is not possible. Furthermore when it does, we have ample notice in history, this expression in great and difficult cases may be achieved at a great human cost. In such cases it is especially valuable to be able to discern whether an as yet inarticulate custom provides the outline of a disposition of the issues in the matter, and if so what that is, without waiting to be instructed in a harder, more costly way. For it is not only fools, but also

[8]*Enquiry*, Section XII, Part II.

the heedless, the incurious, and those for other reasons incapable of learning or unable to be taught, whose instruction in these matters must come, if it comes at all, from experience of a less gentle and sometimes harshly punishing kind.

9 The great practical sagacity of Hume enabled him to see that what he had been led by his philosophical theory to view as custom must and does perform not only the main and more common functions in the guidance of thought and action, but is also an indispensable component of that resource that many philosophical views have sought to isolate from it under the name of reason. This perception might have led him to question whether reason is as distinct from custom as his theory made out, might have led him to recognize that internal to what he accorded the deprecatory names of 'custom,' and also 'habit,' was a kind of process that, since it performs so much of the office of reason, should share that significant title. This he sometimes seems on the verge of doing, but always in the end the theory deeply entrenched in his thought, rather than wisdom, prevails. This theory was one that reflected motives and presuppositions that are not essential to the task of philosophical governance of norms of thought and action, and devotion to which interfered with the performance of this task. What Hume was discovering when he proclaimed that reason is not, and by default custom is, the great guide of life is in part just what generations of disgruntled students of philosophy learn in their classrooms. It is that a canon and organon of procedure organized in response to these motives and presuppositions, such as, for example, those entailed in playing and winning the recherché game of skeptical challenges, are not only in the end incompetent for this peculiar, engrossing academic purpose. They are also, from the beginning, as Hume stressed, incompetent in application to 'the first and most trivial event in life.' But if not reason – that is, deductive, probative, applicative procedure – what? One answer to this question which has been given by generations of students for whom the alternative of 'custom' has seemed little better, and an answer which fits better into the individualist orientation of much modern philosophy, religion, and politics, is that of direct, individual intuitive judgment. From Rousseau, through Kierkegaard to the present day, this has been the most attractive alternative guide to those to whom the difficulties of accepted patterns of thought and action seemed manifestly to disqualify custom, while in the frustrations of justification theory they seem to see reason persistently and knowingly engaged in disqualifying itself.

10 It is not that Hume himself, like many others in his philosophical tradition, was not personally and explicitly committed to developing a theory of philosophical processes that would minister to the end of guiding life, both in knowledge and in moral and political practice. It was his early purpose, announced on the title page of his first and most ambitious philosophical work, 'to introduce the experimental [and presumably improved] method of reasoning into moral subjects.'[9] But, again like others, Hume had other purposes, one of which was to have a theory resting upon foundations which could be successfully exposed to the kind of extreme but yet apparently legitimate assaults that are generated by systematic philosophical skepticism. It so turned out that the pursuit of this latter purpose, to which, not uncharacteristically for a modern philosopher, he gave priority, resulted in a theory which was at cross-purposes to that other major end for which it was sought. It was a theory which could not assimilate moral subjects and upon which he was bound logically to conclude that the general intention to found and cultivate moral subjects upon a basis of experimental method rested upon a profound methodological mistake. Retaining his purpose of elucidating critically those procedures which we employ in moral subjects; by which, for example, we judge causes and effects and make relative judgments of worth in moral and political matters; but debarred from doing this in his own theory of reason; he proceeded to do it in alternative language and concepts of very different kinds of resource, of which, in matters of knowledge, custom was the chief, and in morals and politics the passions and moral sentiment.

A principal attraction of the conception of governance embodied in justification theory is that the theory does seem to offer standards of governance that are above and independent of the admittedly imperfect standards provided by the system of custom of any community. But this independence is purchased in the theory at the price of irrelevance, of detachment from and incapacity for the major function for which the standards are needed. But the detachment and incapacity of the theory in no way lessens the need. Recognizing the need, one may nevertheless reject it as a demand upon the theory; one may sanction the detachment of the theory from the performance by adapting for it different ends.

[9] The term 'moral subject' was much broader in Hume's usage than it is now. As the title *A Treatise of Human Nature* indicates, the term included for Hume all those subjects for which an understanding of human nature seemed essential: not only morals, strictly considered, and politics, but the theory of knowledge, including therein the philosophy of science.

The alteration in some degree, and sometimes in a great degree, of the ends for which it is pursued is a natural feature of any extended branch of activity, and one that may sometimes signify growth and improvement in the activity just as sometimes it signifies decadence and deterioration. It is not necessarily a defect of the gourmet that other primary ends have displaced nourishment in eating the meal, nor of the lover that the end of procreation should be displaced by others in that worship of one's partner with one's body which, in the moving words of one of the Christian marriage ceremonies, is a feature of a marriage. Still the need for nourishment in human life and of procreation in human society remain. And if the ends of justification theory, as a theory of philosophical governance, be reconstituted to be in the satisfaction of curiosity, or in learned amusement at what Hume referred to as 'the whimsical condition of mankind' which must believe and seek a kind of grounds for its beliefs which it is constitutionally incapable of finding, still the other, less abstract critical needs with respect to custom and other possible bases of belief remain. One may develop, as Hume did, a theory of morals in which the essential guiding role of persistent, careful reflection, celebrated by philosophers since Socrates, is detached and conferred upon the passions, and one may then draw the corollary conclusion that 'Reason is, and only ought to be the slave of the passions, and can never pretend to any other office than to serve and obey them.'[10] This does not erase the need for what had previously been sought under the title of philosophical governance in morals, but rather leaves the task to be investigated and ministered to under some such misleading and sure to be troublesome title as 'theory of the passions.' Now, for example, to secure a view of the passional grounding and complete subservience of reason to passion in morals, a discrimination will have to be made between the 'violent' passions and those which are so 'calm' that they are mistaken for reason by those 'who judge of things by their first view and appearance.'[11] Similarly, if one agrees with Hume's proclamation so much as to hold that in the determination of proper procedure, not only in the cognitive but in other phases of life, custom is the great guide of practice and judgment, this conclusion of one investigation immediately calls for another. There is need to elucidate how a thesis that fits so well the decisions we make in the settled areas of practice and judgment does also fit the

[10] *Treatise*, Book II, Part III, Section III.
[11] *Ibid.*

unsettled and hard cases which, for those 'who judge of things by their first view and appearance,' it flagrantly does not. It does not seem to fit these cases because they represent issues and questions for which in one respect custom apparently does not provide a disposition. This, it seems, must necessarily be so, since these issues and questions arise, as has already been emphasized, at just those places in which settled ways of proceeding for one reason or other fail to provide clear and definite guides to thought and action.

11 An essential ingredient of the kind of hard cases of governance with which philosophy is perennially concerned is their deductive indeterminacy with respect to the background of accepted norms against which they are judged. Justification theory has moved to deal with such cases, in so far as they are tractable to the theory, by repairing the deductive insufficiency; this, by replacing accepted norms with more sufficient ones derived from some altogether different source: pure reason, pure experience, or a combination of both. It is this move that Hume so destructively criticized, and the reversals of which were strikingly repeated in the history of the most noteworthy effort to carry off this project in recent years, namely, logical positivism. There is no need here to dilate upon the fact of these reversals. They have been repeated enough, and serious enough, to suggest strongly that the time has come to give up the attempt to reduce all governance to its deductive forms. It is time to recognize that a view of the philosophical governance of norms is not possible that does not include the important, indispensable functions performed in governance by processes that are not deductive. Rather than condemning and disregarding ampliative processes because they embody different standards and perform different functions from deductive ones, we need to understand their own proper standards and functions better, and then use this understanding as a means and component for developing a more realistic and effective view of philosophical governance.

Part 2
NORMS

4

Concreteness Restored

Topical Outline

83

mediated through their relations with other norms. Some of these affecting features are features of our human environment and some are non-human. And of both kinds some are and some are not subject to our control. The limitations imposed upon us and opportunities offered us by external and internal nature, and the revelations of nature itself effected by these limitations and opportunities, were grasped and stressed by the adherents of natural law in the long tradition of that name in politics, law, and morals. There are more ways in which our norms of thought and action can reflect features of the human and non-human environment in which they are engaged than those of pointing out, assigning predicates to, or, more generally, enunciating true propositions about these features.

1 It was observed at the very beginning of Chapter 1 that in one respect, namely, the widely recognized failure of justification theory, the present situation in philosophy is similar to that of a hundred and fifty years ago. Then the remedies for the failures of this kind of philosophical theory were sought by a group of philosophers, the most important of whom was Hegel, in the resources of the community and in a re-examination of the relations between reason and social tradition. If the French Revolution may be regarded as, among many other things, a rough expression of that version of justification theory disseminated in the so-called Age of Enlightenment in Western Europe and America, the political philosophy of Burke may similarly be regarded as the somewhat fragmented and unsystematic beginnings of an opposed theory devised in response and for application to urgent concerns in political affairs. And although Rousseau did not conceive himself as propounding a theory of philosophical reflection ('A thinking is a depraved animal'), but rather of simple sentiments uncontaminated by and opposed to what Rousseau himself understood to be intellect or reason, he too, in an unsystematic way did present a view of the cultivation of virtue that sharply diverged from the conventional 'rationalism' of his day in the important role it assigned to the community.

What Hume and the Enlightenment, which was represented in his philosophy, had so forcefully put assunder, Hegel endeavored to put together again. Some grounds for this, in application to political philosophy, lay in Rousseau, though he himself would have rejected this way of looking at these grounds. The situation is masterfully set forth by G. H. Sabine in his treatment of Hume, Burke, Rousseau and Hegel in his *History of Political Theory*. It may be observed in passing that Sabine's own views on the philosophical issues involved were emphatically in agreement with Hume. In consequence of this, like Bertrand Russell, he regarded Hegel's complex social and historical view of reason as one which from the point of view of sound philosophical analysis was fundamentally retrograde, a movement of counter-revolution against what had been a great achievement in reform. Writes Sabine,

> Rousseau's collectivism ... required a drastic revaluation of custom, tradition, and the accumulating heritage of the national culture, without which the general will was nothing but an empty formula. This in turn amounted to a thorough revolution in philosophical values. Since the time of Descartes reason and custom had by common consent been set in contrast to one another. The proper work of reason had been to release men from the bondage of authority and tradition, in order that they might be free to follow the light of nature.... The idealism of Hegel tried to weave reason and tradition into a single unit – the expanding culture of a national spirit or consciousness.... What Hegel's philosophy professed to offer, therefore, was an enlarged conception of reason that should overlap and include what had been separated by the analysis of Hume and Kant.[1]

The celebrated (or notorious) dialectic, the new intellectual method which Hegel worked to systematize in his logical writings, was advanced as a means by which reflective philosophical processes – call them 'reason,' for short, in this context – could perform certain operations of which, according to the analysis of Hume, they were in principle incapable. Among these was the extraction of intellectual, moral, and political standards from a study of historical development and the heritage of that development. In the rubrics of the Humean philosophy this meant endeavoring to derive 'ought' from 'is,' 'value' from 'fact.' Some of the philosophical presumptions embedded in these

---

[1] Revised edition (1950), pp. 594, 620, 621.

apparently transparent, innocent distinctions will be discussed in a later chapter.[2]

2 The disagreement over reason and custom in philosophical governance is an aspect of the clash between a view of acceptable governance that is strictly deductionist and one that reserves an essential place in that governance for non-deductive, ampliative processes. The inclusion of ampliative processes among acceptable ones eliminates the possibility of continuing to view governing processes as ones engaged in exclusively by individual agents, rather than as ones that in many important cases are essentially social.

In its formulation by Descartes, justification theory was embedded in a larger metaphysical view, little of which would be agreed upon by those who either by profession or, mostly, by their procedure as philosophers, express their adherence to the theory. It is remarkable, after over three centuries of metaphysical change, how faithful the theory remains to that aspect of Descartes's vision which conceived of philosophical reason, the capacity to effect acceptable philosophical governance, as *lumen naturale*. Fundamentally in the theory this reason is conceived to be an individual endowment, and what the empiricist versions of the Cartesian philosophy did in revising the philosophy at this point was to enlarge greatly the reliance in it upon one aspect of the endowment, namely, the capacity of individuals to receive instruction from nature through the avenues of the senses. The distributed endowments of the natural light, '*la chose du monde la mieux partagée*,' was conceived in its operation as paying more attention to the nature and order of sensations, of ongoing sensory experience, than to the nature and order of developing ideas. More important than the differential emphasis upon sense and intellect in the two versions was their joint agreement that this endowment, cultivated in philosophical education and exploited in the philosophical governance of norms of thought and action, is made distributively to individuals rather than to groups or communities, and imparted to groups or communities through its exercise by these primary individual legatees. Individuals of course live and engage in reflective thought in company with each other. But in the performance of the function of critic, judge, and curator of norms, the resources an individual must call upon are ones accessible to him as standards, as authoritative, independently of his social inheritance and surroundings.

[2] Chapter 7, §§13–22.

These resources lie in the capacity of each of us to be aware of and record both the nature and connection of things in the natural world revealed to us in experience, and the nature and connection of our ideas. In these ways the archetypes or standards of norms are accessible to us: to us as individuals operating for the purpose in isolation from the influence of 'what others have thought' (Descartes, *Rule III*), or said, or done; relying solely upon what it is in our power as individuals to grasp alone; trusting that, however limited the instruction available to us from these sources may be, it will be, in Locke's words, 'suited to our state and concerns.'

The particular special standards, as they are grasped by us and included in our philosophical repertory, are not engrafted in us by tradition, social custom, or culturation. As grasped and adopted, they are original in each of us, though also remarkably congruent. What those other sources – tradition and the rest – may provide, and it is indispensable that they do so, is an awakening to the need for such standards, and clues to the sources wherein they can be found. Reflective philosophical governance proceeds in the persistent search for and employment of such standards. Only in relation to them can any accepted or proposed norms attain philosophical accreditation. In consequence, in its relation to accepted practices of thought and action, philosophical reflection performs exclusively as judge and teacher, never as the subject of judgment or instruction by practice, never as pupil. There is no effrontery or presumption or disqualification in the behavior of those whose grasp of these standards has been cultivated in seclusion from practice, in purporting to judge authoritatively concerning the practices in which they have not been cultured and indoctrinated. There is no impropriety in these prophets of reason proceeding, without benefit of this culture and indoctrination, to stipulate for science what shall be rationality in that field, what shall count as justification or confirmation in scientific theories, as proper explanation in history, psychology, or other social studies, or as good reasons in ethnics. There is not impropriety, for the voice that speaks this way speaks from authority; though it is, indeed perhaps because it is a produce of the cloisters, it may now speak *ex cathedra* as the voice of reason.

3 A contrary view is that when we engage in any substantial way in the reflective philosophical governance of norms or practices, as in reflection generally, we draw upon capacities of greatly various kinds developed in us by nurture as we are formed into civilized human

87

beings. We develop these capacities very early out of potentialities with which we are endowed as members of this species. We learn to think and act, and to choose between competing possible ways of thinking and acting. These ways are possible partly because we have a biological inheritance of a certain kind: one which, given a certain kind of teaching and experience, makes all of a plurality of ways possible but no one of them necessary. Without this inheritance they are impossible; and likewise impossible with that inheritance unrefined, undeveloped, uncultivated. It is by benefit of this inheritance that certain questions arise. The inheritance makes the questions possible, rather than precludes them or predetermines their answers. For example we are able to deliberate concerning the performance of a certain action, such as speaking in opposition to or in support of a motion on the floor of a meeting, *because* we have such resources. The resources (physical ones of brains, lungs, and mouth; cultural ones of language, understanding, and the rest) make it possible for us to speak. It is a curious conclusion that because the question of what we shall say presupposes a mouth and language, that the mouth and language therefore determine what we shall say. The insufficiency of such necessary conditions to determine answers is emphasized by Socrates in his well-known comment in the *Phaedo* upon the insufficiencies of the physical theories of which he as a young man had been a student. Whatever these theories may do, Socrates says, they do not identify the kind of cause needed in the present circumstances to explain his action in submitting to the penalty of the Athenian court rather than, say, saving his life by fleeing to Megara or Boeotia. The primary cause of this, Socrates says, is his own judgment of which among the possible courses of action open to him is the best. Exponents of these physical theories, he says are like someone who would try to explain why he (Socrates) sits here rather than escapes by showing that he does:

> because my body is made of bones and muscles; and the bones, as
> he would say, are hard and have joints which divide them, and the
> muscles are elastic, and they cover the bones, which have also a
> covering or environment of flesh and skin which contains them;
> and as the bones are lifted at their joints by the contraction or
> relaxation of the muscles, I am able to bend my limbs, and that is
> why I am sitting here in a curved position – that is what he would
> say; and he would have a similar explanation of my talking to you,
> which he would attribute to sound, and air, and hearing, and he

would assign ten thousand other causes of the same sort, forgetting to mention the true cause, which is, that the Athenians have thought fit to condemn me, and accordingly I have thought it better and more right to remain here and undergo my sentence.[3]

4 A broad theory of the processes, ampliative and otherwise, by which governance of norms is effected, has to begin with and take account of the ways in which we acquire those norms that now have become the objects of criticism and possible change. We come to such situations, can indeed come to them, only because, as has long been recognized in the field of moral philosophy, we are equipped with a complex body of norms that enable us to make more or less secure judgments on matters that come before us for decision. That is to say, we can come to situations in which our task is criticism and possible emendation only because we are already so equipped that for most situations these are not called for. Expanding the notion of *conscience* beyond its customary restricted application to moral matters, we may say that for most situations in which we need to make decisions on how to think and act, we are equipped, not necessarily with algorithms or other more or less automatic decision procedures, though in some cases we do have these, but with *consciences* that are competent for the task. Certainly we should have no such consciences were it not for various native endowments of mind, brain, and central nervous system. But whatever may be their bases in our mental and physical structures, consciences we do have. A theory of governance of norms or practices need not be concerned directly with those features that, arising out of our common endowments, all our consciences necessarily have. These features are chiefly important for governance as being beyond its reach. Governance is directly concerned with those features that are not so determined for us, with norms or practices that are open to our criticism and appraisal, and that it is sensible for us to try to affect either by promoting or by resisting change. These features are not implanted in us, once and for all, like the Kantian forms of perception and understanding. They do not subsist in all of us, fixed and absolute, the forever unchanging standards, buried treasures in our nature, hard diamonds of reason which we can mine, recognize, appreciate, and come to know better, but cannot, either as individuals or as communities, create, alter, or destroy. Rather they are formed in us by what are surely our proximate

[3] Steph. 98–99 (Jowett trans.).

creators, if not our final ones, namely, the communities of which we are members in family life, in schooling, in vocation, in religious practice, in political affiliation, and in other areas of communal living. Like a kind of collective mother, these communities nourish us and form us by imparting to us aspects of themselves, by creating in us a variety of more or less well-composed miniature reflections of themselves.

Implicit in the norms we follow in the more or less routine guidance of thought and action are ideals, models, visions of life that, aborning, are resources for both the reinforcement and refashioning of these norms themselves. Each individual is a vessel, holding, expressing, utilizing, and often altering in use some portion of the entire corpus of communal practices. That any one of us may develop and commit ourselves to standards which diverge from those of the communities which formed us is misunderstood by some as evidence that there is in us a capacity to discern standards that is quite independent of the communities. But just as the capacity to produce genetic change is a character of, not alien to or separate from, biological species, so the capacity to develop divergence is a character of social standards themselves, considered not as quasi-linguistic, abstract platonic entities, but as aspects of practices joined in more or less competitive and also more or less cooperative ways in the lives of communities. Considered as an abstract rule, as a formula congealed in some symbolic medium, a standard can no more generate change than, as Parmenides said, 'what is' can become 'what is not.' Considered as a feature of practices more or less composed with others in communal life, liability to change becomes natural and indeed essential to it.

In an address to a Phi Beta Kappa society over half a century ago J. E. Creighton made these same points while speaking of the life of the scholar, 'the life that concerns itself with ideas,' in relation to what, as expressed in the title of the address, is 'The Social Nature of Thinking.' The often expressed view that the scholar's life isolates the individual from his fellows derives its appearance of plausibility, he said,

> from a false and antiquated theory of the nature of thinking and a misconception of the conditions under which it takes place ...
> [from, among other things] a popular idea that thinking is a process by means of which the individual evolves ideas in some mysterious way from the depths of his own consciousness.

On the contrary, Creighton argued,

the life which concerns itself with ideas involves the closest union of the individual with his fellows. .... 'Without society no individual,' is a statement that applies to man as thinker no less than to man as a moral and political being. ... Intelligence is not a private endowment that the individual possesses, but rather a living principle which possesses him, a universal capacity which expresses through him the nature of a larger whole of which he is a member.[4]

5 Before proceeding to elaborate further the character of ampliative processes, it is perhaps worth repeating that what is opposed here on behalf of these processes is not deductive processes in themselves. What is opposed is a view of rational governance of norms of thought and action that is strictly *deductivist*, that excludes from the class of processes that need to be attended to, employed, and relied upon, those that are ampliative. It is not necessary to slight the importance of deductive processes in rational governance in order to insist that they are not sufficient for all purposes, for all cases. A view of what the general processes of governance are like, and what professional philosophers and others do when they participate in such processes, is one-sided, warped, and inadequate if it concentrates solely upon the deductive of these and neglects those that are non-deductive or ampliative. This is a primary lesson to be learned from the unhappy career of deductivist Cartesian or justification theory in modern philosophy.

6 The distinctive characteristics of ampliative process both within and without philosophical thought and the limits of purely deductive ones have been emphasized by a variety of writers in English and American philosophy in this century. Some of these writers were surely as guilty of maintaining the hegemony of ampliative processes as their deductivist counterparts were in behalf of deductive ones. Various writers, in treating ampliative processes, emphasized different characteristics of them. In the paper just quoted (1918) the American philosopher Creighton stressed the social matrix and processes upon which we depend when we engage in thinking of even the most private, secluded kind. The small book, *Implication and Linear Inference*, by the English philosopher Bernard Bosanquet, published about this time

---

[4] *Studies in Speculative Philosophy* (1925), H.R. Smart, ed., pp. 46, 47, 51, 57.

(1920), drew the contrast between what Bosanquet called 'systematic' and 'linear' processes of thought, much to the disadvantage, in his judgment, of the linear ones. The apparent linear character that deductive processes seem often to manifest, and which Descartes had so strongly emphasized in the *Rules* and *Discourse on Method*, Bosanquet regarded as a kind of logical illusion generated by a neglect of the onmipresent interactive effects in reasoning between premises and conclusions. Among figures in American philosophy in addition to Creighton, who stressed the social and what has been called here the 'generative' and 'defining' aspects of some forms of reflection were C. S. Peirce, Josiah Royce, and John Dewey. Some particular works stressing in various degrees and in various ways the indispensability of ampliative processes in thought were C. I. Lewis's *Mind and the World Order* (1929), Brand Blanshard's *The Nature of Thought* (1939), and various works of Dewey from the early *Essays in Experimental Logic* (1916) through the *Logic: The Theory of Inquiry* (1938). Dewey's *Logic* was the last of the line of systematic logics produced in the Hegelian-idealistic tradition, beginning with those of Hegel himself and continued in English philosophical writing by F. H. Bradley and Bosanquet. Lewis, like another figure who deserves to be mentioned in connection with the dependence of deductive processes upon ampliative ones, namely, Wittgenstein, exhibited in his philosophical writing a reversal of thought concerning the closely related question of the feasibility of the deductivist, foundational program in the philosophy of knowledge. In Lewis's case the reversal was from the obstacles to such a program regarded as residing in the possibility of alternative conceptual schemes, in *Mind and the World Order*, to the foundational program strongly defended in *An Analysis of Knowledge and Valuation* (1946). In the case of Wittgenstein the reversal was from the foundational, asocial doctrines of the *Tractatus Logico-Philosophicus* (1929) to the strong social and pragmatic emphasis of the later philosophy, particularly in such works as the *Philosophical Investigations* (1953) and *Remarks on the Foundations of Mathematics* (1956). The absence of a positive doctrine of the role of ampliative processes in the governance of norms (forms of life) in Wittgenstein's later views may be largely explained by the fact that, having given up the foundationism of the *Tractatus* and the aspiration for a logically ideal language capable of serving as the central instrument of philosophical governance, he did not regard that governance as a function that philosophical reflection is in general competent to perform. There is much in Wittgenstein's later philosophy that is Hegelian in doctrine, though evidently not in origin. But in contrast with the main current of Hegelian tradition one thing that is not in this philosophy is a theory or program of positive philosophical governance.

7 A necessary component of an understanding of the processes of governance of norms is an understanding of norms themselves. And a great obstacle to understanding norms in contemporary philosophy is the prevailing tendency to think of them, for philosophical purposes, in distortingly abstract ways. So many influences converge in support of this tendency that the project of weakening it in any marked degree is a formidable one. The supporting influence of logistic eidola as they bear upon the replication view of the employment of norms, were discussed in Chapter 2 (§5). The logistic view of norms and of the guidance of thought and action by them is a particularly prominent and important present example of the general abstraction which, when unrelieved by wider philosophical consideration, obscures the effects upon norms of the ampliative processes to which from time to time they are subject in various degrees. One aspect of these ampliative effects, namely, the effects produced in norms by their subsumptive application will be treated in some detail in Chapter 5. An exclusively logistic view of the subsumptive process obscures what may be called the 'reactive' effects, both mutational and stabilizing, upon norms of the immediate conditions, the 'instances,' to which they are applied.

Obscured also by a different abstraction are the important effects upon particular norms of other norms with which they are more or less intimately related, and the effects through these of the wider existential conditions under which these related norms are applied. However valuable it may be for certain scientific purposes, for philosophical purposes it is detrimental to think of norms exclusively as individual patterns connecting specific responses to specific stimulating conditions. Norms are not such patterns, abstracted from each other and from the communal life of which they are features. A norm neither represents nor prescribes a pattern of action or response that can be thought of as existing independently of its relations to other norms though capable also of being brought into relation with them. A norm is not just a form of action. It is a form of appropriate action, of appropriate response; and this appropriateness is something that is determined in its relations with, among other things, other norms: by the role which this or that mode of action or response plays in the constitution of

93

individual and communal life. Ampliative effects consequent upon these wider relations of norms will be illustrated extensively in the ensuing detailed discussion of ampliative processes. A brief specimen illustration of such effects is the development in Greek mathematics by which the norms defining numbers were expanded to include that famous non-rational, the square root of two. Here the connections between numerical norms and others applying to measurement yielded the untoward effect that so long as numbers are conceived in the manner to which we now define rationals, the diagonal of the square is incommensurable.

8 One of the more troublesome consequences of an abstract view of norms in a theory of the governance of them is that generated by the attempt to absorb in such an abstract view a recognized interdependence of norms, as these operate in the guidance of thought and action. The consequence is that of conceiving governance as a process directed at achieving some kind of coherence or harmony among abstract entities. This way of conceiving governance invites the kind of objection, based largely upon misunderstanding, that was often made against what was commonly called the 'coherence' theory of truth. When one thinks of coherence as a relation among mental or logical entities called 'judgments' or 'propositions,' conceived to have an independent life in the realm of mind or of the intellect, it is not difficult to show that such coherence can provide no adequate account of truth. Coherence of abstract thought can easily be shown to be no adequate substitute for truth, and the same holds for coherence of abstract norms as a substitute for governance. But just as it was an important part of the contention of the criticized philosophers, which they were generally at fault in not making clearer, that the thought of judgment to which the term 'coherent' could sensibly apply was not a kind of thought abstracted from life and action, from connection with things, states, creatures, persons, and whatever else we live with in our environment, so it is essential here to the thesis about governance and norms that the latter be conceived concretely as features of actual life, not as formulae that could be fitted together at will into various compositions, as in imagination we fit abstract possibilities together when we invent a new kind of game or a new pattern of dance.

The term 'coherence' is unquestionably a bad actor in these contexts, one which had better be avoided when possible, since it so generally seems capable of imposing upon critics a caricature of the view they are disposed to criticize. It seems worth repeating that to say that a norm cannot be genuinely conceived independently of its relations with other norms, is not to say that abstract patterns of response or action achieve governance by being combined with other similar patterns in suitable relations and in a suitable critical mass. What we pick out as norms, what we formulate as norms, are features of the life which they compose. Selected, abstracted from that life, like organs from the surgical patient, they are always to some degree denatured. To think, therefore, of governance as the installation among such items of suitable relations, is like thinking of forming a human being, as Frankenstein's monster was formed, by a proper assembly of denatured parts. The parts in question are not organs, members of a body. No amount of other relations with similar parts will make them such. They are organs, members only when together, each in its own way, they contribute to the living body which is individual and communal life. As soon as one is abstracted from that life it is, as a norm, in some degree deformed. The price of separate identity is some distortion as a norm, since by itself it cannot be a norm, cannot perform that function in life which is essential to a norm. The chief reason why the term 'coherence' has been so disadvantageous in discussions of reflective governance is that commonly among critics, and sometimes even among advocates, norms have been conceived in this particular way. Given elements of this sort, the infusion into them of coherence will not suffice. So that any such view of the governance of norms must in a relatively obvious way prove unsatisfactory.

9 The interrelations among norms, their various forms and degrees of interdependency, are essential parts of their character, which must be explicated in a view of the governance of them. A further and likewise essential characteristic is their relations with and dependency upon features of their environment, both human and other, by which they are constantly conditioned. Though in their effect upon norms these features are inextricably combined, it is important to keep in mind, in thinking of the governance of norms, that some of the features determining the character of norms are, and some are not, in us; some are and some are not subject to our control; and some of those that are not subject to our control are among those that lie in us. Some of the conditioning features to which norms are constantly responsive are those present in the immediate context of their application. Norms are constantly molded, strengthened and weakened, refined and degraded, by the objects, the particular situations, the 'instances' to which they are applied. This is the aspect of the determination of them that will be

treated immediately in the next chapter. To these immediate determinations of the character of norms may be added the whole complex of mediate ones to which they are subject: not through direct use, but in consequence of their association with other norms and of the indirect effects upon them of the determination of these, including the reactive effects of their own use. As has been emphasized, norms exist in life. They are interrelated in various ways because aspects of life are so interrelated. When norms collide and abrade each other, aspects of our life are similarly colliding and abrading; practices, habits, customs are colliding and abrading because they are somehow ill-adapted, ill-suited to the life in the world of which they are a part. And one reason for this lack of fit in such cases may be that the norms, to speak in a hyper-intellectual way, themselves embody false assumptions about that segment of the world with which they are engaged. That we are able by reflection to effect governance of norms does not mean that such governance is thereby divorced from natural and objective conditions in the world. Since norms are integrally related to the world, reflective governance is likewise. The achievement of governance is the achievement of a kind of life in the world. It is an achievement in which our environing world plays a necessary part, and, further, an achievement in which in some domains, such as in scientific research generally, the main end in view may be the discernment of features of the environment which effective governance can provide. The progressive elaboration, refinement, and adjustment of norms is in scientific research the primary way in which the general character of the world for which the norms are designed is explored and determined.

10 Appreciation of the influence upon the development and criticism of norms exerted by the conditions under which thought and action take place is confirmed and enriched by a recognition of the variety of ways in which this influence is exerted and in which the relations between thought and action and their existential conditions may be explored. The dominant model in Western philosophy for exploring the relations between thoughts and those objects, states, and so on – the character of which act as constraints determining the correctness or incorrectness, adequacy or inadequacy of these thoughts – has been one that seemed to fit the kind of relations explored in science, both ancient and modern, and a logic that could trace its origins back to the origins of science. Much attention has been given to the topic of names (expanded in recent philosophy to the category of referring

expressions), to terms, and to propositions, judgments, or statements ascribing monadic or polyadic predicates to these terms. So dominant has been this way of conceiving the relation between thought and those constraints upon it which, in order to fulfill its purposes it must somehow reflect, that tractability to this mode of conception has often been used as a criterion of whether in any given way of thinking there are any such constraints, reflections of which in the thinking may, in their manner and degree, be determinative of the acceptability of the products. Thus the question of whether there are such constraints in moral, ethical, and political thought has often been reduced to a question of the discernibility in our environing world of something corresponding to the predicate 'good' in the way that there are correspondents to such predicates as those of colors, shapes, and so on.

Comment upon this matter here must be limited to an expression of misgiving about the inadequacy of the choices which adherence to such a model presents to one interested in exploring without prejudice the ways in which norms of thought and action need to be articulated with conditions in which that thought and action is conducted and to which that thought and action must somehow conform in order to achieve success. For example, one need not suppose that because nothing determinative in the conditions of political life of man can be formulated as an unrestricted universal proposition about political life, or as a law-like statement of the form that is employed in the sciences, that therefore the emphasis upon the articulation between the conditions of political life and political arrangements which has been a central feature of the tradition of natural law is without foundation. A conviction that in this tradition there has been a sound and valuable recognition of conditions beyond our wishes and wills revealed in the elaboration of moral and political arrangements does not commit one to the view that in elaborating and criticizing these arrangements one is describing these conditions. There are a variety of ways in which our thought and action can reflect – clearly, distortedly, or mistakenly – characteristics of the domains in which they are carried on besides pointing out, naming, assigning predicates to, or more generally, speaking falsely or truly about these domains. There are, for example, more choices in ways of understanding our evaluative thought than that of viewing it either as expressing personal or group predilections and incitements to response, or as attributing to the objects of our evaluation special, elusive, non-natural properties. The employment of accepted norms in praise or dispraise of human actions reflects in indirect ways characteristics of human life and of the conditions in which that life proceeds. It is important to understand that an appreciation of this aspect of thought in reflecting the conditions under which it occurs may be maintained without assimilating this to thought and speech *about* these conditions, without viewing all thought as the idealist philosophers have, as judgment, as discrimination of the character of the 'real,' which in turn upon their view comes to be regarded as but one phase, in us, of a process of self-discrimination, self-determination, and self-realization carried out in many ways by a larger, cosmic subject much grander than we.

5
Replication and Subsumption

Topical Outline

the special service of discrediting deductivism at a place of its greatest strength.

In addition to such thought-experiments, history is a rich source of illustration of the resources for philosophical governance of norms that reside in their aspects as components of wider activities, practices, institutions, and communities.

These aspects are extremely wide in most cases that fall within the jurisdiction of reflective philosophical thought. The constitutional character of such cases. And the indispensability to competent governance by philosophical thought of a broad and deep understanding of the norms with which it is engaged.

1 The elaboration of the deductivist view of the employment of norms of thought and action in Chapter 2 began by calling attention to a central component of this view that may be called 'replication theory.' This theory itself was described as a resultant of the interweaving of a variety of influences – metaphysical, epistemological, logistic and other – some of which were briefly commented upon. The general view embodied in replication theory takes on a different form from time to time as one or other of the different influences upon it is dominant. Thus recently prominent is the logistic form the theory assumes under dominant theoretical linguistic influences.

To this form of the theory, criticism in the present chapter is directed. The target of the criticism is not replication theory in all respects, in all contexts, for all purposes. The replicative view of the employment of norms, in its logistic form, as in others, neglects certain aspects of this employment, among them the ampliative ones. And for many purposes this neglect is extremely valuable, indeed indispensable. But, as is often the case, neglect that is indispensable for some purposes may be seriously harmful for others.

2 Common to replication theory in its various forms is a commitment to what may be called a 'monadic,' which is to say, an atomic view of norms and of their employment. In its logistic form emphasis is upon the linguistic forms in which the normic atoms and molecules are represented. The presumption is that norms are capable of being represented, with no significant loss or distortion, in compound symbolic expressions that syntactically connect expressions signifying conditions of response with others signifying appropriate responses. By

these connections various relations between conditions and responses are represented: relations of necessity, possibility, permissibility, likelihood, and the rest.

3 The amount of abstraction entailed in this presumption is considerable. Excluded from the theory embodying this abstraction is a place for those determinative relations between norms themselves that cannot be refunded in terms of such elementary relations between symbolic expressions, and likewise those determinative relations between norms and their conditions of application that similarly cannot be so represented. Widespread abstraction of this general sort has persisted through centuries of modern philosophy and through a variety of idioms, at first largely mental (ideas, concepts, judgments, beliefs) and more latterly linguistic (terms, propositions, sentences) in which this general theory has been couched. The objective and result of this abstraction is thus a view of norms, and of the philosophical governance of them, in which norms themselves are conceived as entities that have and retain identities that can be discriminated and treated independently of the matrix in human life in which they are found and which they serve to inform. It is helpful in appreciating the degree of abstraction thus affected to keep recalling the aspect of norms that this platonism tends to suppress, and that the alternative term 'practice,' in comparison with the term 'norm,' tends to emphasize, namely, that they are ways of thinking and acting embodied in human life.

4 When the presumptions embedded in these abstractions are imported into philosophical thought, in particular, when the methods of analysis implementing the presumptions are taken to be a sufficient basis for a comprehensive view of philosophical governance, various inadequacies emerge as philosophical problems. The two closely related inadequacies to be briefly examined here are (1) those associated with what may be called 'problematic subsumption' (§§5–16) and (2) corresponding ones associated with understanding the force of logical necessity in the routine, non-problematic cases of subsumption in which this necessity is commonly taken to be exhibited in paradigmatic form (§§17–32).

5 The versions of norms treated in monadic replication theory are in the interest of that kind of analysis somewhat truncated and denatured. Commitment to analysis of this kind was supported by the successful way it seemed to apply to the large segment of our norm-guided actions that are routine. It is the practices embodied in highly routine action

that for many purposes lend themselves to representation by symbolic formulae specifying by the proper descriptive expressions certain key features of an action following the practice. For these purposes the formulae specify adequately the conditions of the action conforming to the practice, and the action itself. It is possible to skim off these key features and through them represent action conforming to the practice, because in practices of an extremely routine character much, both in the background of the action and in the action itself, may be neglected. But for other purposes what is neglected in this abstract representation is of great importance; and this applies eminently to the topic of subsumption, of following or employing a practice, of subsuming instances under a rule. Subsumption has a very different look, when one thinks of it concretely, as exemplified in action, from the way it looks when one thinks of it symbolically as merely a matter of effecting concrete expansion of a general formula by the substitution in it of proper specifying expressions for the variables employed in signifying the conditions of application. The easy way with which, given the rule that the Achaians are proud, we manufacture the expression 'Achilles (or Agamemnon, or Menelaus) is proud' masks some of the features of the more concrete process, not of substituting a name for a variable, but of applying in thought the rule about pride to individual Achaians. Thinking of the rule exclusively as it is expressed in the monadic formula, and subsumption as merely symbolic expansion like the above, one is encouraged to conceive of following practices, of applying rules in concrete cases as similarly an easy, automatic, and likewise all-or-nothing procedure.

Action following a routine practice, routinely subsuming instances under the rules of the practice, whether the action is overt or is only an action of thought, may be called 'routine' subsumption: this in contrast with those in which the appliction of rules is in some degree problematic. Routine subsumption is widespread, and unquestionably an essential part of human life. That it is widespread and essential does not justify the concentration upon it, indeed the almost exclusive preoccupation with it, that has prevailed in modern philosophy. One important reason for this concentration has been the success attained in the theoretical development of symbolic analogues of this process. So successful has been the collective analogue as a theoretical model of the process, that it has effectively graduated from its position as analogue to that of philosophic definition of the process itself. Just as among some enthusiastic psychologists the success of the model of the conditioned reflex led to the elevation of that model to the status of a definition of learning itself, so among many philosophers the admittedly valuable analogue of routine subsumption came to be taken for the process itself, and, in consequence whatever in the original process could not be reduced to the model was extruded from this refined philosophical conception of it.

6 Several things, be it noted, are being distinguished here: first, the general process of subsumption; second, two sub-species of the whole process denominated respectively 'routine' and 'problematic'; and, third, the symbolic analogue of the routine process. The thesis being developed here is that the great success of the symbolic model in illuminating the routine sub-species led to the mistaken identification of the subsumptive process with this model and with the routine processes of which it is a surrogate. In consequence of this the vast body of non-routine, problematic, less symbolically tractable subsumptive processes was excluded from the philosophically oriented study of rules and practices, and the wealth of illumination that may be developed from the study of them thereby lost. In particular, the consequence of this for the understanding of the warrant for change of practice has been that one of the major sources of change, and of the warrants for such change, has been on principle excluded from the consideration of practices in use and the sources of change and warrant in that use. An example of this in the area of cognitive practices has been the development of a theory of inference that concentrates upon determinate validating relations holding between premises and conclusions – the kind of relations that are characteristics of routine subsumption – and neglects the rich store of much less definite relations that hold between practices and conclusions drawn through them when following the practice is not routine, but requires in the following a kind of crafting of the practices themselves.

7 Applied to the simpler, more elementary components of practices, namely, rules, the point concerns the character of rules and of action following rules. A conception of following rules is seriously inadequate that does not include the problematic, as well as the routine forms of this activity, and that hence excludes from its purview of the whole process the function performed by the problematic forms in generating change and developing warrants for change. Valuable as it is for certain purposes for us to distinguish sharply our action in following a rule from our action in discerning the need for change in the rule and in moving to effect this change, for other purposes the distinction is

extremely unrealistic and the source of much theoretical as well as practical difficulty. For one of the most important sources of change of rules and of detection of warrant for change in them is our action in following them, and our alignment, while engaged, of the action with the ends that the rule is employed to serve.

8 It is important, then, to recognize the largeness of the role played in our lives by the mutant-producing capacity of problematic subsumption, to recognize the prevalence, proximity, and normality of this mutational effect. This effect pervades all domains of thought and action, from the most homely situations in daily life to corresponding ones in the physical and social sciences, including both the abstract mathematical ones and, of course, such extremely concrete ones as law, politics, religion, and morals. But it may be quickly observed that this recognition is not enough. Granted the prevalence, etc., of these mutational processes, what shall we make of them? Where shall they fit in our view of practices and rules, and of action guided by these? Upon what has in general been the majority view, these aspects of subsumption are not essential to it, are to be conceived rather as perturbations of the process due to imperfections of the practices or rules involved. When subsumption is viewed through the paradigm of symbolic expansion there is no place for, no need for recognizing these aspects of the process. Concretely, when applied to action governed by rules, this means that there is no place in the conception of rule-governed action for these same aspects, no place for the adaptive, adjustive, redefining, reconstructive processes that commonly in many areas of life are essential features of such action. Correspondingly, though for present purposes it is of less importance, there is no place for the stabilizing, fixing, and entrenching processes that similarly and as commonly accompany action. Upon methodological principle, the effects of use upon practices and habits are rigorously excluded from our view of action guided by these practices and habits; on principle we are prevented from recognizing in the action important sources of both change and stasis, and of warrants for each of these, as they bear upon the practices and habits themselves.

9 It may be helpful here to underscore some features of the terminology used so far in the discussion of norms and their employment, and now to be applied specifically to the topic of the subsumption of instances under rules. The logistic view of the application of norms, interesting and important as it is in itself, is more interesting and important for the topic of norms and rules as one

particular form taken by the more general monadic or atomic view of these. Incorporated in the replication theory of the employment of norms, such a view is a major component of deductivism.

A contrary view is one that emphasizes the concrete thought-and-action-informing functions of norms, rather than the operations of their symbolic analogues. Such a view may properly be termed a pragmatic one. Explicitly rejecting the monadic and replicative presuppositions of deductivism, as these are exemplified in the logistic view, a pragmatic view is more adapted to assimilating the holistic aspects of norms, and more capable of employing both the mutative and stabilizing effects of the processes employing norms in the illumination of the general topic of philosophical governance.

10 The roots of the divergence between these two views run deep. It would be rewarding to explore here the personal and social grounds to which the roots are attached and from which they derive sustenance. These grounds include dispositions and attitudes, and deep commitments and presuppositions, both ethical and metaphysical, through which these dispositions and attitudes are intellectually articulated. All these things seem to be implicated in these contrasting views of what rules of human practice are like, and how we can best understand what we do when we follow rules and thus, in thought or action, subsume instances under them. But the interest here is primarily on, and needs to be restricted to, a different facet of these contrasting views, namely, their consequences: and, among these principally, but not exclusively, the consequences for understanding the warrant of change of practice.

The consequences of the pragmatic view in this regard are the major advantage urged here on behalf of it in comparison with its logistic alternative. At the heart of the logistic view lies a conception of a process that has been described here as a symbolic analogue of routine subsumption. This analogue is seriously misconceived when it is taken to be a critical paradigm of subsumptive processes generally. For not only is it but an analogue, but also our employment of rules is by no means always routine. The routine cases – those in which the application of the rules is determinate – are complemented by a rich population of problematic cases in which application is more or less indeterminate. And depending upon many things in these cases – the degree of indeterminancy, the importance of the rule, the ends for which it is employed, and so on – the result is not always a failure to employ the rule to guide action. It is sometimes a revision or adaptation of the rule to make it apply, and hence guide.

Surely, one may think that there is little here that anyone, however logistic his proclivities, would object to. The controversial issue is not whether the employment of rules is always routine, nor whether the admitted non-routine cases shall be awarded the title of 'subsumption,' nor whether the title should be extended to cover the adaptive effects that so often accompany the non-routine cases. The issue is by no means exclusively or primarily a verbal one, but one concerning the significance that these admitted facts about subsumption have for our conception of what action following a rule is. To begin with the matter of the mutational effects, when they occur do they constitute something that is foreign to the subsumptive process? Are they perturbations of a basic process, the model of which can and should be conceived without them? Or are they one form of a more general effect – call it a 'reactive' effect – that is itself an essential feature of the process, so that what needs to be accounted for is not the presence of such effects in some cases but their apparent absence in others?

11 There is on the one hand a conception of following a rule as replicating a mode of action stipulated by the rule. The rule says, 'Slow traffic keep right,' and the slow driver replicates this in his response. The rule is an archetype. A person following the rule conforms to the archetype, exhibits in behavior an instantiation of it. Following is conforming. This view may be contrasted with one in which a rule is seen, not as an archetype to be replicated, but as one of a variety of components out of which the action governed by the rule is formed. For rules do not govern individuals in a monocratic way. They do so in company with other and often competing rules, and in a great variety of circumstances that can and do affect the action that is a response to the rule. The slow driver does not respond to but one rule, but to others that take into account the condition of the road, the state of the traffic, and so on. This latter view of action following a rule differs from the former archetypal-replicative one in being, rather, compositive or organic.

If the subsumptive process is regarded as a purely replicative one, the mutational effects that sometimes are generated in applying a rule to instances will be regarded as external to it. But if the heart of the process is not replication-in-act of a character already present and predetermined in the rule, but is rather the generation, creation, or composition of a character of which the rule is one major, but not the sole component, then an access otherwise lost to understanding these effects is provided. Thus, rather than a purely nominal point about what we shall choose to call 'subsumption,' the point is about the character of action following practices or rules, is about how action is informed by them. The reconception of these that is implicated in the assimilation of mutant effects to the subsumptive process is a considerable one. Having included these effects in the process and begun to understand the generation of them in individual actions, one is prepared to begin similarly to understand how, over extended time, these effects may be accumulated and stabilized. One who is most interested in the matter of change of practice, and in the warrant for change, will naturally be most interested in those effects that serve this end. But as the evolutionary model reminds us, the effects of use, of application, need not be mutational in character. The same forces that in some circumstances work for change of practice, in others further stability. The latter effect is especially pronounced in the forms of subsumption that have been called routine. In them the effect, over time, is to stabilize practices, and forms of action governed by them, so that altogether some practices are modified by the reactive effects of use; some are stabilized; some are eventually extinguished; and in the processes new ones are generated and refined. Routine subsumption, it now appears, should be viewed, not as a form of subsumption from which the general reactive effects of use are utterly absent, but those in which these effects are rather stabilizing, not mutational, and much less prominent than mutational ones.

12 Consider, for example, that subsumption to which J. S. Mill devoted much valuable if inconclusive effort in his discussion of the syllogism.[1] The application of the rule of human mortality to even so redoubtable a figure as the Duke of Wellington, is routine, as it would be if the subject were George IV or that king's valet. Nothing in the circumstances of drawing a conclusion about the mortality of these men is problematic; nothing suggests a question about whether each is an individual to which the rule of mortality properly applies, or similarly whether the termination of the mortal career of each properly qualifies as death. Nothing adaptive, accommodative, or generative in the way of reactive effects upon the rule is entailed by the application of the rule to the Duke.

Contrast with this our situation if we set out to apply the rule to such extraordinary individuals as, say, Elijah of Old Testament

[1]A System of Logic, Book II, chapter III.

theology (remember the chariot of fire), the mother of Jesus in modern Roman Catholic theology (think of her Assumption), or King Arthur ('I pass, but shall not die'). These eccentric examples illustrate the possibility of difficulty arising in the application of so routine a rule as that concerning human morality. For such out-of-the-way difficulties we have a ready supply of means that render them tractable without denying the reality of the instances from which they derive. A much richer supply of subsumptive difficulties would be required to lead to the revision of such a deeply entrenched rule as this. Such a supply might have seemed available to one of the early Christians of the first century expecting an imminent return of Jesus Christ, as it might now seem to a member of a Christian sect committed to some version of the millennial eschatology.

13 The possibility of problematic subsumption and hence of mutational effects in the following of rules involving terms or concepts extends to all those types of case that Friedrich Waismann made familiar some years ago under the title of 'open texture'.[2] The '*Porosität*' that according to Waismann inheres in all of what he referred to as 'empirical' concepts is essentially the possibility of borderline cases, this possibility residing in the circumstance that Waismann, evidently following Wittgenstein in the matter, described as our not having rules ready for the application of these concepts in all imaginable situations. If Waismann's judgment of the extent of this phenomena is approximately accurate, one must judge the possibility of mutational phenomena in the application of rules embodying these concepts to be equally extensive.

If all my large drill bits are in the black drill case, and if what I need to drill a hole for the bolt is one of my large bits, then the bit I need is in the black case. The rule, 'for large bits, black case' tells me where to seek such bits among my tools. Is there any way in which the application of this rule to bit-seeking could lead to some warranted change of rule? Obviously, if in following the rule I persistently do not find the large bit that I need. How could that occur? For one thing, my craft as a mechanic may develop in such a way that I use larger and larger bits, so that eventually a one-fourth inch bit, which once counted in my practice as a large one, and is normally the largest bit in an assorted pack, now counts as small, or perhaps intermediate.

[2] 'Verifiability,' *Aristotelian Society Supplementary Volume XIX*, 1945, pp. 119–50. Reprinted in A. Flew, ed., *Logic and Language* (1951), pp. 117–44.

A likely response to the portrayal of such a homely example of reactive change is that the proper employment of the subsumptive technique embodied in the example presupposes that descriptive expressions like 'large' do not undergo a shift in meaning in the process of delivering the intended conclusion. 'All you need to do,' it is commonly said, is 'define your terms' and proceed faithfully according to the definitions. The confidence of this remark is reminiscent of that of Achilles in Lewis Carroll's celebrated imaginary colloquy between Achilles and the tortoise. For just as Achilles is revealed there to be reacting to a kind of supposed incompleteness of premises in a simple deduction that cannot be remedied by the adduction of further premises, no matter how far this process proceeds, so anyone who supposes that the reactive phenomena can be eliminated from subsumption by a program of definition does not understand the character and hence the necessary limits of this latter procedure. There is a deep, basic reason why in the case of most if not all the terms we employ in subsumptive processes, we are not provided with rules ready for all imaginable circumstances. Or, more accurately, there is a reason why our rules of application for these terms do not provide answers to questions of application in all circumstances. For that is the kind of extreme sufficiency that rules of application alone are, in principle, unable to provide. This is what the open-texture of concepts teaches us. Rules of application of such concepts achieve definition of them in contexts in which for a variety of reasons all those disturbing imagined possibilities ('cats' that grow to the size of bears; 'goldfinches' that recite passages from Virginia Woolf) may be neglected. 'Sufficient unto the day is the definition thereof' is a rough rule of parsimony that is by no means limited to juridical practice.

14 Indeed, juridical interpretation, especially of items of constitutional law, and similar activities in other fields, provide some of the most striking of the readily available examples we have of the defining effects of reactive subsumption. From the time of John Marshall, for example, the subsumption by the United States Supreme Court of problematic instances under the famous Commerce Clause of the Federal Constitution giving Congress power 'to regulate Commerce ... among the several States ...' has repeatedly led to the refashioning of this grant of power. This reactive activity was most pronounced in the fourth and seventh decades of the present century. In the earlier period, after some years of increasing political friction, a Court that had been attempting to preserve a long-time, precedent-honored distinction

between 'manufacture' and 'commerce' in the interpretation of the clause, moved, in a widely celebrated (and bitterly criticized) set of reversals to greatly dissolve this distinction, and with that to affirm the power of Congress to intervene widely and actively in the regulation of the economic life of the nation. A generation later a succeeding body of judges on the Court effected a similar refashioning of the clause when that clause, as hitherto interpreted, abraded against a rising tide of sentiment in the nation to ensure to all persons, regardless of race, certain fundamental rights in public accommodations, employment, and in the possession and use of real property. At the present time the best known of recent juridical reactive subsumptions is perhaps that in which the Court in another celebrated reversal employed the equal protection Clause of the Fourteenth Amendment of the Constitution to invalidate the practice of regulating attendance of pupils to individual units of the public school system on the grounds of their race. This large quantum movement in the interpretation of this particular clause has so dislodged it from its traditional moorings in legal practice as to stimulate an avalanche of attempted expansion of its application that still continues, and in view of which it is impossible to say with any confidence what it will eventually be when legal interpretation and legislative attempts to influence that interpretation once more reach a state of relative quiescence.

Essentially the same capacity of a rule or practice to be remolded in subsumptive use was illustrated in an extremely rudimentary and personal way in the earlier example of the drill bits. A final, less rudimentary and more social example wculd be that of a university senate, previously composed of all faculty of the rank of professor, proceeding to interpret its own resolution to alter its composition to that of a number of representatives elected in a scheme of proportional representation from and by the full-time faculty members of the rank of instructor or above in the various academic units of the institution. The general rule of proportional representation of faculty has already undergone some reactive definition in the exclusion of staff members on part-time appointment and those below the rank of instructor, for example, graduate assistants. Further definition will be required when the rule of suffrage-cum-representation encounters units that have hitherto been classified as academic though members of them did not participate directly in the great teaching and research functions of the university. For payroll purposes, for union membership, or similar reasons, it was by and large more convenient to count them on the academic rather than the non-academic side of membership in the university family. An example of such a unit would be a large staff of permanent professional workers required to operate a large library, or collection of libraries, and the supplementary information retrieval agencies that are naturally associated with such institutions. The *Porosität* of the term 'faculty' begins to be apparent to the constitutional congress when subsumptive application of the proportional representation rule yields the result that the large staff of such a unit, most of whom have no formal teaching or research responsibilities, will now have a much larger voice in the determination of educational and research policy of the university than most of the academic departments that are directly engaged in performing these basic teaching and research functions of the institution.

15 The view of subsumption to which the logistic model is central is by design isolated from all those cases of the process in which mutational effects of some sort are realized. By design it is not competent to account for the ways in which rules and practices are remolded by their application or for the particular forms that the remolding in the various circumstances takes. Likewise it is unable to account for the omnipresent potentiality of mutational effects that resides even in those cases of subsumption, like that in the rudimentary deduction about the Duke of Wellington, that have commonly served as paradigms of the process generally. This last capacity seems seriously defeating. Some indication of the seriousness is given in one of the common moves made to avoid it, that is, by translating the subject from one of concrete subsumption to a subsumption of a more abstract symbolic kind, namely, of instances under rules for the management of signs, for the algebra of the permutation and combination of signs.

The uncovering of the potentialities of mutational effects in what may be termed the inner sancta of the logistic view supports the pragmatic view by making it now appear that those forms of subsumptive procedure that have usually been considered to be irreducible obstacles to it can be assimilated by it. These forms then serve to confirm rather than weaken the view. Where they once seemed to be the very models for a purely logistic conception of subsumptive processes, they are disclosed now to be rather special and misleading forms, in that in them the reactive effects are confirming and stabilizing, and in consequence inconspicuous. It is such subsumption that we are engaged in when we apply the rule of mortality to Socrates, the Duke of Wellington, or Prime Minister Thatcher, implicitly excluding Elijah, Arthur, or the Virgin Mother. Similarly it is such when, in certain circumstances we confidently apply such elementary logical rules as that of *modus ponens*, or the transitivity of the if-then relation, which we are nevertheless prepared to suspend in domain or situations, sometimes very concrete and sometimes highly theoretical, in which the conditions of application are seriously problematic.[3]

16 The exclusion of reactive effects from the logistic conception of subsumption is one of the sources and reinforcements of that celebrated puzzle concerning 'is' and 'ought' that was given classic formulation in Hume's *Enquiry Concerning the Principles of Morals*. How, the question may be put, by acting according to a rule (or practice), by means of a procedure conforming to and warranted by that rule, can we possibly arrive at a form of activity that deviates from the rule and to that extent is contrary to it? How can the 'ought' of the new procedure be generated in a logically defensible way from the 'is' of the original one?

Much of difficulty suggested by these questions is due to the abstraction by the logistic view of the reactive aspects of subsumption. The restoration of these aspects to this process is no small thing, no simple ad hoc revision for the purpose of easing the view past an embarrassing difficulty. It means revising our understanding of the process in a substantial way. It means breaking out of the confines of the traditional idiom of deduction and debate: of premises, and conclusions erected upon premises, deriving their stability from these premises, and therefore weakened by any tendency of the premises to move beneath them. It means, not rejecting the model of subsumption represented by these conceptions, but assimilating it into a wider view, the more basic units of which are not propositions, statements, sentences, not linguistic or quasi-linguistic entities of any sort, but ways of behaving, or proceeding in thought and action. Within this wider view provision can and must be made for the possibility – sometimes great and sometimes small – that in the very process of following these ways of proceeding, the ways undergo change, redefinition and reconstruction. The signs are now strong that what is needed is not more assiduous application of an old paradigm, but the elaboration of a

---

[3] The converging views of R. Nozick and F.I. Dretske on the matter that Nozick refers to as the 'failure of knowledge to be closed under known implication' is a striking example in recent theory of knowledge. Nozick, *Philosophical Explanations* (1981), pp. 204–11, 896–90.

new one, in order to understand the dynamic of practices in use, and with it the sources and nature of the warrant of practical change.

A variety of aspects of change of practice will be found to be more tractable to philosophical investigation when the reactive effects of subsumption are no longer repressed by our logistic super-egos. Detailed investigation of these effects and of the variations in the processes by which they are generated, should contribute richly to our understanding of changes of practice in general. Further related topics upon which investigation guided by an altered philosophical framework may fruitfully proceed are the extent to which reactive changes are essentially communal, and the extent to which they can be carried on by the relatively independent thought and activity of individuals; and the closely related topic of the extent to which and the most effective ways in which deliberate control of them may be effected. Cast in a new and helpful light also are two unrealistically sharp contrasts that have impeded progress in the theory of knowledge generally, and in the philosophy of science in particular, namely, that between the contexts of discovery and justification, and that between the intra-paradigmatic activities of problem-solving and the inter-paradigmatic ones of crisis management or conflict resolution.

17 It has not been much noticed that similar lessons subversive of replication theory and the logistic view of the subsumption exemplifying this theory can be drawn from certain matters emphasized by Wittgenstein in his reflections on rules and logical necessity. Attention to Wittgenstein's thought on these matters has been revived recently by Saul A. Kripke's discussion of these reflections in *Wittgenstein on Rules and Private Language* (1982). Kripke interprets Wittgenstein as presenting a paradox about meaning and then advancing a 'skeptical solution' of the paradox, much in the manner in which Hume formulated a paradox about causation and then proposed a skeptical solution of it.

18 The alleged paradox bears closely on deduction because it raises questions about how our thought and action are determined by rules and how necessary consequences in thought and action issue from such rules. With startling intellectual penetration Wittgenstein posed the following question about our proceeding according to rules. How, in following a rule, is action determined to follow the course that we commonly think of as conforming to the rule, when, if we consider just an individual who has learned the rule, and his subsequent action, there

113

is apparently no end to a number of contrary courses of action, any one of which may be conceived to conform as well as any other to the rule. For example, consider a person instructed to produce a sequence of numbers in the following way. Beginning with the early positive even integers we teach him to add 2 at each step, thus producing 4,6,8 and so on. But then rounding the turn at 1000, he produces the numbers 1004, 1008, 1012, and so on, rather than the expected 1002, 1004, 1006. We naturally say that at this point he ceased to follow the original rule, that the rule determined that the numbers go on in the way we expected rather than in the way in his thought they actually did. But how does the rule determine this? What is it about the person's performance that makes it a violation?

19 A primary object of criticism in Wittgenstein's reflections at this point is, of course, the notion of a private rule, and with that, of a private language. If one thinks of a rule as a mental or even cerebral construct that serves as a template for action, it is difficult to see how the idea of such a private template can be elaborated in such a way that in a case like this the rule itself determines the next response after 1000 to be 1002 rather than 1004. How did we, in teaching this person the rule by exhibiting applications of it at steps less than 1000, produce such a template in him that faithfulness to it required him to proceed in one way rather than another? What was the cue that he missed as he proceeded beyond 1000? How was 1002, 1004, already in the rule, as it were? And if it was, how did the subject miss it, especially, if, when taken to task, he insists sincerely that he was carefully following the rule? We protest, 'But after 1000 you were supposed to do exactly what we taught you early, namely, to add 2.' He replies, 'Yes, that is what I am doing. Doing exactly what I did before, at this point, is proceeding 1004, 1008, 1012, and so on.'

20 A central point of these and other similar examples discussed by Wittgenstein in the *Philosophical Investigations* (1953) and *Remarks on the Foundations of Mathematics* (1956) is the indeterminacy between anything in our personal equipment, conceptual or linguistic, that we might have conceived of as the model or template of action and that action itself.[4] It is not that the rule 'Add 2' does not determine us at the juncture of 1000 to proceed in a way that excludes as next items 1004, 1008, 1012; it is that it excludes it in a different way. And that

---

[4] *Investigations*, Part I, Sections 143–243; *Remarks*, I, Sections 1–5, 113–69, etc.

means that accordingly we have to understand rules in a different way.

21 In a paper, 'Wittgenstein and Logical Necessity,' some years ago Barry Stroud showed how attention to the interdependence of our rule-conforming activities illuminates Wittgenstein's emphasis upon the dependence of exemplifications of this activity upon forms of life in communities in which the activity takes place.[5] An analogous case conjured up by Wittgenstein in the *Remarks* was a people who in selling timber calculate the price of a pile of it by the area covered by the timber when piled together even though the timber may be piled together in any one of differing ways, yielding arbitrary different areas.

22 Emphasizing the element of custom in our methods of calculation, Wittgenstein asks how one might show such a people that they don't necessarily buy more wood by buying a pile covering a bigger area. One might

> for instance, take a pile which was small by their ideas and, by laying the logs around, change it into a 'big' one. This *might* convince them – but perhaps they would say: 'Yes, now it's a *lot* of wood and costs more' – and that would be the end of the matter. We should presumably [*wohl*] say in this case: they simply do not mean the same by 'a lot of wood' and 'a little wood' as we do; and they have a quite different system of payment from us.[6]

23 Stroud questioned whether such striking examples are as intelligible as they seem at first. Consider the hypothesized wood-sellers:

> Surely they would have to believe that a one-by-six-inch board all of a sudden increased in size or quantity when it was turned from resting on its one-inch edge to resting on its six-inch side. And what would the relation between quantity and weight possibly be for such people? A man could buy as much wood as he could possibly lift, only to find, upon dropping it, that he had just lifted more wood than he could possibly lift. Or is there more wood, but the same weight? Or perhaps these people do not understand the expressions 'more' and 'less' at all. They must, if they can say, 'now it's a lot more wood, and costs more.' And do these people think of themselves as shrinking when they shift from standing on

[5]*Philosophical Review*, vol. LXXIV (1965), pp. 504–18. Reprinted in G. Pitcher, ed., *Wittgenstein: The Philosophical Investigations* (1966), pp. 477–96.

[6]*Remarks*, I, Section 149 (Ital. orig.).

both feet to standing on one? Also, it would be possible for a house that is twice as large as another built on exactly the same plan to contain much less wood. How much wood is bought need have no connection with how much wood is needed for building the house And so on.

24 Stroud's general suggestion is, then, that

the initial intelligibility and strength of Wittgenstein's examples derive from their being severely isolated or restricted. We think we can understand and accept them as representing genuine alternatives only because the wider-reaching consequences of counting, calculating, and so forth, in these ways are not brought out explicitly. When we try to trace out the implications of behaving like that consistently and quite generally, our understanding of the alleged possibilities diminishes.[7]

25 This seems right. Further, it does seem to call for some recasting of our ideas of rules and our action in accordance with them. The reason that Wittgenstein's hypothetical rule-followers begin to fade in plausibility when the consequences of their aberrant rules are traced out, is that rules about measuring, pricing, selling, and using lumber are aspects of a large and interconnected set of human practices apart from which we cannot understand well how rules do determine action in the way that they do. A fixation upon rules of measuring, apart from the practices in which they are embedded and the ends they serve in the wider life of a community, will yield an abstract object which for some purposes rewards investigation, is enlightening, but for other purposes is obscuring to the point of paradox. Unhinged from its basis in the life of the community it loses its power to guide action, loses the power it would have and does have in actual life, a power so great that it takes a genius like Wittgenstein to imagine it dispelled.

26 Rather than requiring a skeptical solution to the problem of how a rule can determine action in accordance with it, these reflections help us understand how in fact this determination is realized. The rule of adding 2 does not guide a being who, like a newly created Adam, is without tradition, company, practices, and institutions from which our rules of calculation are generated. The rule guides beings like us, with all these developed resources. It is these that perform the function of

---

[7] 'Logical Necessity,' pp. 487–8.

ballast, providing the kind of responses that we count as steady performance. And it is these too, in a somewhat different social context, that render the lumber-measuring practices so wildly inappropriate to their larger social function that the response of the imagined lumber pilers, 'Now it's a lot of wood and costs more' cannot be 'the end of the matter.' This seems an eminently plausible way of reacting to the suggestion about beings that construct sequences or manage lumber transactions in the above aberrant ways. Stroud commented that in both cases the supposed beings would be 'different sorts of beings from us, beings which we could not understand and with which we could not enter into meaningful communication.'[8] This seems understatement. Rather it appears that the more we try to understand in detail the action of such beings, the less we succeed. The same fundamental obstacle, namely, logical incoherence, that would prevent our communication with them, should they exist, prevents our succeeding in imagining them to exist, when we understand what we are trying to do.

27 In his monograph Kripke aptly compares Wittgenstein's views on rules and meaning with similar views of W. V. Quine and Nelson Goodman: Quine on indeterminacy of translation and inscrutability of reference; Goodman on the 'new riddle of induction.'[9] Both analogies are apt, but the one with Goodman more striking and for present purposes more rewarding. One cannot help being struck with the similarity of the predicament of the putative mathematical thinker who is unconstrained at any point in the development of the sequence, and the inductive thinker who in applying predicates to emeralds is unconstrained to the extent that he may as well term them 'grue' as 'green.' Goodman's new riddle was among other things a further nail driven into the coffin of deductivism. For Hume, as for John Stuart Mill in some phases of his thought, the deductivist program seemed to be frustrated by the incapacity of the recursive model to explicate how the governing process could deal with such seemingly indispensable first principles as that the future will be like the past or that nature is uniform. Goodman's examples showed clearly that the adduction of such principles is insufficient to assimilate inductive generalization to the deductive model. Even given such principles there remains in such cases a further indeterminacy in choice of predicates to which these

[8] Ibid., pp. 492.

[9] Kripke, pp. 14–15, 20, 55–8.

principles are applied. For example, the term 'green,' as we ordinarily construe it applies to all observed emeralds, and so also does the term 'grue,' which we might construe as meaning 'up to the present, green; after that blue.' In the abstract, the principle of uniformity between past and future applies to emeralds equally well when the past ones are termed grue and when they are termed green. But they yield of course contrary conclusions concerning future emeralds: in the one case that these will be what we could commonly term 'blue,' and in the other what we would commonly term 'green.' 'Nothing so like as eggs,' wrote Hume, 'yet no one, on account of this appearing similarity, expects the same taste and relish in all of them.'[10] Similarly one may construe Goodman as saying, that nothing is so like as grue emeralds, yet no one on that account expects future emeralds to be blue, just as no one supposes that the pair, 1004, 1008 conforms to the rule for constructing the sequence in the way of the pair, 1002, 1004. Or, as Mill in other phases of his thought wrote,

> Every person's consciousness assures him that he does not always
> expect uniformity in the course of events; he does not always
> believe that the unknown will be similar to the known, that the
> future will resemble the past. . . . To look for constancy where
> constancy is not to be expected, as for instance that a day which
> has once brought good fortune will always be a fortunate day, is
> justly accounted superstition.[11]

28 Mill's point may be regarded as a specification, in one particular kind of application, of a more general point about action according to rules or norms that can be abstracted from Wittgenstein's reflections. 'Every person's consciousness assures him,' to use Mill's phrase, that acting in accordance with norms is not an empty notion, that as in the case of laws, there are definitely actions that conform and others that conflict with existent norms. If in the project of understanding these relations we are led to conceive norms and actions in such a way as to obliterative these relations altogether, we then have strong reasons to conclude that our conception is radically mistaken.

29 The more abstract grounds for the infeasibility of the deductivist program, ranging from those of Hume, Mill, Wittgenstein, and others, were complemented at a more concrete level by the historical work of

---

[10] *Enquiry*, Section IV, Part II.

[11] *A System of Logic*, Book III, Chapter III, Section 2.

Kuhn. A rich supply of further concrete grounds is furnished by the historical experience of the program in a variety of areas, not only scientific ones, but also in morals, law, and politics. Examples of this experience were given in Chapter 2.

30 Experiences in these latter fields strikingly illustrate some of the practical ill consequences of philosophical views and programs that seriously misunderstand their object. Difficulties and frustrations are natural in philosophical thought engaged in the governance of norms. But these are immeasurably increased when the nature of governance is fundamentally misunderstood, as it is on many occasions when the employment of norms in the guidance of thought and action calls, not for more intense and rigorous application of accepted norms, but for a reappraisal of them and, out of the reappraisal, the generation of revisions and replacements.

31 Commitment to deductive, applicative procedures as the exclusive legitimating ones effectively obscures the need for the ampliative, generative ones. Those whose commitment to deductive procedures is combined, sometimes in equal strength, with a conviction of the legitimating incapacity of these procedures, are naturally led to skepticism of the possibility of philosophical thought fulfilling to any extent the governing functions traditionally assigned to it. Decades of turbulent and often bloody contention over norms and ideals proper for human beings in the twentieth century amply testify the readiness of other less diffident and often less benign agencies of governance to assume these functions.

32 The obscuration of the need for ampliative governance more commonly has its effects among those whose engagement in philosophical reflection and governance is guided by an as yet unimpaired confidence in the sufficiency of deductive processes for the purpose. In philosophical thought concerning norms in everyday life, science, morals, and elsewhere, the frustrations encountered by the Cartesian deductive program in its more abstract exemplifications (material objects, other minds, inductive generalization) have their more concrete counterparts in controversies that are deeply rooted in opposed norms taken as basic, absolute, and as hence immune to either criticism, revision, or reconciliation. In such circumstances the shielding of controverted norms from the effects of ampliative processes – reflective, conscious ones as well as otherwise – is a shielding of controverted issues from the means of their resolution, and an intensification of frustration, hostility, and intransigence in dealing

119

with them. Examples in recent and contemporary thought are controversies over methodology in the physical and social sciences (indeterminism in physics; behaviorism in psychology) and in morals, law, and politics (human rights, abortion, various facets of race relations, and self-determination in international affairs.)

33 Various considerations, both abstract and concrete, thus reinforce and expand conclusions urged earlier concerning the indispensable role of ampliative processes in the governance of norms. As some of these considerations indicate, ampliative processes, or phases of processes, are not opposed to the deductive, applicative ones, but rather are complementary to them. Indeed from a broad point of view the two are indispensable to each other. They represent two factors at work in the employment of norms, both of which determine the manner and result of each employment, but often in greatly differing degrees. In routine, customary employment of norms in everyday life, or in the routine formalized procedures of logic and mathematics, the applicative factor is dominant and the ampliative minimal, while the situation is reversed in the redeployment of concepts in the reorganization of a mathematical field (for example, the development of the set-theoretical formulation of probability theory) or in the reinterpretation of fundamental legal norms in constitutional law. From time to time the mutative effect of employment is sometimes great and sometimes little. Heightened mutative effects signify a tension between the narrower and the wider aspects of norms: between their aspects as patterns of molecular segments of thought and action and as components of wider activities, practices, and institutions through which individual and communal life is realized.

34 The two mathematical examples discussed strikingly illustrate one side of this interdependence. In both the procedure of constructing the sequence, and that of calculating the price of the lumber, the dependence of the applicative employment of the norms upon their wider, ampliative aspects is striking. This dependence is ignored in the imagined response of those interlocutors of Wittgenstein who say, 'Yes, now it's a lot of wood and costs more.' Only by ignoring it can these *Holzhändler* philosophers insulate their norms of wood-handling and wood-pricing from the wider relations that wood-piling and wood-measuring have with other norms practices, institutions. Only by ignoring it can Wittgenstein himself, that one-time house builder on the Kundmanngasse, accede to their response, 'And that would be the end of the matter.'

35 In addition to such thought-experiments there is history. The historical experience of the West in various areas – in everyday life, in mathematics, science, morals, law, politics, and religion – is rich in illustrations of the valuable resources for the philosophical governance of norms that reside in the ampliative aspects of their employment. From time to time the conduct of governance in various of these areas has been referred to in preceding chapters. Ironically, it is the same aspects of governance that according to the view advocated here are resources for philosophical governance, that according to the view of many are in principle obstacles to such governance. Clearly the division between the views embodies a difference of opinion of what philosophical governance, the kind of governance that is possible by philosophical reflection is like. And at the heart of the division lies a difference over the philosophical theory and practice of what has been referred to as deductivism.

36 From the point of view of an opposed philosophical theory the task in the debate with the deductivist is not that of enabling such a person to see the resources of governance in these cases, but enabling him to see them *as* resources. This is no uncommon situation in philosophy. Many times in the analyses of perception philosophers have cited aspects of this experience as showing that its object is not fully real, which rather support a contradictory conclusion. It hardly shows the table that I see to be not a real table, that I do not see every aspect of it, or that what I am directly aware of in the way of color depends upon the light, the angle from which I view it, and so on. If what I am directly aware of in sight, if what I can visually inspect of the table did not so vary, but remained unchanged even when the light was extinguished, then I would begin to doubt that I was seeing a real table.[12]

37 The thought-experiments perform the special service of discrediting deductivism at a place of its greatest strength, namely, the abstract and

[12] 'The table ... appears to be of different colours from different points of view ... and we know that even from a given point of view the colour will seem different by artificial light, or to a colour-blind man, or to a man wearing blue spectacles, while in the dark there will be no colour at all.... Thus colour is not something which is inherent in the table.... But the other colours which appear under other conditions have just as good a right to be considered real; and therefore, to avoid favouritism, we are compelled to deny that, in itself, the table has any one particular colour or texture, or shape.... But if the reality is not what appears, have we any means of knowing whether there is any reality at all? ... Doubt suggests that perhaps there is no table at all.' Bertrand Russell, *The Problems of Philosophy* (1912), pp. 13–14, 24.

highly replicative operations of arithmetical construction and calculation. Once a disruption of the hegemony of deductivism has been created in this apparent fortress of strength, it is much easier for its one-time staunch supporters to begin to recognize more widely the limitations of a theory built squarely upon the replicative model. Recognizing the ampliative and hence governing potentialities of the effects produced in the activities in the community by the imagined practices of measuring lumber, it is not so difficult for one to see similar capacities in the ampliative aspects of other often much more concrete norms of thought and action.

38 Of course in most actual cases that fall within the jurisdiction of reflective philosophical thought the ampliative aspects are extremely broad and deep evaluation much more controversial. Controversial issues are of constitutional dimension, each side appealing to features of a constitution that as it stands supports, opposes, or leaves open contrary determinations. Such situations exemplify the unrealism of the often unthinking supposition that Dewey referred to as a 'hallucination – that all the questions that the human mind has asked are questions that can be answered in terms of the alternatives that the questions themselves present.'[13] Deductive processes by themselves in such situations, however acute and ingenious, are insufficient to deliver secure, acceptable determinations. These require acquaintance with and attention to ampliative aspects of the norms under adjudication, among these the human interests that the norms represent, the concrete ways in which these interests are pursued, and the institutional structures in which the norms are incorporated. This is not to say anything about the competence of philosophical thought in general to effect governance. It is to recognize only the indispensability to competent governance by philosophical thought of a broad and deep understanding of the norms with which it is engaged.

[13] *The Influence of Darwin on Philosophy* (1910), p. 19.

6

Norms as Universals

template view of norms and Oakeshott's criticism of
what he calls 'rationalism in politics.' But
understanding of ampliative processes and the role
they play in governance is better served if one
conceives the difference between ampliative processes
and deductive ones as residing in two different ways
in which norms are employed, rather than in two
different kinds of norms.

§§13–17   In learning to think and act one learns norms. And in
learning norms one does not simply assimilate
patterns of response. One assimilates with these
patterns a sense of propriety. For this sense is part of
the norms themselves. The sense of propriety is like a
cultivated taste, like conscience. Thus the resources
for scrutiny and criticism of norms need not be
invented and imported *for* norms. They reside *in*
norms. This theory has features of both intuitionism
and naturalism in moral theory.

§§18–20   A further metaphysical issue impinged upon here is
one of great implications for logic. Organicism in
Oakeshott's views criticized by Franklin. It is alleged
to lead a view of politics in which reasoned argument
is impossible and is replaced by 'some form of
divination or subjective intuition.'

    Organicism and logic. What is to be opposed is the
complete dominance of monadic, atomistic logic. We
all do think organically at some times. We are
justified in doing so. Indeed we must do so.

1 It was emphasized in Chapter 4 (§§7–11) that essential to an
understanding of the rational governance of norms is an understanding
of norms themselves. A few further features of norms need to be
recognized in that understanding.

The term 'norm,' like 'practice,' has been used here to refer to a
highly heterogeneous class of features of life and knowledge: settled
concrete practices, rules of thumb, scientific rules, laws, principles and
theories, logical and moral precepts, civil laws and rules of procedure,
and so on. The justification of treating all of this heterogeneous group
under this one title is that they all do represent norms of thought and
action, standards of procedure. In a variety of ways these rules,

principles, and so on, help to mold our thought and action by providing guides to what is proper, what is improper, and what is merely permissible. And in a variety of ways, and in various degrees, these norms, guides, standards, practices, come within the reach of governance.

Essential to their capacity to perform as guides in thought and action is an element of generality which has been discerned and treated by various writers in various ways. This element was a central feature of a relation which Hume postulated as fundamental in all of what he called 'reasonings concerning matters of fact,' namely, the relation of cause and effect. Upon the necessary generality of this relation Hume erected that skeptical paralogism that came to be known as the problem of induction.[1] Two hundred years later C. I. Lewis, with very unskeptical designs, followed Hume in discriminating as basic in our knowledge of objective reality something that he called a 'terminating judgment' and which he argued was essentially, if usually implicitly, general.[2]

2 This is not primarily a book on metaphysics. But a metaphysically sensitized reader will notice that several very fundamental topics in that field are being impinged upon. While extended discussion of these is not possible here, two of the most important of them deserve brief notice. They are the topics of (1) universals and (2) the determination of human conduct. Adequate treatment of the topic of criticism and change of norms involves one in thinking in a certain way of universals and of the way, in the form of norms, universals can guide human action.

3 The view of universals is by no means a new one, reaching back in modern philosophy at least as far as Hegel. Hegel's own views on the matter are not easily assimilable without some considerable linguistic indoctrination. They were expressed by him most explicitly in connection with the doctrine of the transcendence of the abstract universality of the representations of the understanding by the concrete universality of the notion (*Begriff*). This contrast was elaborated by Hegelian writers in Great Britain in the late nineteenth and early twentieth century in the linguistically simpler opposition between the 'abstract' and the 'concrete' universal.[3] A more assimilable version of

[1] For example, in *Enquiry* Book I, Section IV.
[2] *An Analysis of Knowledge and Valuation*, chapter VII, §8.
[3] A brief introductory bibliography on the topic of the abstract and the concrete universal is given by John Passmore in *A Hundred Years of Philosophy* (1957), pp. 66 n.

the aspect of these views that is most relevant here may be extracted from the teaching of Wittgenstein and Waismann concerning the open-texture of concepts and their definition. The bearing of this teaching upon norms is perhaps most obvious in the application made by Waismann in elucidating the relation between a scientific law and what he referred to as 'the experiential evidence' for the law. Against the positivist doctrine on this point Waismann argued that 'a law is not a sort of universal statement from which particular statements follow.' It is a mistake, he urged, to describe in logical terms, like 'entailment,' the relationship between a law and what serves to verify it. This would be correct if and only if it were possible to state accurately and completely all the conditions upon which the result of even the simplest experiment depends. This is not possible. The vague supposition, upon which we proceed from law to experimental result, to the effect that this is 'a normal situation,' that 'no disturbing factors are present' is one that 'cannot (in principle) be split up into clear and separate statements.' Put in other terms, a scientific law never states a sequence or concomitance of observable phenomena which, if it occurs, is a full realization, a full translation in the medium of phenomena, as it were, of the law.[4]

Waismann's interest in the implications of this doctrine were somewhat diverse from those that prompt reference to it here. He was, for example, more interested in the destructive bearing of the doctrine upon certain positivist views about language, theory, and experience that were widely accepted at the time he was writing. The positive, constructive implications of the doctrine with respect to universals, and norms as embodying universals, are very important. Some of these were touched upon by Wittgenstein in some very striking passages in *Philosophical Investigations* dealing with common names and rules for their application.[5] It seems possible that both of these men and their followers were unaware that the view of universals implicit in what they were urging was, in its rejection of platonism and what has come to be known as essentialism, coincident with views of Hegel. These views themselves had some limited precedents in the philosophy of that staunch formalist Kant. He had concluded that since 'to *define* ... really only means to present the complete, original concept of a thing ... an empirical concept cannot be defined at all, but only *made*

[4] 'Verifiability.'
[5] Pp. 31-8.

explicit.' A word like 'water,' he said, 'with the few characteristics we attach to it, is more properly to be regarded as merely a designation than as a concept of the thing.'[6]

4 Neither Wittgenstein nor Waismann proceeded to draw the conclusion that since empirical concepts must be incapable of complete definition of the kind Kant had in mind, they are not properly concepts. Agreeing both on the necessity and incompleteness of a large body, if not all, of such concepts, Waismann preferred to speak of this body of concepts as 'porous,' as having open-texture. But if so large a body, including all material-object concepts are necessarily incomplete in definition, one must wonder at the standard of completeness by which they are being judged. One alternative response to the state of affairs exposed is that if empirical concepts by and large (leaving aside the question whether there are any non-empirical ones) are and must be incompletely defined, this may reflect as much upon our view of what concepts are as upon our views of definition. What indeed would a non-porous concept be like, and why should we be in any way surprised by a discovery that they are much rarer than we thought, and perhaps even non-existent?

5 The answer of Wittgenstein and Waismann to this question is that a completely defined concept is one for which we are 'equipped with rules for every *possible* application' (Wittgenstein, emphasis added), for which we have 'rules ready for all imaginable possibilities' (Waismann). The reference to rules in both cases is a sign of how closely connected the linguistic topic dealt with by these men is to the topic of norms. Some readers may think that in this remark there is too much attention to sameness of words, and a neglect of difference of concept: a neglect of the radical difference between such things as scientific laws, mathematical rules, civil laws and moral rules – all of which may be plausibly thought of as dictating proper ways of thinking and acting – and mere linguistic rules defining the use of a word. Most readers, however, will understand this comment to issue not from an oversight but from a philosophical judgment, and to be indicative of difference in principle between – to put the matter in summary fashion – the view of this book and one which regards linguistic, and particularly, lexical rules, as purely nominal and ontologically innocent conventions and stipulations.

[6]*Critique of Pure Reason*, 'Transcendental Doctrine of Method,' Section 2, A727–28/B755–56. N. Kemp Smith trans. Italics in original.

NORMS AS UNIVERSALS

Divergence from this latter view is implied throughout the opening chapters, most explicitly in the discussion of the term 'concept' in Chapter 1 (§§7–10) and of the intimate relation between custom and reason in Chapter 4 (§§1–4). Difference of philosophical opinion upon this matter in Western thought extends as far back as Plato's *Cratylus*, even to Herodotus. In the late eighteenth century and early nineteenth century it was a subject of contention between the positivist leaders of the Enlightenment and that strong counter-revolution against Enlightment hopes and principles that characterized what might be called the Hegelian century. It remains a subject of voluminous discussion and contention today over such subjects as linguistic determinism, the cases for and against a universal grammar, indeterminacy of translation, conceptual schemes, and epistemological and ontological relativity. In the interest of completing a general discussion of criticism and change of norms, these and other closely related topics may not be ventilated here. Upon the particular point of issue of whether linguistic rules of grammar, semantics, and of general development and use of linguistic terms may be treated as mere linguistic rules, the position taken here is that there is no 'mereness' about it, and that the unknowing Hegelian dictum early in the *Philosophical Investigations* (Part I, §19)) is a fundamentally sound one. To imagine a language *is* to imagine a form of life.

6 Once one has concluded that concepts must be thought of in a different way, a natural move – and once one has surmounted the distinction between what used to be called the 'material' and the 'formal' modes of speech, an obvious move – is to the further conclusion, corresponding to that about concepts, that the objects of these concepts, the denotata of the terms must likewise be thought of differently. This move was made by writers in the Hegelian tradition under the formula of identity-in-difference. To these writers the view, presently advocated by some, that in place of one universal character exhibited in the objects one should think of the group of objects as marked off from others by their family resemblance to each other, would have seemed to be a relapse into a discredited and intellectually enervating nominalism. Rather than abandon the view of the reality of universals, in consequence of such phenomena as the open-texture of concepts, they proposed that we think of universals differently and also differently of the way in which they are realized in particular instances. These writers were thus not, either in intention or accomplishment, advocating a family-resemblance theory in a confused and antique way.

128

Their differences with such a theory were real and profound. The move to such a theory, from their point of view, would have to be regarded as an unsatisfactory half-measure, dictated by the incapacity of many philosophers to make the profound and radical revisions of well-entrenched metaphysical and logical theories that fuller, more satisfactory measures require. For what was called for on the side of metaphysics was the kind of transformation of our view of what we pick out and refer to as objects, real entities, creatures, persons, etc., that came to be known in much debate earlier in this century as the theory of internal relations. On the side of logic this in turn called for what to most who have been brought up in the Anglo-American tradition an intolerably agonizing reappraisal of principles of accepted logic centering upon the interpretation and application of the Principle of Identity.

7 It is the view of universals emerging from this reappraisal to which the doctrine of the concrete universal applies. The general doctrine was exploited by idealist writers for the purpose of supporting an array of broad metaphysical, logical, ethical, aesthetic, and political conclusions. What is most pertinent here is the bearing of the doctrine upon the relation between norms, as universals, and the particulars to which they apply. Hegel expressed the point in question in his lectures on logic by saying that the generality of universality of the notion is not a set of common features (*ein Gemeinschaftliches*) abstracted from the particulars which have their own independent existence. Rather than 'the common' abstracted from the independent particular, Hegel said, the true general is to be thought of, in its relations with its particulars, as *particularizing* itself (*specifying* itself) in them and remaining by itself in them without, as he put it, 'any disturbances of its clarity.'[7] Put more prosaically this seems to mean that it is the nature of the general to particularize itself, that particularization, realization in differing in differing instances, is not contrary to, but in accordance with, its identity. Neglecting here most of the large metaphysical and epistemological iceberg that lies below and, for Hegel, supports this visible tip, one may notice that in this explicit pronouncement he seems to be saying that, in accordance with the doctrine of identity-in-difference, just as it is of the nature of the general to particularize itself,

[7] *System der Philosophie*, Erster Teil, Die Logik (The 'Lesser Logic'), §163. *Sämtliche Werke*, H. Glockner, Hrsg., Band 8, pp. 358–61; W. Wallace trans., *The Logic of Hegel* (1892), pp. 291–4.

so it is of the nature of the consequent particulars to differ from each other; and this, of course, not just numerically but qualitatively. So J. N. Findlay, in his comment upon this passage, interprets Hegel as saying that rather than being 'merely common to the species and individuals it informs, the universal is *differently* realized in each of them' (italics in original). There is, Findlay adds, no more mystery or problem here than there is 'in seeing how a Universal like "being greater than ten" can specify itself in different numbers, or how a Universal like "man" can specify itself in the various sorts and conditions of men.'[8]

8 The second metaphysical topic mentioned above as being impinged upon the treatment of norms is that of the determination of human conduct. Some points of impingement have already been alluded to. In Chapter 4 (§§7–10) it was emphasized that it is a misconception to think of norms as entities capable of having existence apart from things: that, instead, they exist in life, and are interrelated because aspects of life are interrelated. Corresponding to this misconception of their nature, a misconception of their employment in the guidance of thought and action has been identified as replication theory (Chapter 2, §§1–5); and two respects in which the inadequacy of the replication model generates difficulties for logical theory have been elaborated upon (Chapter 5). Rather than independent templates determining the character of appropriate thought and action by dictating reproductions of themselves in these media, norms serve as components out of which, with other materials, instances of thought and action, which are no mere replicas of themselves, are constituted. What is to be observed here, in further elaboration of this view of the employment of norms, is that action in accordance with norms is not to be conceived on the model of pre-established and automatic responses to stimuli. The most influential paradigm in the study of human behavior during the past hundred years has certainly been that of Pavlov: that of the conditioned reflex, itself a modification of a simpler neuro-behaviorial conception, that of the reflex arc. Entailed in the view of norms and of rationality in thought and action advanced here is a rejection of this general model for the understanding of human action. Rejected therewith is the general assumption that human action can be adequately understood when the exclusive model employed for

[8] *Hegel: A Re-examination* (1958), p. 226.

understanding is that of those simple causally conceived connections discernible in human action which are regarded as the paradigms of understandibility in human action because they are in no characteristic or essential way human. Rejected is the assumption that human action can be comprehensively understood as a kind of grand mosaic of self-dependent instances of action of this kind, the analogues in this medium of the particulars, which, Hegel said, on the abstract view of universals are taken to have their own independent existence. Abandoned is the conclusion, drawn from the discoveries of modern natural science, which the economist-philosopher Frank H. Knight some years ago formulated ironically, as 'an inference, characteristically drawn by the "best minds of our race", that since natural objects are not like men, men must be like natural objects.'[9]

Accordingly, with respect to norms and the way in which the actions of human beings are guided by these norms, to be rejected is the view that this guidance takes place in a piecemeal, fragmented way, that norms guide human action by providing fixed templates which serve in the manner of a mechanical die or mold to produce as replicas atomic bits or episodes of action. This misconception concerning norms and action is as basic in its own sphere of influence as are its readily perceived analogues, for example, the nominalist view of universals and the inductivist view of the growth of knowledge. According to it one thinks of human beings as, by learning, having internalized within them these templates of action which now supplement such templates already engraved in them by nature as the well-known pupillary and patellar reflexes. Guidance by such templates is, with minor variations, an all-or-nothing affair; one conforms, or does not conform, by acting, or not acting, within the parameters set by the template. To the extent that one acts according to a norm, in that action one follows the path, the route, the course laid down by the norm. In the graphic if inelegant words of the well-known limerick, one moves 'in predestinate grooves ... not even a bus, [but]...a tram.[10]

---

[9] *Freedom and Reform* (1947), pp. 226–7.
[10] Here, for those not familiar with the limerick:
There once was a man who said, 'Damn.
It is borne in upon me I am
An engine that moves
In predestinate grooves;
I'm not even a bus, I'm a tram.'

M.E.Hare

131

9   One important recent philosopher who on occasion opposed this misconception was Dewey. Beginning with his very important criticism of the reflex arc concept, in 1896, in the course of developing his functionalist theory of mind, Dewey came to the conclusion that many psychologists and educators radically misunderstood the character of habits and other forms of learned responses in human beings. They misunderstood individual forms of response by thinking of them along the lines of the stimulus-response reflex model, a consequence of which, he said early, was to make activity 'a patchwork of disjointed parts, a mechanical conjunction of unallied processes.'[11]

An alternative view of habit emphasizing with Dewey the flexibility of conscious behavior guided by habit, the interdependence of habits, and the aspect of purposeful action in habit, was elaborated by Boyd H. Bode, a contemporary and follower of Dewey who was very influential as a teacher and writer in the philosophy of education. In books on psychology and education Bode argued that habits rarely attain the fixity of the reflexes commonly employed for understanding them; that they serve as the vehicles for all kinds of adaptive behavior; and that they do not function in isolation from each other or from other activities to which they must somehow become adjusted.[12] 'In order to understand conscious activity.' Bode said, 'it is necessary to deal with habits, not in isolation, but as elements in adaptive behavior.' Conscious acts

> are guided by the perceived situation, which directs them towards an end. Habits enter into such activities and make them possible, but the habits are combined into wholes which as wholes are not mechanical at all, but flexible, so as to suit the circumstances of the moment. The final act is an integration of habits and is a new thing.[13]

[11] 'The Reflex Arc Concept in Psychology,' *Psychological Review*, vol. 3 (1896), p. 358. See also *Human Nature and Conduct* (1922), Part One, Section I; Part Three, Section I. In the Schilpp volume on Dewey, Gordon W. Allport observed that Dewey did not consistently adhere to this conception of habit, sometimes attributing to habit, in Dewey's own words, 'machine-like repetition, a duplicating recurrence of old acts,' *The Philosophy of John Dewey* (1939), p. 272.
[12] These views were a marked shift from Bode's earlier view expressed in *Fundamentals of Education* (1921). There (p. 150) he said of habit, 'Its outstanding characteristic is not flexibility but fixity of response. Habit is just an acquired reflex.'
[13] *Conflicting Psychologies of Learning* (1929), pp. 270–1.

That part of the total act which consists in steps taken to achieve integration, Bode said, 'is what we ordinarily call intelligence.'[14]

10 The bearing of all this upon norms is direct. The rigid, reflex view of habits, which Gordon W. Allport referred to as 'the ball-and-chain' conception, is a version of the same fundamental misconception of norms which views them as strict templates for action. The separation of habit from intelligence against which Dewey and Bode argued is fundamentally one with what, adopting a Deweyan way of speaking, is a mischievous dualism separating reason from norms. One would be duplicating this dualism upon a large scale if one attempted to draw as sharp a contrast as that urged by Kuhn between normal (habitual) science and science of a revolutionary (basically innovative) kind. It is not a question of there being some contrast here, but rather of how sharp and fundamental the contrast is taken to be. Kuhn's general exposition and conclusions concerning scientific revolutions called attention to the serious ways in which actual scientific development and practice in modern times has diverged from the canon of legitimate development and practice prescribed by the one-time well-entrenched positivist philosophy of science. This was a most valuably illuminating contribution. But to the extent – and it is not minimal – that Kuhn was led to draw disturbing agnostic conclusions about science from these discrepancies, the conclusions reflected less upon the discrepant scientific processes than upon the background of philosophical presumption that dictated that the discrepant characters were flaws. Kuhn's interest in scientific work has been primarily historical, and primarily directed to episodes of broad change in theory and practice in the course of development of the physical sciences. His depreciating remarks about certain aspects of these episodes need to be evaluated, in relation to his major interests, as the collateral comments, the obiter dicta of one whose acquaintance with and influence by the current positivist orthodoxy led him to expect otherwise. Similarly his supposition that in the periods of great change the sciences have a manner of development that is radically different from that in the more static ones seems to be in part a gesture of compensatory justice to that orthodoxy, for which, though displaced from revolutionary periods, great application is to be found in the more enduring and more characteristic periods of normality.

[14]*Modern Educational Theories* (1927), p. 198.

11 There is some substantial agreement between what have been identified here as weaknesses of the template view of norms, and weaknesses identified by Michael Oakeshott in what, in his book of the same name, he called 'rationalism in politics.' Writing in 1947 Oakeshott estimated that at that time almost all politics in Europe and in culturally closely related regions of North America had become Rationalist or near-Rationalist. The Rationalism to which he referred distinctively with the upper-case letter is not a view characterized merely by some general allegiance to reason or rationality, but by allegiance to reason conceived in a quite particular way, namely, one that coincides substantially with what in its application to reflective thought in the governance of norms has been called here 'deductivism'. Noting the Cartesian, individualist, and skeptical features of this flood of Rationalism in which we are all but inundated, Oakeshott found that the pre-eminent source of its endurance lay in a doctrine about knowledge which can be outlined by first making a distinction between two kinds of knowledge, namely, technical and practical. What distinguishes technical knowledge from the practical kind is that it is susceptible to formulation in rules, principles, directions, maxims, in short, 'in propositions.' By contrast, practical knowledge is not susceptible to formulation of this kind. 'Its normal expression is in a customary or traditional way of doing things, or, simply in practice.' 'Technical knowledge can be learned from a book ... [or] in a correspondence course.' 'Practical knowledge (speaking strictly) can be neither taught nor learned, but only imparted and acquired.' Though distinguishable, these two kinds of knowledge do not in fact exist separately, and both are always involved in any actual activity. The doctrine of Rationalism, then, is that what has been discriminated here as practical knowledge is not knowledge at all, that instead all knowledge is technical knowledge. Thus, 'the sovereignty of "reason", for the Rationalist, means the sovereignty of technique.'[15]

12 Translated into the terminology of norms Oakeshott's doctrine is that there are two kinds of norms, knowledge of which issues in the two kinds of knowledge just outlined above – kinds which are discriminable though sufficiently interdependent that they cannot exist separately. Writing in reaction to and criticism of a generally positivist view of politics that overemphasized the claims of technical

---

[15] *Rationalism in Politics* (1962), pp. 7–13.

knowledge, Oakeshott naturally responded by stressing what to him were the equally legitimate claims of practice, of the kind of knowing that practice itself represents. There is some considerable agreement between Oakeshott's stress on practical knowledge in politics and the stress of this present book upon ampliative processes in which we are engaged with norms. Perhaps the most important difference, beyond the obvious one of generality, is that it appears that an understanding of ampliative processes is better served if one conceives the difference between ampliative processes and deductive ones as residing, not in two different kinds of norms, but in two different ways in which norms can be and are employed. Among the advantages of this way of discriminating technical from practical, or deductive from ampliative, is that, granted that these processes are so interdependent that they cannot be separated, conceiving the difference to be in a different use of norms rather than in a difference between two kinds of norms is extremely helpful in enabling one to understand the interelations between the processes and, among these, the distinctive role that the ampliative ones play in the generation, definition, criticism, and reconstruction of the norms that come to be employed in both types of use. While much of what Oakeshott calls 'technical knowledge' can be understood without regard to ampliative processes affecting the norms involved, what cannot be well understood is the ways in which, under philosophical scrutiny, the norms themselves display their liability to reinforcement or alteration, and their need for activity directed to one or other of these ends. The interrelations of norms, and the rationale for imported governance that takes place through these, is best understood first, not at the complex and rarified level at which philosophical governance intervenes, but at the simpler, more homely level of everyday life of which governance is a constant ingredient.

13 A person learns to act and think in a variety of ways, in a variety of roles, as a member of a variety of communities. In a modern civilized society a person is normally a member of a family; a practitioner of some single occupation or profession, or a combination of them; a member of a variety of political, religious, cultural organizations; and so on. A person learns to act reasonably in these roles by engrafting onto his inherited equipment, by assimilating, by being indoctrinated in, a large and complex cultural inheritance which contains rules, precepts, maxims, patterns of action, a variety of cultural entities which have been referred to here as norms. And of course pre-eminent among the norms with which one is inculcated are those of morality,

those which are taken to apply to each person, not as teacher, doctor, or mechanic, but as a human being. Expanding a term employed by Toulmin to refer to the set of concepts representative of a historically developing discipline, one may refer to this cultural inheritance, on the analogy of physical inheritance, as collectively forming a 'transmit.'[16]

It has been urged above, in the somewhat abstract and general vocabulary of 'habits,' that it is a serious mistake to think of the enculturation of a person into these norms as a process in which he is equipped with a repertory of fixed, unthinking modes of response. A person who was so equipped, in whom the norms of his social environment had been absorbed as if they were such modes of response, would not pass for long as a person trained in a certain discipline, occupation, or craft, or as a responsible moral agent.

It is not, of course, that a person learns norms as fixed paths of action, and learns also an independent, supervening craft, namely, how to judge. Rather, one learns to judge in learning how to act, in being educated in norms of action; and learns to judge only in relation to patterns of action. One who separates these in thought under the rubrics of 'habit' and 'thought' is in this medium executing the bifurcation executed by Descartes on a grand scale, and like Descartes is doomed to a vain effort to assemble together aspects of human activity which, with the best of intentions, have drastically and unhappily been put asunder.

14 In the face of much inclination to think otherwise, it is hard to emphasize too greatly the integral relation between these two aspects of norm-guided human action: patterns of action, procedures, on the one hand, and scrutiny, judgment, criticism applied to these procedures, on the other. Neither can be conceived adequately when divorced from the other. A part of procedure learned, a part of a norm of action, is some sense of propriety concerning the pattern of action represented in the norm. And a great deal needs to be packed into this conception of a sense of propriety. It embraces a sense of the relative importance of different modes of procedure and, with this, of the purposes in the life of the community in which a judgment guided by this sense is made. An excellent example of alertness to the wide sweep of social significance relevant to such a simple practice as that of grading of students' papers is the discussion of this matter by Arthur E. Murphy in his Carus lectures, *The Theory of Practical Reason*.[17] One can

[16] *Human Understanding*, p. 158 ff.
[17] Chapter 3.

participate in such a practice as this with very little appreciation of the wide significance of what one is doing in, say, assigning numbers to the answers made by students to examination questions, just as in the familiar case treated by J. O. Urmson one can participate in the grading of apples with little understanding of the significance of the labels or classifications employed in effecting this particular partition in the collection of the fruit.[18] But, save in some Pickwickian sense, save as a mechanical analogue of an overt phase of some larger social function one cannot be thought of as engaged in grading or evaluating. The sense of propriety developed by one in learning to act in accordance with approved procedures is part of that general knowledge that one has of what he is doing which, as a variety of writers have emphasized, is an essential feature of intentional action, as it is a kind of knowledge that is capable of great variation in degrees of adequacy. Terms like 'sense' and 'intuition' apply well to this knowledge, so long as one remembers that what is referred to here is not some altogether inborn and perhaps also infallable faculty. The sense or intuition in question is not of this character; it is more of the character of cultivated taste, or judgment, or conscience.

15 The analogy with moral judgment suggested by the word conscience is helpful. As a child grows to maturity, becomes a socialized human being, he absorbs more and more of the moral standards of his community, or of the various communities of which he is a member. And, to be sure, the standards which he absorbs in school, church, or synagogue, may diverge widely from those derived from older associates in work or play or in other forms of leisure activity. One may think of these standards in a very simple way, as incorporated in maxims like those of the Ten Commandments or the Golden Rule, or like that to the effect that what matters most is how you played the game, or, by contrast, that there is no substitute for victory. Or they may be such complex systems of standards as those of the Talmud or of the moral teaching of the Catholic Church. In the case of any particular precept such as the compressed Golden Rule, or the commandment not to bear false witness, understanding the rule entails a sense of propriety with respect to the formula of response encapsulated in the rule or commandment, the conditions under which and the way in which it is applied, its importance in relation to other ways of proceeding, and so

[18] 'On Grading,' *Mind*, vol. LIX (1950), pp. 145–169. Reprinted in A. Flew, ed., *Logic and Language*, second series (1953), pp. 159–86.

on. Over two millennia ago Plato made the point, in the opening Socratic dialogue of the *Republic*, that the act of telling the truth or paying one's debts does not by itself constitute a just (or righteous, *dikaios*) act. Overall there is a significance in justice which extends to the whole nature of a just man and to that of a society in which he lives, since a thoroughly just life can be lived only in a society which is itself just. Thus when one pays back a debt under ordinary circumstances, but refuses to give back arms to the rightful owner who comes to claim them when he is not in his right mind, one illustrates in a striking and extreme way that by itself the act of paying a debt does not constitute a just act, but does so only when the act of repayment is in keeping with a broad sense of justice which could be described as a sound moral and political conscience. One expects a person who has been brought up properly in the morality of paying one's debts, to refuse to give back arms to the non-competent claimant, not because beyond morality there is moral theory in terms of which he can be expected to weigh the merits and demerits of returning property in this case and come to a sound conclusion, but because a man who learns in a proper way the norm of paying one's debts learns with it, indeed in it, a sense of propriety with respect to claims, rights, and duties which permits him to withhold what in many other cases he would be obliged to relinquish. It was a lack of this sort that President Calvin Coolidge many years ago noteworthily displayed when, asked to comment upon the complex and vexing problem of the repayment of loans to the United States by economically distressed countries which had incurred large debts to this country during World War One, he said simply, and, as Murphy tartly observed, simple-mindedly, 'They hired the money, didn't they?'[19] And it is similarly an unusual contravention of such a sense of propriety which the authors of the musical comedy contrive for our amusement when they have the girl of somewhat easy virtue offer to justify what might seem to be delinquent behavior by recounting how in moments of moral stress she thinks of the Golden Rule and then does for an ardent lover 'what he would do fur me.'

16 The sense of propriety with respect to modes of proceeding that is part of the norms passed on from generation to generation, from teacher to student, from upperclassmen to their juniors, from master to apprentice, and so on – like the various languages each individual speaks, including whatever attached technical terminologies he employs

[19] *The Theory of Practical Reason* (1964), p. 117.

– is a somewhat idiosyncratic and somewhat eclectic reflection of a composition or systematization of norms achieved and maintained in change by the various communities of which each individual is a member. This aspect of the composition of norms, that it becomes internalized in individuals, is obvious and needs little emphasis in comparison with the internality of compositions with respect to norms themselves. The authority of the composition and the sense of propriety that reflects that composition derive from norms. These norms, in joint consequence of their positions within the compositions and their employment in the guidance of thought and action, are subject to change. The changes, when they occur, are themselves capable, in greater or less degree, of effecting change in the composition itself. The composition of the norms affects life for the individual and the community, just as the character of the norms, and life lived in accordance with the norms, affect the composition. And as a consequence of this both composition and norms in the community, sometimes gradually and sometimes abruptly, undergo redefinition.

17 The resources for the scrutiny and criticism of norms thus need not be invented and imported for norms. They reside in norms themselves and in the ongoing compositions of which they are components. And since the process of scrutiny and criticism is one of mutual interaction among norms themselves, rather than of the employment of any norm or set of norms as a standard to which all others must conform, rational governance achieved in this manner is critical rather than foundational. Rather than being invented, the resources of scrutiny and criticism need to be exposed and understood, understanding being an obvious condition for exploiting the resources and guiding the process, where this is possible, in an understanding manner; and exposure being required because both the resources and the process have been greatly obscured by the models of these resources and processes which have dominated modern philosophy. These models have effectively led us to neglect resources constantly present, though not always in the same degree, by blinding us to a process constantly going on, though not always at the same speed, right before our eyes.

18 A theory designed to reflect these resources and processes as they are rather than as philosophical preconception dictates they must be, and that views the processes of scrutiny and criticism in individuals and communities on the analogy of character formation, conscience formation, will formation in the moral life, has features of both

intuitionism and naturalism in moral theory. With intuitionism the theory recognizes that an indispensable feature of our employment of norms is a sense, like that of conscience, of their proper relation and coordination. It holds that apart from this sense, rules, maxims, or formulae do not function as norms. On the other hand, this sense is related to norms in a reciprocal way. Consequently, while norms without sense are barren, as intuitionism emphasized, so sense without norms is empty, as was emphasized by naturalism. Since both norms and sense, internal to each other as they are, are necessary, the truth lies with neither of these theories taken as exclusive alternatives. But when these two theories are themselves composed to each other, they both are altered. The ways in which we think of moral norms and of conscience are changed.[20]

19 Implicated in this view of norms in relation to their composition in human life is a further large metaphysical issue, which also is of great significance for the philosophy of logic. As before, the issue is not a new one, having been joined a hundred and fifty years ago by Hegel himself and raised intermittently by generations of more or less Hegelian metaphysicians and logicians. In a very useful and strongly critical review of Oakeshott's *Rationalism in Politics* Julian Franklin called attention to the issue under the title of 'organicism.'[21]

In spite of Oakeshott's admittedly sincere disclaimers and efforts to the contrary, Franklin argued, he was committed by his 'organicist' view of politics to the conclusion that substantive political judgments are fundamentally and in a wholly undesirable way intuitive. They are such that between two fundamentally opposed judgments 'no reasoned argument is possible.' In short, as Franklin saw it, Oakeshott was committed to opposing rationalism, not merely to the extent that this term refers pejoratively to some extremist view in which an appreciation of formal rules and principles has expanded like a cancerous growth into idolatry, but also to the extent that it refers to any view which conceives of fundamental political questions as falling within 'the field of knowledge properly so called,' as capable of being answered by reasonable procedure, argument, and logic, without

---

[20] A similar but somewhat divergent composition of these two contrasting moral theories is presented and elaborated, with special emphasis upon the historical contexts in which these theories flourish, in A. O. Rorty's 'Naturalism, Paradigms, and Ideology,' *Review of Metaphysics*, vol. XXIV (1971), pp. 637–67.
[21] *Journal of Philosophy*, vol. LX (1963), pp. 811–20.

dependence upon 'some form of divination or subjective intuition.'[22]

Franklin's route to this conclusion in his review is more interesting and, up to a point, sounder than the conclusion itself. He sees with admirable clarity that to the extent that organicism holds for any domain, be it politics or whatever, there are limitations to the adequacy for that domain of what he calls 'ordinary logic.' Since what is referred to as logic in the ordinary language is formal, atomistic logic, it surely follows that in the respects in which, and to the degree which, any subject-matter is 'organic,' that logic will be distorting and, if taken too seriously, misleading. This raises the question which Hegel faced, of whether there is not, for the purpose of dealing with concrete wholes and internal relations, a more appropriate way of thinking, 'a higher and more reasonable logic in which ... the limitations of ordinary logic are shown to be transcended.

20 The reader is not left long in suspense over whether that higher and more reasonable logic is forthcoming. 'It can readily be shown,' Franklin avers, 'that Hegel's dialectic, like any other dialectic of this sort, being devoid of any formal principle, itself depends on intuition.' And just as readily demonstrable, surely, is the simplistic manner in which any organic view of politics or any other subject is convicted by Franklin of a dependence upon intuition, and a commitment to all those unattractive features, for example, 'divination,' 'subjectivity,' and presumably also thinking with one's blood, which he conceives intuition to have. Of course, if the only alternative to a formal and atomistic logic is a *Schwärmerei* of undisciplined thought, is 'wallowing,' to borrow Peirce's phrase, 'in the rich mud of conceptions,' then there is no acceptable alternative to rationalism in politics or any other subject. But surely this is an altogether false, unrealistic choice.

There are times when it is appropriate and necessary to think abstractly – to use a Hegelian phrase – and there are times when concreteness in thought has equally valid claims. In the latter kind of thought we do not treat the objects of thought as atoms or monads; whether we are aware of it or not there are aspects of these objects to which the celebrated rules or principles of monadic thought – like the celebrated Principle of Identity – do not apply. To many, the thought of this is alarming, reinforced as it is by that stern warning of J. E. McTaggart to the effect that no one went about to break logic, but in

---

[22] *Ibid.*, pp. 814–16.

the end logic broke him. Concern about this is natural but unfounded. First, because the departure from abstract logic against which they are warned is not something altogether novel – which they now have the opportunity to consider embarking upon or refraining from. Whether we recognize it or not we all do commonly and fortunately think concretely of concrete things, organically of things, which in their relations with each other form organic wholes. The habitual practice of concrete thought seems to have the same capacity to surprise many of its practitioners that the practice of speaking prose had for Moliere's bourgeois gentleman.

Secondly, in this practice there is no necessary fault. What is faulty is not thinking organically *simpliciter*, nor is it thinking monadically *simpliciter*. It is, rather, thinking organically of monadic matters and monadically of organic matters. No sensible person, for example, would try to think of the United States House of Representatives, in its capacity as a legislative body, apart from its relations with other branches of the government and the functions it performs both with them and complementary to them. Similarly, no one would try to think of a word, say, an ordinary descriptive word like 'brown' or 'cow,' in utter abstraction from everything else, the language in which it functions as a word and the kind of functions which in the language it performs. To try to do these things is to 'break with logic' in just as real though not so blatant a way as to try to think of a cube that does not have twelve edges or of a man who both is and is not thirty years old. It is not a break, of course, if the only principles of reasoning to which one accords the title of 'logic' are monadic ones, but a break surely with principles of reasoning which in their own way, and for their own purposes, have equally valid claims. That we all do naturally and necessarily, in dealing with some matters, think organically, is no sign that – heirs of some intellectual original sin – we are condemned to fall short of some ideal which is impossibly elevated. It is, rather, a sign that the ideal, though understandable as an expression of a kind of intellectual puritanism, is itself impossibly foolish.

Part 3

AMPLIATIVE GOVERNANCE

7

Sources and Modes of Governance

1 The materials are now at hand, and the manner of using them already suggested, for a more detailed account of the operation of ampliative processes in the governance of the norms of thought and action. To this end the present and immediately succeeding chapter will be devoted.

How, if in all proceedings in thought and action we are guided by norms, do we proceed in thought and action to criticize, revise, and, in short, govern norms? One way of putting the answer succinctly, if somewhat cryptically, is that it is a necessary character of norms that they be subject to, be formed by governance.

How is change possible? Again, norms of the kind that are under investigation here are norms only to the extent that they are liable to change. Governance of norms, and their liability to change, are entailed by an aspect of them that is essential to their function as norms. This aspect is that they are constituents of a composition, which itself may be thought of as an individual or interpersonal character, will, or conscience. Consequently, as was argued in the preceding chapter, it is a fundamental error to think of norms as templates of action or response. Norms inform and guide action of individuals and communities in their capacity as members of a corporation of patterns of action, as features of a corporate character, will, or conscience. It is hard to overemphasize the significance of the two correlated errors: first, that of thinking of norms as independent entities, abstracted like Platonic forms from the world of change and becoming; and, second, that of thinking of actions as fragmented acts or responses of organs, members, or faculties themselves abstracted from the *person* for whom these are organs, members, or faculties. Norms guide the actions of persons; it is the actions of such beings, not the responses of legs to electric shock or of eyes to a flash of light, which are guided by norms. It is a person responding, not an abstract organ or member. And in the responses of a person, norms, as a patterns of response, have always their places in relation to other patterns, in consequence of which they are necessarily, to some extent, subject to governance.

2 Though it is somewhat redundant, it seems necessary to emphasize that the composition is itself always liable to change through the interaction of its components. Indeed, it is not just liable to change; it is to some degree always the locus of change. To the character, will, or conscience of a living person or community of persons, change in various degrees and at various rates is endemic. One does not need to suppose, as Hegel seems sometimes to have done, that the impulse to

change in the consciousness of a person or community realizes itself always in the fixed pattern of a dialectical waltz, in order to recognize, as Hegel to his great credit did, that in persons or communities there are always, and bound to be, both forces leading to the maintenance of achieved composition and forces tending in some degree to its dissolution and transcendence. It is the nature of norms and the compositions of which they are constituents that, so long as life according to and through them proceeds, no composition is final. Each is subject to internal and external forces productive of change. Some of the source of change of norms, and, through them, of composition, were treated in Chapter 4 (§§7–11), where they were divided into the following three main classes.

- First, the direct reactive effects of the application of norms to more or less tractable instances.
- Second, the conditioning of norms through their interrelations, both reinforcing and conflicting, with other norms in the various bodies or compositions of which they are constituents.
- Third, the less direct more general effects of the existential conditions under which norms are employed that, unlike the direct reactive effects of their application, are mediated to them through their interrelations with others.

A consequence of these sources is that the compositions achieved in bodies of norms always exhibit, in some degree, the complementary characters of incompleteness and inconsistency, of under-determination and conflicting over-determination. A composition is incomplete because there are substantial areas of possible thought and action for which at any time there are not ready at hand accepted, settled modes of procedure. And it is inconsistent because there are again substantial areas for which there is a plurality of accepted procedures ready to apply to individual cases and leading to widely disparate, conflicting results.

3 Among the internal sources of conflict among norms, and hence of inconsistency in their composition, is one which deserves to be remarked because it has been widely neglected. This source is a dispersed, heterogeneous exemplification of what might be called, with a nod to Kuhn who called attention to some of its broader, more global exemplifications, the 'paradigm effect.' In *Induction and Justification* it was observed about truth claims that the effect of what Kuhn called a 'paradigm' is realized in less striking ways throughout the institution of knowledge. 'The investigation of the grounds for any truth claim

and the formation of a judgment on the acceptability of that claim,' it was said,

> is never restricted in its effect to just this claim. Every successful inquiry leading to the fixation of a claim somewhere in the constellation of facts, beliefs, opinions, and so on, is always to some extent a pattern for further inquiries about other claims. Every successful claim, however modest its scope, is to some extent striving to be a paradigm in its own world, a leader in its family.[1]

The point can be generalized to apply to norms. There is in our modes of procedure a natural imperialism, a natural tendency of accepted practices to expand their spheres of influence. This leads them to conflicts over territories whose present governments, like the governments of many lands that were enveloped by Western imperialistic expansion, are weak. The expansionist impulse which is so unmistakable in large-scale paradigms – such as gravitation theory, mechanics, and evolution theory in science, the germ theory in medicine, parliamentary procedures in government, vertical, steel-skeletoned structures in architecture, and dam building in the management of rivers and water resources – is reproduced on a small scale in our inclination as individuals or communities to transfer and expand beyond their original scope of practice, ways of thinking and acting to which we have become habituated in more or less successful use. Our actions betoken recognition of this tendency on a minute scale when, in applying varnish with a brush, we curb a natural tendency to duplicate the strokes we learned and successfully employed in brushing paint.

The disturbing effect of the collision of expanding practices is one source of criticism and change in compositions and norms, as norms are put into practice and life is lived in accordance with an achieved composition. It is not enough to recognize that norms are always open-textured or incompletely defined in the sense in which Waismann used these terms to apply to concepts, that hence the employment of norms in composition may always lead to the uncovering of borderline cases illustrating the incompleteness of the norms and the consequent need of redefinition. Rather than just a possibility, the generation of hard cases, of cases that are hard because they are borderline ones, is, in general, a natural consequence of norms in use, as is the redefinition of

[1] P. 268.

norms which use thereupon calls for. Since this redefinition can be achieved only by some redefinition of the composition of which the norms are constituents, out of composition arises change in norms, and reciprocally out of changes in norms change of composition itself.

4 Much of the appeal of foundation theory lies in the directedness and definiteness of the answer it offers to the question posed at the beginning of this chapter about how governance is possible. How, since governance, considered as a process, is itself carried on in accordance with norms – itself employs norms – can it ever succeed in being thoroughly legitimating? The answer of foundation theory is, in effect, that there are some norms that in one way or other are immune, as objects, to governing processes. In consequence they are fitted to serve as ungoverned governors upon which the totality of governing processes can be conceived to be grounded. Over the years – now centuries – the prima facie appeal of this answer has been dissipated by a mounting tide of considerations, the moral of which was expressed in the form of a dictum in the Introduction and elaborated upon in opening this chapter, to the effect that an uncriticized, ungoverned norm is a contradiction in terms. There are not, because there cannot be, among norms ungoverned governors. Essential to a pattern of action's being a norm is that it be a constituent of a composition, more normally a multiple of compositions. Being such a constituent it is necessarily in some degree the object of governance in response to the influence of all three conditioning influences discriminated above.

By itself a pattern of action lacks the definition that is necessary to its being a norm; and it achieves this definition in comparison with, in contrast and collision with other patterns of action, and as a result of various direct effects of its own use and that of others. It is in response to such influences that patterns of action represented by injunctions to tell the truth, to desist from cruel and unusual punishment, not to abridge freedom of speech or of the press, to insure for every person equal protection of the law, and so on, become the norms that they are. It is in a competition with other norms which is necessary to its identity as a norm that the injunction about freedom of the press comes to exclude, at least in normal cases, prior censorship, or crying fire falsely in a crowded theatre. And it is similarly that the injunction about equal protection comes to cover a black child's entrance into a school in Topeka, Kansas, but not the entrance of a woman to a Turkish bath in Ypsilanti, Michigan on a night reserved for men, and not the freedom of an employee of the city of Chicago, in opposition to a regulation imposed by the city council, to maintain residence outside the city limits.

It may be thought by some that it is highly inflated speech to speak of governance in this way, to assimilate under the title of governance influences and processes of this wide kind with those exemplified in reflective philosophical thought. Of course in practice we adopt and adapt patterns of action which we deem appropriate to the circumstances. One even curbs one's inclination to smile, sneeze, or cough in view of the circumstances and of the bearing of other patterns of behavior in these circumstances.[2] But is it not perhaps inflated and seriously misleading to think that our disinclination to applaud the invocation at a public meeting displays the effects of governance of the norms of applause?

The justification of speaking and thinking this way does not lie in common habits of speech and thought, but in a philosophical view: a view arrived at in an attempt to understand among other things how one may think of the norms of thought and action in a way that emphasizes their social character without being committed to some kind of stifling social determinism. It was such a commitment which Peirce was expressing when, in arguing the uselessness of ethical science as normally pursued, he said that without the aid of studies of the philosophical basis we all know what morality is, namely, 'behaving as you were brought up to behave ... [obeying] the traditional maxims of your community without hesitation or discussion.'[3]

According to the view advanced here no one is or could be brought up *just* to obey the traditional maxims of his community. And, *a fortiori*, neither morality nor rationality consists in this. In community life and in the lives of individuals, maxims function as norms, which themselves are not simly formulae for response, but features of larger compositions. As Darwin found the rudiments of rationality among lower species, so we may find governance in rudimentary form widely distributed in everyday life. Reflective governance in its more overt and noticeable forms is a continuation, at a high level and in a more complex, prominent, and self-conscious way, of a procedure that

[2] In the preface to *Scepticism and Animal Faith* (1923), George Santayana wrote, in anticipation of the temptation that the reader might have to smile at the offering of 'one more system' of philosophy: 'In the first place, *my system is not mine, nor new* (italics in original). I am merely attempting to express for the reader the principles to which he appeals when he smiles. There are convictions in the depths of his soul, beneath all his overt parrot beliefs, on which I would build our friendship.'

[3] *Collected Papers*, 1.666.

goes on at much lower levels in a largely unself-conscious way. This holds of reflective governance in both its deductive and ampliative forms, or, to speak more precisely, in both its deductive and ampliative *phases*. For, as has been stressed, one aspect, and often initial step, in the illegitimizing of ampliative processes of governance, is the separation in thought of the deductive phases from the ampliative ones and the employment of these abstracted objects, considered as independent processes, as models for a theory of philosophical governance. An initial step in the contrary legitimization of ampliative phases is the understanding that – valuable for certain purposes as the separation of these phases may be – for the understanding of philosophical governance, the interdependence of the two has to be recognized and exploited. To speak Hegelese for a moment, since the deductive processes so discriminated require for their own development, for their own self-realization, to be combined with and enriched by their ampliative complements, in the broad view of these matters required by an investigation of philosophical governance the opposition between them must be overcome. And, if the lesson needs to be spelled out further, the same may be said of normal and revolutionary science, of established and innovative constitutional law, of habit and intelligence (Dewey), or (Hegel again) 'understanding' and 'reason.' If without the nourishing sources in ampliative processes, deductive ones wither, no theory of governance can be adequate that concentrates upon the deductive alone.

5 All this bears upon the how-possible question to which foundation theory in its various forms is an elaborate response. In contrast to that response, the view advocated in this book does not accept this question in the sense in which it is posed in that theory. Rather it seeks to transform and rectify the question. For the question as traditionally posed, arising out of the indispensability of norms as means employed in the governing process, itself rests upon the presupposition of the fundamental rightness of deductivism. With the rejection of this presupposition, the question is altered. Governance is no longer problematic. It is not only possible, and actual; it is necessary, omnipresent, and inescapable.

To someone strongly influenced by deductivist foundation theory such a response to the original question will seem unsatisfactory. What is offered to him under the title of governance are processes with which he was already familiar, whose reality he never thought to doubt, but whose relevance to the original question he is ready to dispute. What the original question asked about, he may point out, is not the possibility of these omnipresent and often commonplace processes that are urged to be essential to the character, the identity of norms. It did not ask about just any processes whatever that might with some propriety be accounted governing ones, but about governing processes of a kind that are instantiated in philosophical thought. How are the kinds of governing processes possible that we need to engage in in such thought: when the norms of thought are broad and deeply entrenched; when the activity is in a high degree reflective; and when the character of processes is such as to help us discriminate what we do well and also what we do ill in our engagement in these processes?

6 This not unreasonable rejoinder deserves some reply. First it may be observed that if the special kind of governance intended is deductive governance, if that is the only kind that will be accepted as genuinely reflective and philosophical, then of course the deductivist, foundationist position is presupposed at the outset and with it the irrelevance of ampliative processes in general. Such is the result of elucidating governance by employment of concatenated 'What justifies you?' Socratic questions that more subtly presume a deductivist answer to the 'how possible' question.[4]

Secondly, we have here an illustration in philosophical thought itself of the way in which any considerable transition in theory entails ampliative processes and a concomitant recasting of conceptions. These occur in the present case as in thinking about governance one moves, often slowly with difficulty and with the ever-present possibility of relapse, from the framework of forensic, individual deductive processes to that of often social, testive, and generative ones. In this governing process itself the ruling consideration will not be internally in one or other of these two frameworks, in what points can be made forensically and probatively with the means supplied in each. The inclusion of the widely instanced non-philosophical and non-reflective ampliative governing processes with the reflective, philosophical ones in a view of philosophical governance must establish its superiority over the more restrictive deductivist view of philosophical governance by its superior capacity to illuminate these processes for those interested in them and

---

[4]A more detailed discussion of the philosophical presuppositions implicit in these apparently innocent justification questions is given in Chapter 6 of *Induction and Justification*.

provide understanding guidance for those having occasion to engage in them. The illumination and guidance it will provide will not be in the form of a canon of method. It will, on the contrary, emphasize the wideness, variety, and complexity of consideration that enter into the search for composition of norms of the kind with which philosophical reflection is characteristically concerned. It will emphasize that in this wideness, variety, and complexity, and, more importantly, in the very nature of the compositions striven for in philosophical governance, there are fundamental and conclusive reasons for abandoning the supposition that the needs can be met by deductive processes alone.

7 The hunger for ungoverned governors is hard to dispel. Dissipated in one form it tends to reconstitute itself and appear in another. So one common response to the kind of view advanced here is a disposition to look for the ungoverned governors hidden in it. These it will suppose it has found in the characteristics sought in the composition of norms: characteristics like harmony, coherence, conservatism, and simplicity. Still somehow committed to the deductive mode, one seeks to find in characteristics such as these the materials for the final governing principles of governance. And of course there is little to be found. Such broad, abstract, and desiccated characters can quickly be shown to be poor candidates for the sovereign throne of deductively governing principles.

One must resist the urge to extract supreme governing principles from such characters, as one must resist generally the urge to search for ungovernable governors. The contrast between these two views at this point is not over the location of the basic governing principles necessary for the deductivist program to be a feasible one. One who seeks for such principles, and who judges the adequacy of the view presented here by its capacity to provide them, must surely judge the view severely. For these characters are not suitable for the purpose, nor are they intended to be. In them one has not found at last the fugitive first premises that a non-deductivist view must *malgré lui* eventually own. These are not premises, first or succeeding ones. They are not candidates for the throne, for it too is abolished in the achievement of constitutional reorganization that the abandonment of deductivism entails.

8 Conservatism combined with open-mindedness; harmony combined with healthy competition; simplicity combined with sensative complexity; these and others are all characters that are entailed in composition. They are dimensions, variable determinables, in terms of which from time to time, in various degrees, and with various weights

154

we judge compositions, both achieved ones and ones recommended for achievement. They are dimensions in which compositions extend, not themselves criteria of the magnitude of the extension. Only in a concrete case, for example, is it possible to make any sensible judgment of the manner and degree in which simplicity is desirable, and likewise complexity. Indeed only in reference to concrete situations can simplicity, complexity, and the rest be given any but a most general, empty and honorific significance. Compositions should be as simple, and as complex, as they need to be. Truisms like this are little guide in dealing with the varied concrete issues over governance that arise in conduct of and reflection upon affairs in mathematics, the natural and social sciences, morals, law, politics, history, religion, and various other domains of public and private affairs. Appreciation of the variety of norms that from time to time call for composition in these and other domains, and of the variety in the compositions they call for, discourage the thought that somehow embedded in the concept of composition lie ready to be exposed the absolute unowned premises of a philosophy that presumes to operate without them.

9 Philosophical sagacity in the governance of norms is possible. But it does not consist in a set of first principles that like a collective intellectual touchstone, preserved and polished by the philosophical priesthood, stands as the ready fixed universal criterion of governance in whatever fields issues concerning governance may arise. It is the beginning of wisdom to come to understand that philosophical sagacity does not so consist: that *general* sagacity itself about governance consists more in understanding the directions in which compositions are to be sought and the means by which they are produced than in particular expertise in knowing how successful compositions are to be achieved or are achieved in any specific domain. As the particular manner and forms in which composition is achieved are not fixed in general for all occasions, so likewise not fixed for all are the relative roles played by deductive processes in that achievement. Both surely are generally necessary, though sometimes what is pre-eminently called for is more intense and strict application of accepted norms, and sometimes less strict, more liberal, expansive employment of them. And frequently it is only due to some increased intensity in the deductive application of norms that the need and directions for their expansion are disclosed. Part of the general sagacity about governance that general philosophical reflection can provide in the various areas of practical and theoretical life in which it is pursued, is that in that pursuit neither one of these

155

broad ways of employing norms may on principle be excluded. Neither by itself will suffice.

10 The term 'composition' has been used here to express a view much wider though somewhat analogous to that expressed by W. V. Quine in writing of the corporate rather than individual way in which 'our statements about external reality face the tribunal of sense experience.' That norms face the tribunal of life corporately of course does not deny the reality of the facing process but rather characterizes it. But this characterization is not sufficient by itself to define for philosophical purposes the goals of the process or the criteria by which success in it may be judged.

11 Nevertheless, and especially in the present philosophical situation, the emphasis upon the corporate character of the norms that come under the jurisdiction of reflective philosophical governance is not inconsequential. The emphasis is a facet of the opposition of a contextualist, pragmatic view of governance to a deductivist, foundational one. The division between these views, according to what has been said, is deep and extensive, affecting in important ways how we think of norms, practices, habits, rules, and action guided by rules or norms. Through these it affects further our views of the character of human action in all the various humanistic disciplines in which the basic character of that action is focal. With respect to reflective philosophical governance of norms, recognition of the corporate character of the aspects of governance, and hence of the governing process itself, is an essential first step in the development of a theory of governance that is based not upon antique preconceptions but rather upon a realistic understanding of actual governing processes. Such a theory offers relief from the persistent compulsion to carry out governance only by means of a set of narrow, recursive steps, and to neglect the complementary processes of wide progressive adjudication. Contextual, pragmatic, systematic theory provides an intellectual constitutional stance upon which we can proceed to do in reflective philosophical governance what we all to some extent do naturally, upon which we can proceed to do openly, without intellectual misgivings, what otherwise philosophical preconceptions may force us to do under the cover of some distorting and often impeding intellectual disguise. The theory assists us in diverting intellectual energies from the centripetal patterns of expenditure that much academic custom has imprinted upon us, to the centrifugal patterns which in many cases are indispensable to the achievement of a

legitimate and secure governing result.

12 A stage of composition achieved by governance, philosophical or otherwise, is not necessarily a new stage, though it often is. Sometimes the result of governance is properly more conservative than innovative. But it can be genuinely the latter. Recognition of and emphasis upon this distinguishes a view of governance incorporating ampliative processes from a deductivist one, since a defining characteristic of the deductivist view is the claim that all legitimate governing results are the results of the application of already installed, pre-existent established norms. The opposing claim is that not all new norms are merely ostensibly new, the applicative offspring of norms already established. There are indispensably others that are genuinely new in the precise sense that they cannot be derived from already established ones in a strictly applicative way. Offspring of established norms, their relation to these is that of legitimate successors to them, their legitimacy residing, not in their recursive derivability from them, but in their capacity to perform the function of guiding thought and action in situations in which their predecessors have become deficient. Commonly norms of philosophical breadth and depth do not wait upon reflective recognition of their deficiences in order for these deficiencies to make themselves felt. Nor do they wait upon reflective creativity in order to begin the process of generating remedial successors. But it is a presupposition shared by both deductivist and non-deductivist theories of governance that attentive alertness to the deficiences of composition in accepted norms and deliberate intelligence devoted to the task of repairing them can often improve our governantial experience and performance.

13 Philosophical understanding of the ampliative phases of governance offers as dividend, then, no organon for the conduct of these processes. It offers instead grounds for holding that the development of such an organon is not only not to be expected but also not to be desired. These grounds lie in aspects of norms, their concrete character and their corporate interrelations. They lie in the way in which they do actually guide thought and action; in the bearing of these upon the effects that guided thought and action have upon norms themselves; and in the reconsideration of reflective philosophical governing processes to which an appreciation of these things leads.

14 In view of the massive and corporate character of norms of thought and action that from time to time come before the tribunal of reflective philosophical judgment, it verges upon the quixotic to

suppose that in the philosophical criticism of them an understanding of these complex entities and the roles they play in the lives of communities could be replaced by some ready intellectual standard that can be employed without such understanding. To someone confirmed in the expectation of such a standard, a philosophy excluding its possibility will seem defeatist and skeptical. But upon a more balanced view it appears to express, rather than skepticism, a proper regard for informed judgment in contrast to uninformed substitutes. Just as ampliative reasoned elaboration of law requiring careful, refined understanding of accepted law cannot be replaced by deductive, applicative procedures, however ingenious and refined, so it is generally when in philosophical governance deductive procedures need to be supplemented by ampliative ones. The broad and deep understanding of the norms subject to governance by ampliative processes is not a sign that on this occasion proper philosophical procedure is being diluted by the infusion of an inferior substitute. Rather it is a sign that the means of governance are responsible to its needs, and that further, as in the legal case, in assessing the needs of governance in norms there is no substitute for a wide and deep understanding of accepted norms themselves. Understanding of this sort is indispensable in order for reflective philosophical governance to be a kind of activity that, in addition to challenging one with many delectable intellectual puzzles, also qualifies, to adapt words used by William James nearly a century ago, as a study worthy of serious men and women.

15 The primary focus of attention in the present study is governance of a particular kind, namely, reflective philosophical governance, and with that the differences and relations between the ampliative and the deductive phases of this general process. But as has just been emphasized, an important part of understanding ampliative governance as it is realized in reflective philosophical thought, is understanding governance more generally: not only its *deductive* but also its *ampliative* forms, its *non-philosophical* as well as its *philosophical* forms; and its *non-reflective* as well as its *reflective* forms.

The three characters, 'R' (reflective), 'D' (deductive) and 'P' (philosophical), taken as independent, contingent attributes of governance, yield in the abstract an eight-fold classification: four reflective forms, RDP, $R\bar{D}P$, $RD\bar{P}$, $R\bar{D}\bar{P}$, and four corresponding non-reflective ones, $\bar{R}DP$, $\bar{R}\bar{D}P$, $\bar{R}D\bar{P}$, $\bar{R}\bar{D}\bar{P}$. A brief overview of some of the differences and relations between the species distinguished in this simple taxonomy may be of service in further delineating the character of reflective philosophical governance as it is realized in both its deductive and ampliative forms.

RDP. Ready examples of reflective deductive philosophical governance abound in the dominant Cartesian tradition in modern theory of knowledge. Particularly clear and notable are the analyses of our knowledge of 'external' objects presented early in Bertrand Russell's *The Problems of Philosophy* (1912) and *Our Knowledge of the External World* (1929) and later in C. I. Lewis's *An Analysis of Knowledge and Valuation* (1946). More recent examples are R. M. Chisholm's elaboration of the notion of epistemic justification in *Theory of Knowledge* (1966) and, on the more formal side, J. Hintikka's investigation of epistemic logic in *Knowledge and Belief* (1962).

RD̄P. The classic exemplar of reflective ampliative philosophical governance in modern theory of knowledge is Hegel's *Phenomenology of Spirit* (1807). Braving the entailed anachronism one may say that the primary topic of this work, namely, the logical processes invoked in the evolution of forms of consciousness, was an anticipatory answer to the challenge that many philosophers saw in the view promulgated by Kuhn that such transitional paradigm shifts cannot be rationalized by 'logic and experiment alone.' By means of the ampliative processes of dialectic Hegel attempted to show, contrary to, say, Hume's skepticism on the matter, how a form of consciousness characterized by a commitment to common-sense objects (substances and attributes) develops our prior immediate and in the end self-refuting sense certainties. A fine exposition of this particular transition is given by Charles Taylor's essay on the opening arguments of the *Phenomenology* in the A. MacIntyre collection *Hegel* (1972). Readers of the moral and political writings of John Rawls will have made the acquaintance of ampliative governance in political philosophy in the processes and products embraced by Rawls under the concept of 'reflective equilibrium.' A close relative in the philosophy of law is the process of legal interpretation for which Henry M. Hart and Albert M. Sacks coined the name 'reasoned elaboration.'[5]

RD̄P̄. Reflective deductive non-philosophical governance is plentifully illustrated in routine normal science, comparable 'normal'

---

[5]G. Edward White, 'The Evolution of Reasoned Elaboration: Jurisprudential Criticism and Social Change,' *Virginia Law Review*, vol. 59 (1973); reprinted in White's *Patterns of American Legal Thought* (1978).

juridical interpretation, and in the routine elaboration of commonly accepted moral rules.

$R\bar{D}\bar{P}$. Contrasting with reflective deductive governance in non-philosophical domains are, for example, expansive elaborations of moral, political, and legal principles. An example of reflective governance of this kind in politics is given in the next chapter (§1, 6–8) in connection with Michael Oakeshott's discussion of the enfranchisement of women in Great Britain in this century. Aspects of the elaborative interpretation by the United States Supreme Court of the important Commerce Clause of the Constitution, already alluded to (Chapter 5, §14), are discussed briefly in both Chapter 8 (§14) and Chapter 9 (§12). Further examples are the decisions of the Court on school segregation, (*Brown v. Board of Educ.*, 347 US 483, 1954), state poll taxes (*Harper v. Virginia Board of Elections*, 383 US 663, 1966), and state laws restricting abortion (*Roe v. Wade*, 410 US 113, 1973).

$\bar{R}DP$. Philosophical governance that is non-reflective is exhibited again and again in the very real though less than conscious penumbras of philosophical reflection where we are unwittingly guided by deep presuppositions the consequences of which we follow without recognizing their source. Unwittingly we suppose space to refer to some receptacle, rather than a complex of relations, and suppose that sensation terms like other common substantives refer to 'things,' albeit ones of a very special kind.

$\bar{R}\bar{D}P$. Non-reflective, ampliative philosophical governance can be discriminated as complementary to the corresponding reflective governance in any of the wide-spread and deep social movements in modern Western history: the rise of capitalism, political individualism, nation states, democracy, and modern science. Various examples from the history of science are discussed in Chapter 10 (§§6–13). Matching the many important non-deliberate, non-reflective, and even non-conscious processes in individual mental life are corresponding social processes. The implicit anthropological rationalism of much epistemological thought concerning social processes needs the counter-balance of emphasis that wide philosophical categories have their evolution, and that much of this evolution is effected by processes that proceed mostly below the level of explicit consciousness. Examples of this emphasis are provided in several essays by F.A. Hayek in the collections, *Studies in Philosophy, Politics and Economics* (1967) and *New Studies in Philosophy, Politics, Economics and the History of Ideas* (1978). Elaborating on the theme 'The Results of Human Action

But Not of Human Design' (*Studies*) Hayek writes in 'The Errors of Constructivism' (*New Studies*):

> we need merely to consider language, which today nobody believes to have been 'invented' by a rational being, in order to see that reason and civilization develop in constant mutual interaction. But what we no longer question with regard to language (though even that is comparatively recent) is by no means generally accepted with regard to morals, law, the skills of handicrafts, or social institutions. We are still too easily led to assume that these phenomena, which are clearly the results of human action, must also have been consciously designed by human mind, in circumstances created for the purposes which they serve (p. 4).

$\bar{R}D\bar{P}$. Non-reflective *deductive* non-philosophical governance is realized as a complement of the reflective species of this governance (#3 above), to the extent, which is not negligible, that some part of the deductive, non-philosophical governance is non-reflective.

$\bar{R}\bar{D}\bar{P}$. Non-reflective *ampliative* non-philosophical governance is illustrated in the simple case of the drill bits in Chapter 5, §13. It occurs widely in all cases in which norms of thought and action undergo non-reflective mutation in employment (mutative subsumption), and thus richly populate governance in law where one is commonly engaged and by no means always with much reflective awareness, with (Levi's phrase) 'a moving classification system.'

16 Various points about the differences and relations between varieties have been stressed, in addition to the primary difference between deductive and ampliative governance. One of these is the continuity between the reflective and non-reflective forms of ampliative governance. Another is the close contemporary relation between the ampliative and deductive forms of governance, in consequence of which the ampliative forms, no less than the deductive ones, are inescapable aspects of governance in general, and of the practices of thought and action of which governance itself is an integral aspect. The inclusion of both the non-reflective with the reflective forms of philosophical governance underscores the disclaimer that implicit in all these forms there is an identifiable organon. Correlatively this inclusion puts in question whether the whole body of governing procedures constitutes what may properly be termed a 'discipline.' Certainly there are aspects of governance that can be learned, refined, and taught. But if referring to these collectively as a 'discipline' suggests, as it often does, strict

161

rules, formulae, techniques, even algorithmic decision procedures, then the distinction between deductive and ampliative processes dictates immediately that disciplinary governance is what is segregated on the deductive side of the distinction, and that ampliative processes, skills, judgment, and understanding must be characterized otherwise. One cardinal point which has been reiterated is that just as ampliative governance in general is an integral part of thought and action employing norms, so, generally ampliative processes, are an integral component of the kind of governance that is philosophical, including both its reflective and non-reflective forms. Ampliative philosophical governance, neither as process nor as product, can be avoided by inattention, studied or otherwise. The processes, both reflective and non-reflective, will occur, and their results ensue. What remains in question, given all this, is how an understanding of both processes and results can be utilized for the purpose of guiding philosophically enlightened thought and action.

17 It may be helpful to mark a further contrast between the views advanced here and those of Toulmin, whose work on conceptual evolution has already been touched upon (Chapter 1, §§7–10). Toulmin's response to what, in his terminology, are the problems of conceptual change is an endeavor to do what it has been urged here ought to be done, namely (if one is going to speak in the idiom of 'concepts'), develop a theory broad enough to embrace both concepts-in-being and conceptual change.[6] The theory Toulmin develops is on the model of the Darwinian theory of variation and selection, with concepts occupying the position occupied by species in the original Darwinian version. His elaboration of this theory is illuminating and valuable, especially the detailed way in which he makes clear the social character of norms (concepts).

Some ways in which his theory is restricted by his choice of idiom were commented upon in the earlier discussion. A further way, and a natural consequence of this Darwinian model, is the neglect of the aspect of norms just discussed in terms of their composition in an intellectual character, conscience, or will. Without recognition of this aspect, Toulmin is seriously hampered in trying to account for the authority that may be claimed for certain judgments *about* concepts in the hard, or, as he calls them, the 'cloudy' cases. The contrast between

[6] *Human Understanding*, pp. vii, x, 84, 83.

two paradigm ways of thinking of development and change – the one Hegelian and the other positivist, naturalist, and Darwinian – is striking here. What legitimating authority there is beyond that afforded by 'existing established rules and procedures' in hard cases has been explicated in this present book in terms of ampliative processes. It is explicated by Toulmin in terms of 'objective restraints' upon judgment in these cases. Employing a kind of distinction between 'is' and 'ought' that was much followed in recent philosophy, Toulmin construes judgments in these cases as falling in the latter category. Within the confines of this distinction he is able to make various sapient observations about the judgments in question, but the overall illuminating effect is somewhat lessened by a comparative neglect, for which the distinction provides theoretical sanction, of both the constraints and positive clues for judgments about what scientific practices ought to be that reside in scientific practices as they are. Attention to these aspects of judgment, as they are exhibited in the compositional, aspect character of norms, could have helped relieve the opacity, and the subjective overtones that Toulmin is obliged explicitly to disown, of his emphasis upon the role in the cloudy cases of the judgments of individuals concerning the degrees and the directions of scientific change.

Toulmin is alert to the broad analogy between judgments or choices of this kind and judgment and decisions in law, particularly those of high appellate courts (the House of Lords in the United Kingdom, the Supreme Court of the United States) dealing with juridical issues of great importance. But in employing this analogy he is unable to use it effectively, as he wishes to do, to show how judgment and choices in conceptual matters are possible that can be preserved from charges of subjectivity and idiosyncrasy. And at the root of this incapacity lies his neglect, in treating the legal analogues, of the role of the composition, which is crucial in the determination of what is the law in controverted cases. Proceeding without benefit of the concept of composition, in speaking of juridical judgments in the hard cases, he is led to identify the law with what, on the theory of norms advanced in the present book, would be norms-in-being considered as independent entities: in his language existing 'established rules and principles.' In the cases in question, however, judgment cannot be reduced to applying accepted rules and principles to new situations. Always to some extent the judgment goes beyond this. Always to some extent the character of the rules undergoes some change in the judgment. How is that to be understood?

If a judgment of what the law *is* is thought of as restricted to an explication of the significance of rules and principles in their routine employment, then judgments in these hard cases will always be to some extent not just about what the law is, but of what it *ought to be*, of what it should become. To that extent a judgment will 'inevitably' be as Toulmin reasons,

> not 'the judgment of the law,' so much as (say) Justice Holmes's or Justice Frankfurter's best individual judgment of the way in which the law should now develop, at this point in historical time, in order to fulfill most completely its general ideals of equity, humanity and certainty.

We are assured that 'such decisions are, in their own way, nonetheless rational, for all that,' but are left still to wonder how, to the extent that the grounds of a decision reside not in the law itself, but in Justice Holmes's individual judgment of what the law should become, this kind of individual, personal ground is to be understood, how it is to be regarded by those whose judgments of what the law should be diverge from Holmes's, and why, except that it has the backing of the police power of the state, it should be accepted as binding upon a plaintiff or defendant in court.

18 The weakness in the treatment of judgments concerning conceptual change in the hard cases call attention to the way Toulmin's Darwinian theory tends to obscure both from Toulmin and his reader the extent to which the evolution of concepts (norms), to continue the biological metaphor, is Lamarckian. A Lamarckian theory of evolution provides a far better model for understanding the selection, and the bases of selection, of certain conceptual variations, because it already provides one with a closely similar account of the origin of the variations. In so doing it helps to reduce what has been in recent years the obstacle to the understanding of conceptual change in science represented by the dichotomy between the procedures of discovery and of justification in scientific inquiry. Neither this dichotomy, nor the deeper one upon which it rests, namely, that between 'cause' and 'reason,' can be maintained in dealing with conceptual change, with change in norms. And, of course, one cannot dissolve in any degree the disjunction between cause and reason without producing a corresponding corrosive effect upon the widely but not universally respected disjunction between 'is' and 'ought.' These results in a realistic theory of the processes by which changes of norms are effected

164

should not be surprising. For at the heart of such a theory must be a recognition of a fundamental fact frequently obscured by mistaken philosophical theory, and often when seen, as in empiricism, utilitarianism, and naturalism, perceived in a crabbed and distorted way. This fact is that ultimately it is from the tuition of 'what is' that we learn what 'ought to be,' learn to discern the right from the wrong, the good from the bad, and the rational in its various forms from the irrational.

19 The bearing of the two related distinctions, 'is' and 'ought,' and 'cause' and 'reason,' upon a sound view of norms deserves some direct attention. Confronted by the problem of how a juridical decision can contribute growth and change to the law, how the law, consequent to such a decision can be different, Toulmin in the passages just referred to makes a natural and popular move. To the extent that a decision has such an effect, it is, according to this account, less a judgment of what the law is, more a judgment of what the law ought to be. More ominously, it is less a 'judgment of the law,' more the judge's individual judgment, the 'best individual judgment' of the judge of what the law ought to become.

20 Here is a striking example of the way in which the most abstract principles can have most important concrete effects. The principle is that everything is what it is, and is not what it is not, or, as Bishop Butler ringingly and famously put it, 'Everything is what it is, and not another thing.' Who can doubt it? No one can doubt that whatever is an identifiable thing, with its own properties and exclusions, is that thing, has these properties and not others. The question is not whether there are counter-examples to this principle, i.e., things that can be marked off, identified, referred to, thought about in the way in which this principle compressedly and cryptically intends, and which yet cannot be marked off, identified, etc., in this way. The question is, rather, whether everything that we need to think about or treat practically can be thought about and treated in this way. This combined epistemic and metaphysical question appeared historically in the thought of many philosophers in the form of questions about the category of substance. How universal for our thought and action is the category of substance and attribute? One kind of answer to the question was given by Descartes and Spinoza in their postulations about substance, and by Leibniz in his theory of monads.

21 The general view of the Hegelian writers upon this matter was radical and similar to that taken long ago by the Eleatics. It was to the

effect that of most we have to think about and deal with we cannot say that the celebrated principle and category hold without qualification. This was the repeated claim of Book I, on 'Appearance,' of F. H. Bradley's *Appearance and Reality*. In Hegel's own philosophy this limitation upon what might be called 'absolute identity' was closely connected with the relativity of the objects of commonsense knowledge and of what Edward Caird, explicating Hegel, referred to as 'that higher kind of commonsense called science.' It was similarly connected with the distinction between existence (*Existenz*) and actuality (*Wirklichkeit*).

Not for our sins, but, more exactly, for our finitude, according to this view, we are obliged for the most part to deal with what is absolute, real, and actual in a more privative and relative way, under the aspect of, in terms of its manifestations as, appearance: as not fully actualized. It is the application of such a view in the domain of human life which is most relevant to the topics under discussion here. Applied to that domain it yields the consequence that a person, an institution, a state may have being under the form of existence without being fully actual. Indeed some deficiency with respect to actuality is a necessary feature of 'existence' and of any entity which we discriminate at this stage in human knowledge. The brighter side of this is that to the extent that we grasp any entity, or more exactly, apparent entity, as actual rather than merely existent, we grasp it also with other such entities that with it show forth the one absolutely self-identical actuality. And grasping an entity in this way we grasp also its capacity to be more than it is under the aspect of existence. We grasp more and more what it is as actual, and as actual also rational.

22   Whatever may be the strengths and weaknesses of the logical and other backing which Hegel endeavored to marshall in support of such a view, the bearing of the view upon the philosophical understanding of human institutions, including therein norms and practices, is fairly clear. There is no gulf between philosophical understanding of the nature of an institution, and criticism of that institution. Criticism grows out of, is itself a part of understanding. In philosophical dialect, 'is' and 'ought' are not distinct, nor even complementary. 'Ought,' the 'ought' of reason, is a necessary feature of a fully developed, i.e., philosphical 'is.' The distinction between 'is' and 'ought,' valuable as it is for common sense and science, is transcended in fuller, philosophical understanding. And this is necessarily so. The institution, in its aspect of existence, as comprehended in the *wertfrei* understanding of the

sociologist, is an incomplete, analytically truncated entity. Out of the wider understanding of the institution, grasping more of its actuality, its rationality, its functions in the life of the communities it serves and its promise, or lack of promise, for future service, derives naturally, without impedance from any naturalistic fallacy, judgment of its *raisons d'etre* and therewith also of the reasons for its maintenance and reform.[7] It was a minute, tell-tale trace of this grand philosophical fact that recently surfaced on a sea of positivist thought when it was noted by a variety of writers that, in a context of certain institutions, under normal circumstances, the fact that a merchant X supplied a customer Y with certain goods entails the further fact that Y owes X payment for these goods.[8]

23 When Hegel expressed this point in his *Philosophy of Right* by saying that what is reasonable (*vernünftig*) is actual (*wirklich*), and what is actual is reasonable, he was misinterpreted by some critics, as he complained in later editions of his *Encyclopedia of the Philosophical Sciences*, of promulgating the horrid doctrine that whatever is, is right, including all sorts of fortuitous, transitory, and degenerate existences.[9] Similarly the reduction of the gap between 'is' and 'ought' with respect to any institution is not to be interpreted as sanctioning as rational what in that institution has merely fortuitous existence and consequently, as Hegel said, 'may as well not be as be.' One thing which is emphasized in this reduction is that our bases for judging the rationality, the broad value and adequacy of the institution in whole or in part, are to be found in the institution broadly considered, as both a natural ('material') and moral ('spiritual') entity. The institution is rational to the extent that it embodies actuality; and the extent to which it is actual is to be judged by the function which it performs or fails to perform, by the contribution it makes or fails to make, in the

[7] How a philosophical 'ought' emerges from reflections upon scientific practice is illustrated in Max Black's discussion of Claude Bernard's proposals for physiology in 'The Definition of Scientific Method,' *Problems of Analysis* (1954), pp. 3–23. Similar relations between 'ought' and 'is' in linguistics and law were emphasized by the present writer in 'Language, Usage, and Judgment,' *The Antioch Review*, vol. XXIII (1963), pp. 273–90; and 'Philosophy, Institutions, and Law,' *Modern Age*, vol. 16 (1972), pp. 379–86.

[8] G. E. M. Anscombe, 'On Brute Facts,' *Analysis*, vol. 18 (1957–8), no. 3, pp. 69–72. For a good introductory bibliography of this discussion see Alan Gewirth, 'The "Is-Ought" Problem Resolved,' *Proceedings and Addresses of the American Philosophical Association*, vol. XLVII, 1973–4, pp. 34–61.

[9] *Philosophy of Right*, Preface; *Encyclopedia* I (The Lesser Logic), Introduction, Section 6.

life of the communities in which it is maintained. In this sense *we* do not tell the institution how it ought to be. Rather, the institution tells us. We discover the norms by which to judge practices carried on in the institution within the institution itself: not the institution considered as existence, as an abstract entity separate from the life of the community it serves, but as actuality and hence in its total context in these communities. Following the same way of speaking and thinking we may likewise say that, in a proper juridical decision, it is not the judge telling the law how it ought to be, but the law, through the judge, expressing its own nature, a nature which in the form of existence is not yet, but ought to be, because in the form of actuality, it is. This is why, in his comments upon the actual-rational equation in the *Encyclopedia*, Hegel emphasizes the identity between Idea and Actuality, and criticizes the analytic understanding, to which the divorce between these two is

> especially dear ... and which prides itself on the ought, which it takes a special pleasure in prescribing even on the field of politics, as if the world had waited on it to learn how it ought to be, and was not.[10]

24 It will surely seem to some as it did to Sabine (above, Chapter 4, §1), that in speaking thus Hegel was recklessly disregarding, obscuring with treacherous rhetoric rather than obliterating, an important philosophical distinction. What more than a verbal preference is being expressed in Hegel's disdain of the '*Sollen*,' which W. Wallace, translating the above passage, renders as 'the imperative ought.' Suppose one follows Hegel's preference in nomenclature, in contrast to that of Hume or Kant, and in the criticism of institutions speaks of what the institution actually is, as contrasted with what of it merely exists. Suppose one speaks in this way rather than of what the institution ought to be, in contrast with what it is. Is one not then recognizing basically the same distinction, between the same things, in spite of the particular linguistic dress in which he now chooses to clothe them? And, having endowed actuality with the same normative implications which are so prominent in the 'oughts' of Hume and Kant, is one not now confronted with the very same problem faced explicitly by Hume and Kant, namely, of how judgments of 'right,' now spoken of as actuality, are to be grounded, since they cannot by

[10]*Encyclopedia*, I, Section 6.

any perspicuous logic be derived from judgments of the 'is' or the existent?

25 Of course they cannot be so derived. And of course that poses a problem for reason in Hume, and for theoretical reason in Kant. But why should anyone expect that these judgments should be so derived? The genesis of this particular problem about critical judgment is in the common-sense and scientistic metaphysic the acceptance of which is implicit in the problem and the general question from which the problem derives. There is no merely verbal difference here, but a difference of the greatest philosophical consequence. There is a fundamental difference of philosophical view – metaphysical, logical, ethical and political – a difference which aptly illustrates some elements of truth in the hyberbolic remark of G. H. Chesterton quoted approvingly by William James in the opening pages of his lectures on pragmatism, to the effect that 'the question is not whether ... one's theory of the cosmos affects matters, but whether in the long run anything else affects them.'[11]

Upon this point the rationalists among our philosophical ancestors were eminently right, emphasizing as they did from Descartes on, the interdependence of metaphysics and the theory of knowledge, and with that the important way in which our conclusions about what we know and can know depend upon what are at one and the same time both premises and conclusions about the skeletal features of what we are interested in knowing about. They were eminently right, too, in recognizing the extremely important bearing in this regard of the rise of modern physical science. A central question for the rationalist tradition, which unlike the empiricist one was not inclined by skeptical leanings to discount the apparently disruptive effect of the new scientific discoveries, was the extent to which those aspects of the world which were being so remarkably disclosed by the new scientific theory could be taken as really definitive of the physical processes, states, and events of which the theory spoke. Concerns about

---

[11] James's quotation from Chesterton's 'Heretics' runs: 'There are some people – and I am one of them – who think that the most practical and important thing about a man is still his view of the universe. We think that for a landlady considering a lodger it is important to know his income, but still more important to know his philosophy. We think that for a general about to fight an enemy it is important to know the enemy's numbers, but still more important to know the enemy's philosophy. We think that the question is not whether the theory of the cosmos affects matters, but whether in the long run anything else affects them' (*Pragmatism*, p. 3).

implications of the mechanical philosophy – for example, about God, freedom, and immortality – led logically to a concern about the metaphysics of substances, the metaphysics of monads conceived in a Democritian rather than an Aristotelian way. They led logically to the question of the broad adequacy of a view of the world the main constitutive feature of which was a pluralism of substances endowed with only the kind of properties – for example, primary rather than secondary qualities – for which there was a place in the flourishing geometrico-mechanical theory. One facet of the general question, which was not long in making its appearance, was a question about the reality of moral, ethical, and valuative 'properties' generally. Hume, for example, criticized in exactly the same manner both alleged ethical and aesthetic properties. Is beauty in or not in the triangle itself? In an account of the non-personal portions of our world, would goodness and beauty, appear or not appear? Must a place be found for a select number of what later came to be referred to as 'non-natural' properties, or, in spite of appearances to the contrary, could these be reduced to 'feigned' properties illusorily conjured up out of personal feelings by entrenched habits of speech imported from our practice with natural ones?

26 Implicit in the view of ampliative processes being elaborated here is a position upon these metaphysical issues. The purpose of the present discussion is not to pave the way for a discussion of them and a presentation of a case for one position on them. Germane as these matters are, concern with them is not urgent. And within the limitations of this book it seems sufficient to call attention to the position and the issues, and to emphasize, as has just been done, that there is a real issue here implicit in the existence/actuality and is/ought distinction. Implicit in the position taken here about what in philosophical terminology would be referred to as the ontological status of normative predicates, is a general outline of a full philosophical view of man and nature, or, more appropriately man in nature. For one most important aspect of the opposition between this view and the Cartesian philosophy which came to full flower in the Enlightenment was the rejection of the opposition between the self and the world and of what was a corollary feature of that opposition, namely, what Charles Taylor, in painting the intellectual background of Hegel's philosophy, refers to as a

vision of the world as [in Max Weber's famous phrase]

170

'disenchanted' *entzaubert* ... or [and partly in consequence of the unremitting efforts of Protestantism, particularly Calvinism, to disqualify the world as a competitor for devotion which should be attached only to God] as 'desacralized'.[12]

Beyond these abstract terms thus live very broad and deep issues, philosophical and religious, about the way in which we should view ourselves and our world. Adherence to is/ought, rather than being merely a matter of linguistic partiality, expresses a stance of man as subject with respect to nature as object, an estranged object. Our relations to it are exclusively relations to an object, an object of our understanding in knowledge and of our will in action. Upon it, as disciples of Bacon, we work our will. It would be benighted and uncivilized for us to suppose that from it, from an understanding of the course of life in it, we could learn what our wills, when informed, are to be. As Dewey said, preaching the doctrines of enlightened instrumentalism to the Japanese in 1919,

In the degree in which the active conception of knowledge prevails, and the environment is regarded as something that has to be changed in order to be truly known, men are imbued with courage, with what may almost be termed an aggressive attitude toward nature. The latter becomes plastic, something to be subjected to human uses.

The attitude of the modern civilized man in contrast to his predecessors or uncivilized contempories, is

nothing less than that the world or any part of it as it presents itself at a given time is accepted or acquiesced in only as *material* for change [italics in original].

Whereas the life of the savage in the wilderness exemplifies 'the maximum of accommodation to given conditions' and the minimum of what may be called 'hitting back,' the civilized man, by contrast in the same circumstances

goes to the distant mountains and dams streams. He builds reservoirs, digs channels, and conducts the waters to what had been a desert.... He imports or creates new plants. He introduces

[12]*Hegel*, p. 9.

machinery to till the soil and care for the harvest. By such means he may succeed in making the wilderness blossom like a rose.[13]

It is from a philosophical and religious stance of this kind, not from some ostensively aseptic, neutral, and quasimathematical 'analysis of concepts,' that commitment to distinctions of the kind just discussed derives. One side of the ontological divide is the world, matter, 'is,' and cause; on the other man, or at least the part of him that is not mere body, his spirit, and with it the imperative 'ought,' and reason. With the installation of these distinctions one affixes one's own signature upon the death warrant of the conception of natural law which Hume early drew up and proceeded to execute. To be sure, since the hunger for ontological backing for our emotive predilections dies slowly, not all will be resigned to the humanism in Hume's position. Denied this backing in nature, some will fabricate it in super-nature, thus disguising for themselves, by taking the source of the imperative ought to lie elsewhere, the *hubris* with which they teach the world 'how it ought to be, yet is not.' The attitudes of 'firm defiance' and 'unyielding despair' with which some confront a desacralized nature were portrayed with almost excessive rhetorical brilliance by Bertrand Russell in the early essay, 'A Free Man's Worship.' Though in later years Russell came to discount the philosophical significance of the point of view expressed in the essay, it would be a mistake to value it, as he then did, as chiefly valuable as an expression of a mood 'useful in times of stress.' For the point of view which is the intellectual substance of the mood is one of genuine philosophical significance.[14]

27 The opposed point of view, which under the name of 'actuality' finds a ground for 'ought' in nature, including human nature, has roots of course in ancient Greek philosophy and one of its classical expressions in the rubric of final causes which early in the modern era were expelled, and to good effect, from physical science. What is being urged here is not the organization of some counter-revolution to reverse this expulsion. It is rather that, whatever may be the case in physics, a puritanic devotion to efficient causes, which has been one of the chief planks in the platform of empiricist philosophy, is a most serious

[13]*Reconstruction in Philosophy* (1920), pp. 114, 116, 85. The irreverent attitude toward nature to which Dewey's reaction to detached, 'spectator' philosophies led him in passages like this is at least somewhat ameliorated, at perhaps some cost in consistency, in *A Common Faith (1934)*.

[14]*Mysticism and Logic* (1918), Preface and Chapter II.

barrier to the full use of the resources which experience itself has for the expansion and improvement of knowledge of living things and, in particular, of human beings in community life. Bound to one of the forms of understanding, we are by its limitations deprived of the instruction available to us in others, and constantly from the course of life in the world, as to what is better and worse for us and other living creatures in the world. For it is as creatures of this world, formed, clothed, instructed, often firmly corrected, and rarely cosseted by this world that the human species and its civilizations have come to be what they are. This does not mean that modern Western man, or modern man generally, may be thought of flatteringly as that far-off event which nature through aeons of time was straining to achieve. It does mean that what we have as human life in its various forms is one of the things which nature in its own way *did* achieve, along with stars, planets, shifting continental plates, round worms, cholera germs, cereals, jaguars, brook trout, and grizzly bears. If, upon the supposition that it is within our power, we entertain the ambition to make some mark upon what has already been achieved, be it in the development of a new form of maize or of some complex institution, we are dependent for instruction with regard to both means and ends upon some understanding of the origins and careers of these forms of life, of the historical processes which have led them to be what they now are.

Whatever alteration we are able, by taking thought, to effect in the character of human life, is to speak in biological metaphor, a variation upon a principal stock already in being. Appreciation of both the opportunities and limits that this entails encourages the kind of realism that the Marxists have liked to call 'historical' or 'scientific' in our decisions about, to use another classic Communist phrase, 'what is to be done.' It is realism broadly of this sort that is aspired to in the theory of governance advocated in these pages. To achieve this aspiration the theory must be, as was urged above, a theory of man and nature, and of what man does when he acts rightly, judges well and truly in accordance with his condition as a human being in the world which for the most part by far he did not make, but which made him, and which, like Margaret Fuller, he must accept in his philosophy, if for no other reason than there is no alternative, only alternative illusions of one. Programs of action in accordance with such a view, especially Hegelian-Marxian versions, have been ridiculed by some as urging individuals or groups to swim with the stream of history. One of the misleading aspects of the metaphor is the external relation it suggests there is between the swimmers and the stream, they standing upon the bank, as it were, debating whether or not to swim, and if so, in what direction. Whatever we are in relation to the stream, we have become what we are by virtue of our relation to the stream and whatever current, or currents, there are in it. Swimming in this stream is internal to our natures. The stream and its currents are the medium not merely for our movement, but for our being. The form of that being is itself a part of the form of the stream. Alterations in one entail alteration in the other. And proposals for significant alterations of the stream, if they are to be informed with respect to either possibility or desirability, require some understanding of the character and career of the stream, and of the land through which it flows.

8

Governance in Practice

Topical Outline

175

political arrangements illustrate the difficulties encountered in understanding ampliative governance of
norms when the actual norms are replaced by
symbolic surrogates, and concrete coherence of norms
in the guidance of thought and action is similarly
replaced by the discernible relations among such
entities. The enfranchisement of women as viewed by
these two writers. Franklin's view on this point is
closely analogous to Hume's about causation.

Cases like this illustrate how reasoned governance
of norms can develop out of and employ as grounds
narrower and wider incoherencies in the norms
themselves, and further, that, so understood, reasoned
ampliative governance is not only possible, but not
even rare. Voting as one institution among others in a
political community. It is in relation to such a complex
of institutions in the life of the community that
reasoned decisions about norms concerning the
franchise can be made. 'Objective constraints' upon
proposals with respect to the legal status of women:
in 1951; in 1791; in Athens in the fourth century BC;
in the Roman Empire in the first century AD.
Another illustration: changes in the interpretation of
the Commerce Clause in the fourth decade of this
century.

§§15–23   Diverse examples of the way in which clues to the
governance of norms emerge from a broad and
concrete understanding of them.

§§24–29   A further dividend of a more realistic view of norms
is the dissolution of a long-standing perplexity that
has haunted philosophy since the time of Descartes,
namely, that of the global governance of the whole
body of norms of some large human enterprise such as
knowing (or moral or ethical judgment, aesthetic
judgment, legal or political decision). Consider, for
simplicity, just one aspect of philosophical
governance, namely, criticism. How does one think
legitimately about the norms of cognition *en masse*?
It appears that in thinking of these norms one must
follow some norms, so that when philosophically one

176

sets out to criticize the norms of cognition all together, one is bereft of norms by which one can proceed. Broad philosophical criticism of norms seems to require at some stage the realization of a situation in which criticism of norms is urgently called for and yet cannot possibly be achieved.

The crucial thing about this imagined philosophical predicament is not so much that it is difficult to extricate oneself from but that it is difficult to get into. The idea of such a predicament is logically incoherent in an extreme degree. E.g., the idea of a person totally bereft of norms. The easiness of incoherent thought and language. Hume on a 'gold mountain' or a 'virtuous horse.' Similar incoherence in the thought of philosophical confrontations with beings with altogether different norms.

§§30–33   The bearing of the concreteness of norms on intended hyperbolic criticism and doubts. The internality of 'things' in relation to 'thoughts.' The unbalanced character of intended hyperbolic criticism and doubt. The temptations against balance, and safeguards against imbalance. It is not the function of philosophy as a discipline to operate in conditions of such extreme intellectual disorder as those represented in these alleged predicaments. Philosophy as an intellectual activity requires for its successful conduct by its practitioners a high degree of mental health, competence to engage in a program of intense, concentrated intellectual activity.

1 The aim of the brief excursion into metaphysics at the end of the preceding chapter was to dispel some of the perplexity which for many attends the thought of norm-governing processes that are ampliative and at the same legitimating. In his essay 'Political Education,' Oakeshott endeavored to give an account of the role of political thought in discriminating possible and desirable steps of political change in terms of the capacity of members of a community conversant with, at home with, understanding the institutions and arrangements of their community, to perceive in these institutions and arrangements what Oakeshott referred to as 'intimations' of their incipient

177

development. Writing, in a manner similar to that exemplified here with respect to norms, of 'the arrangements which constitute a society capable of political activity,' Oakeshott said that these arrangements,

> whether they are customs or institutions or laws or diplomatic decisions, are at once coherent and incoherent; they compose a pattern and at the same time they intimate a sympathy for what does not fully appear. Political activity is the exploration of that sympathy; and consequently, relevant political reasoning will be the convincing exposure of a sympathy, present but not yet followed up, and the convincing demonstration that now is the appropriate moment for recognizing it. For example, the legal status of women in our society was for a long time (and perhaps still is) [UK, 1951] in comparative confusion, because the rights and duties which composed it intimated rights and duties which were nevertheless not recognized. And, on the view of things I am suggesting, the only cogent reason to be advanced for the technical 'enfranchisement' of women was that in all or most other important respects they had already been enfranchised. Arguments drawn from abstract natural right, from 'justice', or from some general concept of feminine personality, must be regarded as either irrelevant, or as unfortunately disguised forms of the one valid argument; namely, that there was an incoherence in the arrangements of the society which pressed convincingly for remedy. In politics, then, every enterprise is a consequential enterprise, the pursuit, not of a dream, or of a general principle, but of an intimation.[1]

Oakeshott's exposition of the matter was weakened in certain ways which Franklin in his criticism proceeded to exploit. Endeavoring to make clear that reasoning in the pursuit and exploration of intimations is complex and informal in the way that the processes characteristics of what he called 'technical knowledge' are not, Oakeshott went on to say that intimations were 'less imposing ... less dignified ... and more elusive, than 'logical implications or consequences,' though 'not on that account less important.' And although he had already spoken (in the passage quoted above) of 'valid argument' in politics, before completing the paragraph he had characterized as an 'illusion' the view 'that politics is ever anything more than the pursuit of intimations; a

[1] *Rationalism in Politics*, pp. 123–4.

178

conversation, *not an argument*' (Italics mine).[2]

2 Franklin's judgment was that Oakeshott was caught up in a predicament precipitated by his need to explicate political reasoning as genuine reasoning, as a kind of activity that cannot be reduced (Oakeshott's own words) to 'acting on hunches' or 'following intuitions,' but that yet transgresses basic principles of ordinary logic. Evaluating Oakeshott's efforts to extricate himself from this putative predicament Franklin concluded that the choice does lie between intuition and logic, that what holds for Hegel's dialectic, namely, that it 'depends on intuition,' holds likewise for Oakeshott's pursuit of intimations.[3] This intrinsic character of Oakeshott's philosophy, which otherwise would issue in 'blatant intuitionism,' Oakeshott was able to disguise from himself by his employment of the equivocal terminology of 'sympathy' and 'intimation.' 'At every critical juncture,' Franklin charged, 'he imports an appeal to intuition, which he has somehow hidden from himself by the use of terms like "intimation".'[4]

This is one way in which the central issue posed here concerning the criticism of norms may be put. Is it the fate of a theory of ampliative processes of governance to devolve into some explicit or implicit form of intuitionism, some view in which governing thought and action under challenge must depend in a substantial way for the validation of their results upon intuition? Is it not the case that at whatever point in the whole governing operation ampliative processes appear which cannot be replaced by suitable deductive ones, there the limits of 'reasoned argument' are reached? There 'no reasoned argument is possible,' and is replaced by judgment which 'must ultimately be defended, if at all, by an appeal to intuition.'[5]

3 Crucial to one's answers to these questions is the way in which certain central terms are construed. If intuition is construed as the complement of deduction in the whole class of reflective philosophical governing processes, then the answer to the question of the inescapability of intuition is of course, Yes. But as so grounded, this is not an interesting answer. So much is now embraced under the title of 'intuition' – everything discriminated by Oakeshott as 'practical knowledge,' a great deal of the sciences, the humanities, and the practical arts, every result that cannot be directly validated by

[2] *Ibid.*, p. 124–5.
[3] *Journal of Philosophy*, vol. LX (1963), p. 815.
[4] *Ibid.*, p. 816.
[5] *Ibid.*

antecedently accepted procedures – that the sting of the charge of intuitionism is effectively removed.

Is 'reasoned argument' not possible? In order to mark the distinctive character of ampliative processes, and not let them be replaced unwittingly by deductive changelings, it has seemed advisable in the discussion of them to avoid the terminology of 'argument.' Not only is that terminology better suited to deductive processes, but also, when extended to ampliative processes it tends to distort our view of them, tends to make us view these processes through the by no means astigmatic lens of the forensic model, with its premises, conclusions, and distinctive applicative derivations.

On this basis it again follows as a matter of course that to the extent that processes of governance are ampliative they will not count as argument, reasoned or unreasoned. This too is an uninteresting result, in comparison with the question that can now be raised in a different linguistic venue, of whether ampliative processes employed in reflective philosophical governance can also be reasoned. More particularly, in so far as the crediting term 'reasoned' is concerned, is it a disqualification in the total activity by which some norm or body of norms is governed, if at any point some processes employed are irreplaceably ampliative?

4 A handicap in the task of exposing and elucidating the reasoned character of ampliative philosophical governance is the protean nature of that character. The complement of the routine is not encapsulable in another routine, nor the complement of the codifiable itself tractable to further codes. For many, the process of coming to understand ampliative governance is itself an ampliative one. The understanding is not achieved by coming to see that the processes in question fit pre-established criteria of what reasoned processes must be. The understanding entails, in the fit between the criteria and the processes, that the criteria be adapted to the processes at the same time that the processes are matched against the criteria.

Thus the task of exposing and elucidating the reasoned character of ampliative philosophical processes is not to be performed by devising a deductive proof that these processes can and do sometimes satisfy some antecedently accepted notions of reason, rationality and the like. It requires proceeding in a more inductive, testive, exploratory manner. It requires making clear – what to many threatens to be literally painfully so – that at the heart of the central predicament with which many modern philosophers have struggled in understanding the reasoned character of ampliative processes is a fundamental antecedent misconception of what that character in general must be. The difficulties encountered in applying the criteria to ampliative processes lie more in the criteria than in the processes to which they are applied. They call for reform of the criteria, a kind of reform that is determined not deductively, applicatively from higher, more *recherché* notions, but rather it takes its cues, its directives, from the difficulties themselves: from the inaptness of which they are signs, from the principled blindness and ignorance incorporated in them with respect to the ampliative processes to which over centuries they have been repeatedly and frustratingly misapplied.

5 A summary rejoinder to the summary change of 'unreasoned' ('intuitive') levelled at ampliative processes is the countercharge 'inapt' directed at the deductivist criteria of 'reasoned' from which the charge derives. The inaptness is exemplified first and generally in the wholesale, indiscriminate derogation of ampliative processes dictated by the criteria throughout all the wide areas of thought and action in which we constantly and necessarily engage in these processes. It is exemplified more concretely and in detail at a variety of points, in a variety of fields – in mathematics, science, morals, law, politics, history, religion – at which the contrast between the dictates of the criteria and what apart from them we accept as enlightened practice is particularly compelling. Two of these areas are referred to most frequently in this study because of their special accessibility to current philosophical reflection. In juridical reasoning in the law ampliative processes are especially prominent and unavoidable. In modern science, though less immediately prominent, they are discernable by study in a wide expanse of historical development, the main outlines of which have become increasingly familiar through much research in the history and philosophy of science.

6 It may be of some help in further understanding and evaluation of the charge of 'intuitive' directed against ampliative processes, to recall the earlier contrast drawn between the testive character of these in contrast with the probative character of deduction. To the extent that the effects of the employment of norms are produced, not by routine, accepted application of them, but by means of significant modifications in them, they lose the compelling power that is characteristic of deductive procedure. Grounds for specific steps in the thought and action that lie *in* norms, individually or in groups, differ strikingly from grounds *for* such norms. In view of the wide variety and wide extent of the grounds affecting norms; the indefiniteness of their

limits; the sometimes indirectness, subtlety and covertness in their manner of effect; and, finally, the way in which norms remain constantly, in various degrees, subject to the ongoing operation of these grounds – in view of all these characteristics of these grounds – the effects of them in the governance of norms must lack the decisive closure that is characteristic of the routine employment of many deeply entrenched norms in the determination of thought and action. A brief review of such grounds, while attesting the complexity of such governance, by its very complexity attests also to the extreme inappropriateness of the philosophical condemnation of all such judgments that is effected by the indiscriminant and eccentric application to them of the term 'unreasoned' and, in that sense, merely 'intuitive.'

7 The tendency to think of response to logical authority as a kind of intellectual submission has no doubt been strengthened in modern philosophy by the extensive engagement of its practitioners, noted above (Chapter 2, §§3–5), with large-scale skepticism. If one thinks of belief, broadly considered, in the manner followed by some medieval writers, as 'thinking with conviction' or with assent, then one way of thinking of logical authority, rules, and principles, is that these compel conviction or assent. Like Hobbes, whose first reaction to that proposition of Euclid was that it was 'impossible,' but then was constrained by the proofs to assent, so in logical argument one submits one's own will to a higher authority which is itself strong enough, as the individual is not, to assume responsibility for this attitude. Nerves sapped by protracted, unrelenting skeptical anxieties are equal to only those assents for which there can be no possible reprehension because there is no responsibility. Here as elsewhere the excuse of 'compelled' serves as armor against incrimination in consequence of 'did.'

In ampliative processes the individual alone or together with others is led rather than coerced, led to change his position, to see things from a different point of view. One adopts one view in preference to alternatives, not because it, rather than they, is altogether extruded from the realm of the doubtful, but because one develops an appreciation of the superiority, which may be slight, moderate, or extreme, of one over the others. Although in some cases this appreciation may burgeon forth in an instant, in others it may require a protracted period of extended, often on-and-off reflection. Thus an individual juror over a period of days or weeks may develop an appreciation of the bearing of the evidence adduced upon the matter of fact assigned to him and his fellow jurors for decision. Thus a judge over a period of months or even years may reach a conclusion upon the merits of briefs dealing upon a point of law which has been brought to litigation. And thus in philosophy, after years of incomprehension, puzzlement, and rejection, one may come to understand, appreciate, and assent to a point urged upon him without seeming effect all this time by one of the great classical philosophical figures – for example, by Locke concerning the concept of power, or by Kant under the title of the postulates of practical reason.

8 The chief cause of experiences, processes, effects like these being dismissed as mysterious, mystical, or (perjoratively) intuitive, and not 'reasoned' thus appears to lie in a narrow, thoroughly scholastic and unrealistic conception of what reasoned processes are. To be sure, the juror, the judge, the questing philosopher ponders, looks at one side and then the other, searches for new alternatives, comes to the point of belief, which Peirce characterized as 'the demicadence which closes a musical phrase in the symphony of our intellectual life,' and may then back away and revive the puzzling, searching, and assessments. To be sure, this kind of pondering, wavering, balancing, readjustment, and reassessment of both grounds and results is not tolerable in probative processes, in which the primary aim is not so much to devise results as to test whether accepted resources suffice to deliver results that are already in some way resident in these resources and hence need to be uncovered in these processes rather than devised. When the requirements of this particular kind of procedure are extended to reasoned processes in general, discredited a priori are the processes of sober, disciplined judgment by which the juror, if he is doing his job properly, comes to make and assesses his decision, and similarly the judge, and similarly the scientist in the processes of elaborating and endeavoring the establishment of a complex theory. Rendered similarly suspect are the processes by which Galileo proceeded from impetus theory to acceleration theory in the investigation of natural motion; those by which Darwin moved from special creation theory through various combinations of natural selection and Lamarckian adaptive variation extending through the sixth edition of the *Origin of Species*; and the almost unbelievably complex planetary orbit Kepler himself followed en route from circular motion to the laws of elliptical planetary motion.[6]

[6] The less well-known reasoning of Kepler upon this matter is clearly and interestingly described by Robert Monk in his paper 'The Logic of Discovery,' *Philosophy Research Archives*, vol. 2.

9 In *The Theory of Practical Reason*, while elucidating the nature of moral reasoning and judgment, Murphy commented favorably upon the distinction made by Pascal between the mathematical and the intuitive mind (*l'esprit de geometrie et l'esprit de finesse*).[7] In a short comment intended as a preface to a treatise on geometry or logic, and now commonly included in editions of the *Pensées*, Pascal discussed under these titles two very different ways in which our minds are capable of employing principles in making right judgments. These ways reflect differences, he said, in the nature and accessibility of the principles upon which judgments in mathematical and in certain other domains are grounded. In its own domain the mathematical mind grasps principles that, though obvious at a certain stage in inquiry, are remote from common use and hence require us to overcome the natural difficulty of violating mental habitude by means of methodological artifices, among which are explicit definitions and orderly demonstrations. By contrast, the intuitive mind employs principles that are 'in common use and plain for anyone to see,' provided as Pascal emphasized, that one is possessed of good eyesight.[8] Continuing the sensory metaphor, he said:

> They [the principles] are scarcely seen; they are felt rather than seen; there is the greatest difficulty in making them felt by those who do not of themselves perceive them. These principles are so fine and so numerous that a very delicate and very clear sense is needed to perceive them, and to judge rightly and justly when they are perceived, without for the most part being able to demonstrate them in order as in mathematics; because the principles are not known to us in the same way, and because it would be an endless matter to undertake it. We must see the matter at once, at one glance, and not by a process of reasoning, at least to a certain degree.[9]

What is particularly relevant to the topic under present discussion is that in Pascal's view the adjective normally translated as 'intuitive' (*fin*: fine, subtle, shrewd) applied to a certain kind of judgment or perception, carried no implication that judgment or perception of this

[7] Murphy, pp. 362–3; B. Pascal, *Oeuvres Completes de Pascal*, J. Chevalier editeur, Bibliotheque de la Pleiade, pp. 1091–3.
[8] *Oeuvres Completes*, p. 1091–2.
[9] *Pascal's Pensées*, trans. by W. F. Trotter, Sections 1–4.

kind is any less than mathematical judgment or perception a function
of intelligence. While it is the case, Pascal said, that mathematicians
make themselves ridiculous when they wish to treat matters of
intuition mathematically, 'wishing to begin by definitions and going
on then to principles,' the laughability is not due to their attempt to
reason about matters which are altogether resistant to reason. It is due,
rather, to their natural disregard of the manner in which reason needs
to be employed in grasping and employing principles in certain matters,
namely, 'quietly, naturally, and without artifice [*sans art*].'

After citing Bertrand Russell as an example of one who mistakenly
endeavored to apply *l'esprit de geometrie* to moral matters and as a
result translated 'the very simple-mindedness which makes ... [that
spirit] so powerful an instrument of theoretical generalization' into a
propensity to deduce 'morally inept conclusions that do not cover
adequately the case at issue,' Murphy went on to observe that the point
that the alternative to codified decision-procedures need not be
undisciplined, unruly decision and conviction was made with respect to
the homely matter of judgment of genuineness of the expression of
feelings by Wittgenstein in the *Philosophical Investigations*. It is a
mark of the captivating power of philosophical ideals that within the
academic theater it often requires a philosophical genius to recognize
and remind us that there is knowledge, instruction and expertness in
such matters.

> Can one learn this knowledge? Yes; some can. Not, however, by
> taking a course in it, but through '*experience*.' – Can someone else
> be a man's teacher in this? Certainly. From time to time he gives
> him the right *tip*. – This is what 'learning' and 'teaching' are like
> here. – What one acquires here is not a technique; one learns
> correct judgments. There are also rules, but they do not form a
> system, and only experienced people can apply them right. Unlike
> calculation rules (italics in original).[10]

'To be content with a philosophy that is in this way indefinite is,' as
Murphy observes, 'not easy for the simple mind,' just as the application
of the lesson to the topic of moral judgment is

> perhaps the most unpleasant truth of all for the morally immature
> to face. They can understand a reasonable judgment only as the

[10] Murphy, pp. 363–4; Wittgenstein, p. 227.

deductive conclusion of a syllogism whose major premise is a 'first principle' they need not think to follow and to understand.[11]

10 Earlier (Chapter 4, §§8) it was explained that one of the difficulties generating puzzlement derives from a particular way of conceiving norms. This source of difficulty is illustrated in Franklin's criticism of what Oakeshott called the pursuit of intimations in the critical examination and reform of political arrangements. In the example of what he called the 'technical enfranchisement' of women Oakeshott spoke of the intimations of the desirability of changes made in the assigned legal rights and duties of women as arising from an 'incoherence [in this regard] in the arrangements of the society which pressed convincingly for remedy.'

How acceptable this account of the matter is depends in a decisive way upon how 'arrangements' of a society, institutions, and the norms of thought and action embodied in these are conceived. With respect to norms in particular, the basic philosophic contrast is between conceiving them as entities abstracted from their environment in individual and communal life, and conceiving them as essentially features of, components of this life. And the basic philosophic question is, 'In which of these ways is the governance of norms, and particularly the role of both deductive and ampliative processes of governance of them, more adequately understood?' For the purpose at hand, can norms be adequately understood when conceived along the broad lines of the logical atomism so effectively promoted by Hume in the now antique terminology of impressions, and simple and complex ideas? Or, to take a more up-to-date rendering of the view, can norms be adequately represented by symbolic counters attached to relatively easily discriminable features of them, and the legitimating philosophical processes applicable to them then represented by regulations specifying permissible and impermissible operations with these counters? Upon such a view of norms Franklin's judgment against Oakeshott will be supported. What more could any sober, reasoned method disclose in the incoherence in the regulations governing such entities than a need for choosing among the indefinitely large number of possible measures by which the need for coherence is to be met.

11 Conceived as a character of systems of judgments, propositions, or proposition-like rules, coherence is clearly deficient as a rendering of

the aim and product of reasoned governance. The divorce of these entities from life and practice – in other words, the consideration of norms as if they were such separable entities – ensures their insulation from influences beyond themselves, taken individually or more or less collectively, which might be thought capable of effecting reasoned criticism of them. This would seem to leave the collection of norms in place in any community open only to whatever rational reform might be produced by the elimination of symbolic inconsistencies and other similar disharmonies, of whatever stresses logical incompatibility and other such disharmonies the norms, considered as abstract entities, may from time to time develop. Modifications of norms, to the extent that they can be elicited from the norms themselves, would be essentially under-determined, being restricted in sanction only to some steps capable of easing these stresses. Talk of discerning and developing intimations that goes beyond this would have to be regarded as misleading, presenting as objects of intellectual clairvoyance what to thoroughly reasoned philosophical processes must be invisible. Wrote Franklin:

> If the given state of women's rights falls short in any way of explicit full enfranchisement we have no reason to conclude that a step toward full enfranchisement is required to make the whole 'cohere.' Since the import of the present state turns out to be completely indeterminate, the given arrangements would cohere just as well with any other alternative it pleases us to sponsor. For example, against the view of coherence which Professor Oakeshott would have taken, it could have been maintained with equal force that there were some respects in which women had not yet been fully and explicitly enfranchised, that there was thus the intimation of a whole in which their inferiority, at least in some respects, would always be acknowledged, and that any incoherence in existing arrangements reflected a too indulgent attitude toward women rather than insufficient recognition of their rights.[12]

12 There are thus fundamental grounds in the view Franklin took of moral, legal, and political norms for his contention, against Oakeshott, that coherent or incoherent as any group of such norms may be, beyond the loose demand for coherence itself there is no basis in them discernible by a reasoned process for their maintenance or possible

[12]*Journal of Philosophy*, vol. LX (1963), p. 816.

reform. 'With any developing totality ...,' Franklin wrote, 'of the unlimited number of conceivable alternatives in any situation, we can never reasonably say [shade of Hume!] of any one that it is either more or less coherent than any other with what has gone before.[13]

Valuable – indeed indispensable as it sometimes is – to view norms in the way illustrated in Franklin's comment, for the purpose of understanding the governance of norms restriction to this way of viewing them is a most serious handicap. Abstract the arrangements determining the rights of women from other arrangements in society and from the communal life which is in part informed by these arrangements and which also in part serve to give form to the arrangements themselves; abstract these arrangements in this way, think of them as being operationally defined by certain patterns of behavior in which they are expressed, and there is then nothing in them that could be discerned as an intimation of proper development. Women vote or do not vote, can execute or cannot execute contracts, can or cannot be obliged to pay alimony in a divorce settlement, and so on. How can one conclude that because one woman can become sovereign of the realm that others should be able to serve in Parliament or to assume command of ships in Her Majesty's navy?

What is chiefly wrong with this line of argument is the basic view of norms which it reflects. If norms were the sort of thing that Franklin takes them to be, then intimations would be as great intellectual delusions as he concludes. But it is as wrong to try to think of the practice of voting, for example, abstracted from the place that this particular form has together with other forms in the life of the community in which the practice takes place. It is as wrong as it is to think similarly of the practice of grading papers in courses in instruction in the university apart from, for example, the function this practice plays in the instruction which the course is designed to give, the place of this instruction in the mission of the institution, the effects which practices like this have upon the relations between instructors and students in the institution, and so on. Whatever intimations one can discriminate in the history and present practices with respect to suffrage, for example, are discernible only as the practices, arrangements, norms pertaining to this institution are understood in relation to the practices, etc., of other institutions and the communal life of which these institutions all are organs. Voting in political

[13] *Ibid.*

elections, referenda, plebiscites, and so on, are not practices that can be understood independently of their relations with other practices and institutions in the communities in which they take place. Voting is not an institution which can at will, even in imagination, be combined with any other institutions whatever; it is not, as Franklin supposed, equally coherent with any others; it could not be the institution that it was, say, in the United Kingdom in 1951 and yet fit with any others equally well.

13 Franklin's comments upon Oakeshott appeared in 1963. If not then, it should be clear now that at that time it was empty and unrealistic to suggest that whatever incoherence there was with respect to women's rights in a society like that of the United Kingdom or the United States could have been taken just as easily to be an intimation that arrangements then in force were too indulgent toward a sex whose proper and permanent position was one of inferiority, as it could be taken as an intimation of a forthcoming and desirable more complete sharing of rights. That there were, as there still are, incoherencies in the arrangements respecting the rights of women in the United States, and that some of these, to use words of Oakeshott, 'pressed and do press convincingly for remedy,' is not in question. What is at issue is whether in the circumstances in which these incoherencies arise there are not inevitable constraints which, by limiting the kind of remedies which are feasible, do positively intimate their relative desirability. These incoherencies have a long history of recognition as well as existence, as the career and opinions of Abigail Adams, the wife of one of our early Presidents and the mother of another, amply testify. Whatever may be said for the Equal Rights Amendment now as a means of dealing with present incoherencies – and upon this matter distinguished experts on constitutional law differ – such an amendment as an additional article in the Bill of Rights of 1791 would have been one for which little merit could be claimed. As a proposal for dealing with one set of difficulties it would have had, as no seer was required to discern, the disadvantage of promising generously to create others. It would have been bound to do so, had any serious attempt been made to put such an arrangement into effect because there was altogether too much in the other political, social, moral, and religious arrangements extant at the time that was contrary to such an arrangement. Put in abstract logical terms, the nexus of actual social relations was such as to forbid the realization of the kind of arrangement which such an amendment proposed. If by some strategy enacted, it would have somehow been nullified in a more

extreme version of the actions by which more recently the Eighteenth Amendment dictating national prohibition was nullified. The manufacture and sale of alcoholic beverages were the seat of unquestioned serious incoherencies in the life of the nation for which this Amendment was designed, as they are now. Those who procured the passage of this Amendment and its satellite legislative acts were deceived, not by the presence of these incoherencies, but by the promise of the measures by which they sought to meet them.

That there are sometimes discernible intimations of the feasible and desirable in the course of historical change is a modest claim. The claim is not that there are always such intimations, that, to speak in Hegelian metaphor, the World-Spirit always shows its hand, or that when it does, what it shows is always easy for the participants in the historical process to read. A mistake in reading intimations, in criticizing and moving to effect change in norms of thought and action, need not be, though it can be, folly. It was apparently not clearly foolish, though surely not well considered, for the elected representatives of the people of the United States and of the individual states, to move to effect change in the way they proposed in the use of alcoholic potables. It would clearly have strained the bounds of good sense to have contemplated such government action in 1791, just as it would have done to propose equal rights and proportional representation in the Athens of Socrates, Plato, and Aristotle, or in the Roman Empire in the first century AD.

14 It has seemed desirable to introduce this much concrete detail in order to explicate in the area in which Oakeshott's views were advanced, what 'intimations,' as he called them, could be understood as being and how, as so understood, what the term stands for is by no means idealistic moonshine, but something real and important. The processes of rational criticism and change thus explicated are basically identical with those identified with respect to legal reasoning in case law, statute law, and constitutional interpretation in Levi's *An Introduction to Legal Reasoning*, to which reference was made in Chapter 2 (§6). At the end of this book, summarizing the development of interpretation by the United States Supreme Court which issued finally in the dissolution of the once canonical distinction between manufacture and commerce among the several States, Levi wrote,

A change in the method of selling and in social life made it hard to distinguish between what had once been the small known group around a seller and the vast outside world. Since the difference could no longer be felt, it fell away. And similarly in the development of a constitution, increased transactions and communication made activities previously remote and local now a matter of national concern. When a wage earner in New York thought his pay was dependent upon the standard of living in Georgia, whether it was or not, a fundamental change had taken place. And with the increased concern for what had been remote and local matters, prior distinctions between neighbors within and without the state began to fall away.

To this Levi appended the following quotation from the Brief for United States in *United States v. Darby* (1939):

As the markets of the manufacturers expanded beyond state lines, the technical processes of production acquired a broader commercial significance. The apprentice to a New York cordwainer in 1800 would have only a disinterested curiosity in the wages paid the Baltimore apprentice. Today the worker in a Massachusetts shoe factory knows that his earnings reflect the wage scales in New York, Georgia, Maine and Missouri. If the result is that the field of congressional regulation under the commerce clause is enlarged, the cause is not a change in what the Constitution means, but a recognition of the vast expansion in the number and importance of those intrastate transactions which are now economically inseparable from interstate commerce – of the unification along national lines of our economic system.[14]

The case against the position so skillfully and persuasively argued by Franklin is, in sum, in its application to norms and their governance, that an adequate understanding of any norm extends by logical necessity to its wider relations, and that by virtue of this critical assessments, proposals for change and development naturally flow. The appreciation of incoherencies, discrepancies, inconsistencies, and incompleteness exhibited in these wider relations is a logical part of the understanding of norms. Intimations are not mystic, illusory epiphenomenal accompaniments of understanding, but logical features of understanding itself.

[14] Pp. 103–4.

15 At the risk of over-emphasis, the point here needs to be driven home. As has been observed, the nub of the philosophical dispute about ampliative governing processes is not the prevalence of these processes but their legitimacy. And a major obstacle to their legitimacy appears to many to be the lack of standards, criteria for discriminating the better from the worse among such processes. Terms like 'composition' or 'coherence' seem hopelessly vague; and so do many of their more recent relatives. *Of course* one wishes to transform a problematic situation into a less problematic one. *Of course* one wishes to meet the needs of the problem, to develop a *modus vivendi* among the opposing claimants; but rules for the direction of proceedings, left at this level of generality, do not go far.

16 Fortunately we do not need to remain at that level, and have little disposition to do so in the concrete situations in which reflective philosophical governance is called for. In the rich matrix of competing, discrepant, faltering, and robust standing norms, phrases like 'the needs of the problem' take on greater specificity. Both the mutative and the stabilizing effects of practice upon candidates for governance – their position in the wider corporate body of norms and in the institutions in which they are bound together; their relation in these corporate entities to various moral commitments, ethical aspirations, metaphysical presumptions, and religious beliefs; their positions in the communal life of which all them are constitutive features, and their positions in visions of further life based upon them – all these and much more in the way of concrete context help to give guidance to the general processes directly at achieving ampliative governance.

17 Levi's above comment upon the governance of the Commerce Clause of the United States Constitution by the Supreme Court is a model of illumination in this respect. Looked upon abstractly, there was little to determine the Court's decision to move toward dissolution of the time-honored distinction between manufacture and commerce rather than toward its preservation. But looked upon concretely there was a wealth of consideration in the economic life of the country which, in the words of the Brief for the United States, lay in 'the vast expansion in the number and importance of those intrastate transactions which are now economically inseparable from interstate commerce.' Upon a deductivist view of the matter one may say, as Franklin said on the matter of enfranchisement of women, that there was 'import' in the increasing inseparability of *intrastate* from *interstate* commerce for either an expansionist or a restrictionist intepretation of

the grant of power given Congress in the Commerce Clause. Only upon such a view can one neglect the positive and increasingly strong grounds that eventually eroded the opposed resolution of the Court on the matter, grounds that had to be steadfastly ignored if one was to hold that with respect to governance in this matter the 'present state ... [was] completely indeterminate.'

18 On a broader social and historical scale similar governance is illustrated in the career of British liberal political thought in the nineteenth century as it moved from the extreme individualism and utilitarianism of the Philosophical Radicals, exemplified by Bentham and James Mill, to the more social views of T.H. Green, Bernard Bosanquet, and L.T. Hobhouse. During the century the ethical, moral, political, and economic norms of this political movement altered in response to a wide assortment of forces, among which were pre-eminently public revulsion to some of the great inhumanities in capitalist development for which *laissez faire* individualism seemed to provide moral rationalizations, and the increasing political power of the farmers and the labor unions. Philosophical norms of thought and action underwent changes in various respects. Prominent among these were norms concerning the nature and function of the state; concerning the relation between the state, and the broader society or the nation; and in consequence concerning the relation between political and economic institutions within the state. These included norms concerning the nature of liberty, the relationship between liberty and coercion, and in consequence the relationship between individual human nature and its social environment. On the more concrete practical side, included were such norms of thought and action as those pertaining to the responsibilities of the government for the protection and welfare of its citizens in a wide range of areas: working conditions in factories, sanitary conditions in populated areas, pensions, and education. Such alterations as these latter ones seem to have been called for from liberalism as a political movement if its own particular celebration of human freedom, in comparison with the welfare provision of the conservative programs of Bismark and Disraeli in Germany and Britain, were not to appear, in relation to the needs of the time (as the Marxists were quick to point out) worse than irrelevant, indeed positively pernicious.[15]

[15] This summary statement of changes is greatly indebted to G.H. Sabine's fuller account of 'Liberalism Modernized' in *A History of Political Theory*, 2nd edition (1950).

19 In both these examples, the primarily legal and the primarily political one, what is of first importance to recognize is that there was in each a great philosophical change, comparable to the changes in the natural sciences that are now commonly discussed as revolutions. Secondly, and closely related to this, the changes exemplified indispensable ampliative processes. They are not ones that could have been effected by the exclusively applicative employment of initially accepted norms. In both cases certain key norms called to be further defined, since under present circumstances they revealed that they were capable of leading to radically different results. What was thought and action in defense of freedom, applied to the activities of capitalist entrepreneurs, seemed clearly to threaten the aspirations of many others in the community who, in the familiar words of Emma Lazarus, were in their own way 'yearning to breathe free.' Similarly, in the legal case, the Supreme Court became a key forum for the definition of norms pertaining to the constitutional power of the United States Congress to regulate, under the title of 'commerce,' the working conditions and other aspects of the manner in which commodities in interstate commerce, or affecting that commerce in important ways, were produced.

20 Further examples of such governance may easily be adduced. It is hard not to mention again one of the most celebrated examples from early Greek number theory, namely, that which over the years produced the enlargement of the theory to include what are now referred to as the non-rational numbers. The norms involved here were principally those associating numbers with countable objects and also with measurable distances; hence the problem about the diagonal of the square in plane geometry. It was pointed out earlier (Chapter 1, §20) that an especially valuable aspect of this episode is its illustration of the mutual dependence of deductive and ampliative processes. Deductive employment of certain mathematical norms exposed the need for ampliative elaboration of them in order for the deductive employment to maintain itself and expand. Some additional examples, this time from modern physical science, are discussed briefly in Chapter 10.

21 One final example, from modern social science, is the still incomplete search for identity engaged in during the past century by the roughly delineated complex of inquiries now embraced under the broad rubric of 'psychology.' By 1890 success in psychophysical experimentation had brought this particular type of research to a dominant position in a field of study struggling for a niche in the intellectual economy

independent of both philosophy and physiology. This dominance was to be challenged on a variety of fronts by other claimants who adduced markedly different grounds for being the models for the new scientific discipline. These were, principally, *Gestalttheorie*, behaviorism, psychoanalysis, and, in America, the kind of functionalism exemplified by Dewey's learning theory and social psychology. In this many-sided *Kulturkampf*, the behaviorists stressed norms of experimentation and theory construction imported from physical science, while the advocates of *Gestalttheorie*, of depth psychology, and of functionalism stressed different ways in which these norms and those of the structuralist-introspectionists needed to be adapted to the role that psychological study might play in a more broadly conceived investigation of 'mental' phenomena concerned with perception, learning, individual illnesses, and social problems.[16]

22 In the conception of reflective philosophical governance as one distinctive way in which individuals and groups participate in this general process are implications concerning what reflective awareness can contribute to the ampliative phases of this activity. At some places in governance deductive decision procedures need to be supplemented by, not further, more refined versions of these procedures, but by what is a complement to that whole species, namely, a judgment of the wider aspect of the norms under governance. Such a judgment encompasses the role that the norms perform, individually and in complexes, in the lives in which they are constitutive components. To make such a judgment in the lives of both individuals and groups by those who are engaged in these lives requires self-understanding, often in a very high degree. For, as has been remarked, such understanding includes not only a view of one's self, or of the community for which one offers judgment, as it is realized and manifest at the time of judgment. It includes also what is always a more or less latent component of one's view of one's self or of one's community, namely, a view of what the self or the community may aspire to be. Both of these components may on occasion becloud the judgment with great and ineradicable indeterminacy; and where this is so, it serves the cause of enlightenment for reflection to disclose this result. In communities riven by controversies which at the time defy composition – whether these be

[16] A brief account by Clifford Geertz of a similar division of opinion and practice in present-day anthropology appeared in the *Times Literary Supplement* of 7 June 1985 under the cover description, 'What are anthropologists doing?'

about the practice of infant baptism, theological predestination, the divine right of kings, or the justification of the abortion of human pregnancies – the supposition that there is one definite legitimate judgment on the issues involved can be a source of great intellectual confusion and also of great public disorder.

23 One way of putting the issue over deductivism in philosophy is to pose the question whether, when deductivist methods fail, reflective philosophical governing judgment is completely indeterminant. This – not the sometime indeterminacy of ampliative judgment – is the major issue. For this reason it is valuable to pay close attention to concrete cases like those cited in this chapter, beginning with the contrasting views of Oakeshott and Franklin on the methodological aspects of judgments concerning the enfranchisement of women in the United Kingdom. Oakeshott's appeal to 'intimations' in this matter may not be as felicitous as possible a way to meet the charge of complete indeterminacy upon such a matter. And there is perhaps overstatement in his remark that the only cogent reason for the technical enfranchisement of women at this point was that in all or most other important respects they had already been enfranchised. But in comparison with the negative assessment of the weight of ampliative processes that ensues from deductivism, the remark is far closer to the truth.

24 Allusion has been made at various points to a further dividend accruing from a more realistic view of norms which recognizes and indeed emphasizes the wide and fundamental way in which implicated in the character of norms, in their very identity as norms, are conditions in the communal life of which the norms are features and in the environment in which that life is lived. That dividend is the exorcism of an apparent difficulty which like a specter has in one form or another been haunting modern philosophy since its conjuration by Descartes and its further legitimatization by Kant in his own version of the critical philosophy. The apparent difficulty is, of course, about the relation between our forms of knowledge, our norms for knowing, our forms of perception and conception, and the objects, events, states, substances or processes which are their objects.

The form in which this difficulty chiefly has attracted the concern of philosophers is as a kind of global predicament that seems to be generated when the idea of governance of norms of thought and action is expanded to philosophical dimensions. In a variety of ways, some much more plain than others, we are asked to consider how a process of philosophical governance could possibly be an effective one, could yield an acceptable product, when its object is not one or another or a limited body of norms, but the whole body of accepted norms of some large human enterprise, such as knowing, moral or ethical judgment, aesthetic judgment, or legal and political decision. How does one think, for example, of the norms of cognition in a legitimate way? How does one think legitimately about knowledge when the object of thought has become the norms of cognitive thought, and when, therefore, every act of thought about the object in question seems implicitly to presume characters in the object that have already been put in question? How does one think of the norms of moral life when similarly the object of thought has become so large as to include any norms of thought concerning this whole field? The broadness of the object of thought postulated seems to require at a certain stage in the proceedings a state of divorcement from norms, of innocence of them, that renders performance of the task of thought quite as impossible as the immersion in that state seems necessary. Consider for the sake of simplicity just one aspect of the entire philosophical governance of norms, namely, that of engaging in philosophical criticism of them. Philosophical criticism seems to require at some stage the realization of a situation in which criticism of norms is urgently called for and yet cannot possibly proceed.

25 The crucial thing about this kind of imagined predicament is not so much that it is difficult to extricate oneself from but that it is difficult to get into. More exactly, it is difficult to understand how there could be a situation of this kind for anyone, in spite of the fact that many have reported this as their own real or hypothesized experience. For example, in spite of the famous Cartesian fable, it is hard to understand how there could be a person in such a situation as Descartes supposes. To be sure we can understand what it means in conditions of doubt, or even simple intellectual or moral decrepitude, to be relatively impoverished of norms of thought and action. For a variety of reasons a person may be less well supplied with norms than he was once, or might be now, or will be hence. But increase the degree of impoverishment in the way stipulated, reduce the stock of norms to zero, and can one still suppose a person? One can suppose a rock on the beach, a wave in the lake, a cloud in the sky as being without norms. But a person is surely another thing. In much less extreme cases, for example where individuals have suffered such severe damage from

disease, accident or senescence that little remains but the waning signs of life – respiration, heart, brain waves – we are insecure in applying to the body exhibiting these remains the title of person. This insecurity is not merely that prompted by a direct intuitive sense of inappropriateness. It is reinforced by a variety of moral, political, and religious considerations. It is easy for one to put words together in combinations which careful thought has the utmost difficulty in endeavoring to construe. This has been one of the great empiricist preachments, and yet one which the prince of empiricists, namely Hume, signally and seemingly without a thought violated in setting forth the bases of his own version of empiricist philosophy.

> When we think of a golden mountain we only join two consistent ideas, gold and mountain ... [and, recalling Gulliver] a virtuous horse we can conceive; because ... we can conceive virtue; and this we may unite to the figure and shape of a horse.[17]

What, then, keeps us from getting, instead of a virtuous horse, equine virtue; or instead of a gold mountain, mountainous gold? There must be much more involved in the formation of such conceptions than Hume's easy talk of joining and uniting suggests. And leaving aside whatever it is that determines that what emerges in this procedure of psycholinguistic permutation is indeed a gold mountain, how shall that phrase be construed? Is a large pyramid of gold bullion reaching an elevation fifteen hundred feet above its base a gold mountain? Or must it have more resemblance in shape to a mountain; and, in conformity with this thought must it be naturally produced, rather than a human artifact? Must it be solid rather than hollow? Pure metal without alloy? And even so, would a huge gleaming mass, though surely gold, but without vegetation or animal life, springs, brooks, and other common features of mountains – and no doubt surrounded and guarded by a well-armed militia – would it still count as a mountain?

26 Easy as it may be, then, to speak or inscribe the phrase 'person without norms,' it is by no means easy to understand what the phrase might refer to. Rather it seems to be impossible. And even if it should not be impossible, if by some stretch of conception one should be able to conceive a being to which the phrase could properly be applied, the possible existence of such a being surely provides no basis for any broad philosophical problem about the criticism and change of norms. If the

[17]*Enquiry*, Section II.

supposed problem is that such a being would be needing to judge and yet deprived of the resources of judgment, it is difficult to understand what the need precipitating the predicament could be. Neither from the point of view of the supposed being, or from our point of view considering such a being, does 'need' seem to apply. Without norms, standards of thought and action, there is nothing internal to such a being that judgment is required. And it seems plainly contrary to the principles of obligation which we apply among ourselves – 'ought' implies 'can,' and the rest – for us to hold from our point of view that such a being needs, is required or obliged to execute actions of which this being by stipulation is quite incapable.

The hypothetical confrontation of alien individuals or groups similarly provides no basis for the construction of a philosophical predicament. The word 'confrontation' was used to refer to such envisioned encounters in order to avoid any suggestion that these could be treated as disputes, controversies, or instances of any similar mode of communication. If two beings are so alien to each other that they have no standards of thought or action in common, they are likewise going to be incapable of communication with each other, linguistic or otherwise. Our inclination to see such possible confrontations as illustrating extremities in which adjudication conducted through the media of common norms is not in principle capable of composing or alleviating a conflict or dispute, feeds upon our failure to follow thoroughly to its conclusion our stipulation of the character of the beings between which the confrontation is supposed to occur. Beings as utterly diverse as these could not communicate as human beings do, or even as many animals far less complex than human beings do, both vertebrate and invertebrate. And should they be able *per impossibile* to communicate in some way or other, they could not dispute or disagree, since the capacity to disagree implies as a basis some kind of already realized agreement. Divergence of opinion however wide is always rooted in some kind of agreement. Two parties can have widely disagreeing opinions of President Ford's pardon of ex-President Nixon only upon the basis of some broad agreement upon certain legal, moral, historical, and political elements in a situation in which both can discriminate the two parties, their relationship with the Presidency, the legal power of the one to grant a pardon for Federal offences, and the capacity of the other to be exculpated by such a grant.

27 The general logical point being urged here is by no means a new one. It may be formulated in traditional terms and in the striking way

of speaking favored by writers in the Hegelian tradition (including, upon this point, Peirce) as the doctrine that doubt implies belief, though the extreme breadth of the terms employed in this formulation give it more the character of a slogan, or a heuristic suggestion, than a doctrine of much precision. And though not exactly the same point, it is clearly related to the thesis, much stressed by Hegelian writers on logic, that 'pure' or 'bare' negation, as a logical operation, is without significance.[18] A version of the point that is closely related to the application of it which has been made here was advanced some years ago by C. S. Lewis concerning quarreling as a form of interaction between human beings. The case, though put with brevity and some necessarily concomitant looseness, was that in quarreling – as we understand this term and apply it to episodes of human life – involves some kind of reference to common standards; that if in any instance of some kind of heated confrontation between human beings it should become clear that common to both parties there were no such standards, we should be logically obliged to withold application of the name 'quarrel.'[19]

28 The answer in brief to the objection that the processes of reflective governance, as they are portrayed here, are not competent to adjudicate disputes or disagreements between parties so utterly alien from each other that they share no common standards whatever, is that there are or can be no such disputes or disagreements. This does not mean that beings of this kind could not affect each other. A person can be affected, and in serious ways, by all sorts of things with which he shares little or no standards. The slate falling from the roof may injure or kill him; the tornado may damage or destroy his home; the buzzing rattlesnake may cause him to cease his harvesting in the berry patch; the blooming of the ragweed at a certain time and place may need to be considered in formulating plans for residence, or travel, or herbicide. But having to deal with the slate, the ragweed, or whatever, is not having to debate or reason with it. Whatever is one's relation with these items of our environment, it is not that of philosophical dispute, or joint philosophical exploration or invention. There is no philosophical issue to be decided between one and the slate, no philosophical perplexity to be resolved, no philosophical reconstruction to be performed. Hence the incapacity of a process dependent upon

---

[18] Bosanquet, B., *Logic*, 2nd ed., vol. I, pp. 279–83.
[19] *The Case for Christianity*, p. 3. One may interpret along similar lines Wittgenstein's 'If a lion could talk, we could not understand him,' *Phil. Invest.*, Part II, Section xi.

accepted norms in this context is no sign of its incompetence. It is not a defect of argument, for example, that by addressing an avalanche in this logical mode one can neither arrest it or alter its path, no more than it is a weakness of thought more generally that merely by taking thought one cannot add one cubit to his stature. The capacity of reflective governance in general to compose or decide issues has its own limitations. There are always some issues, though not always crucially important ones, that are not tractable to such means. It is, however, no deficiency in these means, whatever others they may have, that they are unable to compose or decide issues in contexts in which there are no issues to which they may be applied.

29 Would-be challenges like this about totalities of norms, like would-be challenges about conceptual schemes, are indeed versions of the kind of skeptical attack upon accepted practices and norms that Descartes sought to employ for unskeptical ends, in this respect supposing mistakenly that it would be possible for him to touch pitch without being defiled. Philosophical dispersal of such challenges requires that they be understood thoroughly for what they are, namely, would-be challenges rather than genuine ones, which seem to pose impossibly difficult questions and problems concerning the possibility of reflective criticism because they envision a kind of situation in which the resources of such criticism have by stipulation been logically removed. The principle of dispersal in these hypothetical and hyperbolic cases is that the same means which are stipulated to have removed the resources of criticism from them are also sufficient to remove the conditions necessary for the generation of the intended questions, problems, and challenges. That is why what remain must be accounted to be merely would-be questions, problems, challenges, and doubts, the ghostly grin of these particular logical Cheshire cats remaining after the cat itself has disappeared. In a study devoted primarily to the criticism of this kind of challenge and the self-defeating conclusions of those who accept the challenges as genuine and endeavor to meet them, the principle of dispersal and the argument in support of it have to be elaborated in detail. This was done, in a way which cannot be reproduced here, in *Induction and Justification*.

30 The point chiefly emphasized in the immediately preceding discussions is an application to criticism specifically of the broad thesis advanced at the beginning of Chapter 7 to the effect that governance in some degree – not, be it noted, *good* governance, but governance – is

integral to the character of a norm. Translated into the familiar philosophical idiom of 'thoughts' or 'ideas' and of objects or things to which these in one way or other refer or apply, the doctrine becomes one of the internality of things in relation to thoughts, a doctrine that things are literally, though in a very complex way, integral to our very thoughts. This doctrine was elaborated by the present writer in two preceding publications and its consequences drawn both for skeptical endeavors to raise wholesale doubts about the possibility of our attaining knowledge of things, and for the well-meaning but ill-considered endeavors of those who try to dispel these doubts by providing answers to the apparent questions from which they derive.[20] 'Thinking,' as the matter was summed up in one of these publications, 'is an activity which we engage in not only in the world of things, but by means of things in this world, supported and sustained by them.'[21] They are literally part of the fabric of our thought, though no more for that reason themselves mental, and, if material, no less material. This being so, there is no need to search philosophically for some stage in the procedure of knowing at which coordination can be effected between the order and connection of ideas and the order and connection of things. And those foundationist philosophies for which such a cognitive *place de concorde* is indispensable are destined to frustration in their search for what in the end cannot even be coherently conceived.

31 There is a constant hazard to levelheadedness, when one is thinking about the criticism of norms, in the easy, natural way in which legitimate demands for criticism may expand into illegitimate ones. If criticism of some of the norms one follows in thought and action is good, is not criticism of more of them better, and best of all criticism of all? It has to be granted that this is not at all the way criticism is practiced in everyday life, in the sciences, the humanities, and the practical arts. But may this not be regarded as a concession to practical needs and to other pressing concerns to which a devotion to reflective criticism must often give way? In an enterprise devoted without qualification to such criticism, when the aspiration for thoroughness needs to stop short of nothing but complete fulfillment, does not anything short of complete, global criticism amount to a failure of criticism to be thorough and of governance achieved through criticism to be as fine as it ought to be?

[20]'Thoughts and Things,' *Proceedings and Addresses of the American Philosophical Association*, vol. XLII (1968-9), pp. 51-69; *Induction and Justification*, Chapters 7, 9.
[21]'Thoughts and Things,' pp. 63-4.

The most effective guard against the intellectual hazard represented by these questions is a constant alertness to the fallacious reasoning to which the questions are an invitation. No more may be said here about the incoherence entailed in the grand fallacy of composition committed in such reasoning, a fallacy which has been exposed by a long line of philosophical writers and dealt with in some detail by the present writer in discussions already referred to.[22] It does not follow, to modify the old Lincoln aphorism, that because we may be misled by some norms at any time that we can be misled by all norms all of the time, or even by all norms at any time. It is only in a context of some accepted norms and practices that thought, or more exactly, speech about the misleading capacity of other norms, about error, about mistakes in the use of norms makes sense. To suppose ourselves for a moment released from norms is, to be sure, to relieve us from the possibility of correctness and of the thought to which such terms as 'correct' and 'erroneous' might apply. And of course, just as devotion to thoroughness in the criticism of norms of thought and action does not require criticism of all norms together, so abandonment of that hyperbolic criticism does not require the erasure of all distinctions between superficial, incomplete criticism and that which is thorough and complete. It does require a disjunction between complete and 'all.' It requires that we recognize in thought, as we commonly recognize in practice, that there are no abstract, context-independent criteria as to what constitutes thoroughness in criticism. A thorough physical examination is not an examination of everything in the patient's body, whatever that mind-boggling phrase might convey. Furthermore, a thorough physical examination of an ordinary unathletic patient may be very different from that given an advanced amateur or professional athlete, and that, too, different from the examination of a candidate for assignment to such unusual performance, under such unusual conditions, as that of an astronaut in a long period of work in the gravity-free environment of a space laboratory in orbit around the earth.

32 It is not easy, once one has been brought up and confirmed in the philosophy of hyperbolic criticism, to keep these points fresh in mind and to adhere consistently to the lessons they imply. To what degree the difficulty in this regard is due to the effectiveness of early indoctrination in the long-standing dominant view, and to what extent

[22] *Induction and Justification*, Chapter 7.

to the indirect but very effective influence in this direction of certain features of our language, and to what extent to some kind of natural human propensity, the bit of Descartes in all of us, it is hard to say. From whatever source, there is a strong propensity, once set upon the track, to pursue questions of right, ground, and justification to what appears to be their absolute logical extremity. This is a point beyond norms, beyond human society, beyond human life itself. For by what right do we speak of norms, institutions, and social practices, when we have yet to establish that there are such things, that our trust that there are is a 'belief' which, until it has been 'justified' must like any other belief be forborne? Must we not, like Descartes, establish that we are alive, joined in life with other minds and bodies, all with histories going back beyond the immediate present, extending longer than even five minutes ago?

It is a philosophical question itself whether a proper task of philosophical investigation is to provide answers to such hyperbolic questions as, 'Do I exist?', 'Am I alive?', 'Am I awake?', 'Is there anything in the world besides me?', 'Are there other persons?', and so on. It is a matter of great philosophical significance that intelligent, cultivated people can become prey to doubts and anxieties about such matters, and that the routes by which they come to this state is by reflection upon topics which are obviously central to philosophical investigation, for example, reason, belief, doubt, certainty, and so on. These consequences tell us something of very great importance about the soundness, as well as other characteristics, of the manner in which the reflections have been conducted. Men have sometimes, for example, as a result of intense theological search and speculation come into states of extreme mental imbalance, which express themselves in most eccentric modes of behavior, judgment, and opinion. A man may mis-identify himself as Jesus, and, gathering his family around him and re-enacting the ceremony of the Last Supper may await imminent re-enactment of the sacrifice of the Son of God for the remission of human sins. Such a man is in desperate need of help. But should that help be in the form of a theological argument or treatise? And is it a requirement of a sound theological method that it be capable, if administered to this unfortunate creature in proper doses, of dispelling his madness and restoring him to mental health?

33 The answer to these questions seems obviously to be, no. The function of treatises in theology is not to restore men suffering from religious madness to mental health. Rather, theological arguments,

treatises, and reflections are addressed to those whose mental health and general intellectual competence can be presumed. And it is similarly with philosophical investigations as with investigations in other areas. Treatises on ethics are not designed for the morally illiterate and incompetent, who are wanting, as Aristotle observed long ago, the very basis which the practical virtues provide for the cultivation of virtues of a more theoretical sort. It is not a fault of ethics as a field of philosophical study that it presumes this basis and is not suited for the task of engrafting honesty and loyalty onto Alcibiades, or probity onto Iago. It is not a fault of incompleteness in the mechanics of Galileo or Newton that it presumed that there are bodies that fall and is not competent to the task of demonstrating to someone who professes doubt upon the matter that there are. The intellectual discipline of physics is no more designed to provide cures for men suffering from an incapacity to recognize that there is a world of bodies than the physical discipline of gymnastics is designed to provide cures for those whose disability is an incapacity to realize that they can walk.

Returning to the subject of the philosophical criticism of norms, one may say, correspondingly, that although, as was observed earlier, the generation of hyperbolic forms of responses to the need for criticism is a matter of great importance for philosophical study, it is not the function of philosophy as a discipline to operate in conditions of such extreme intellectual disorder as those represented in these responses. It is not a sign of incompleteness in the discipline, or of investigations carried out within it, that these investigations do not perform this function. Philosophy as an intellectual activity requires for its successful conduct by its practitioners a high degree of mental health, of competence to engage in a program of intense, concentrated intellectual activity. It has to be recognized that a not uncommon side-effect of this activity is the creation of an occasional, and sometimes very protracted, state of mind of such great uncertainty and confusion that, as Hume said of his own experience,

> I am confounded with all these questions, and begin to fancy
> myself in the most deplorable condition imaginable, inviron'd with
> the deepest darkness, and utterly depriv'd of the use of every
> member and faculty.

For reasons already referred to, and which were integral to his own philosophical position, Hume was led mistakenly to regard as a weakness of philosophical investigation, or, as he put it, of 'reason,' that in such cases further engagement with the same queries which had produced the disorder would not homeopathically produce a remedy for it. In doing so he neglected the obvious clue concerning the nature of the disorder offered him by what did prove in his own case to be effective, namely, some natural relaxation of this bent of mind, or some engagement in very different activities – dining, conversation, and backgammon with friends – which in a few hours, could so effectively 'obliterate all these chimeras.'[23]

[23]*Treatise*, Book I, Part IV, Section VII.

9

Stasis and Change

does not signify our necessary imprisonment by them. They can be resources for the promotion of effects in norms that are not merely accumulative, and changes that are not exclusively ameliorative and minor.

§§18–20   The orientation of philosophical governing processes in a wide group of such processes leads to a recognition of a wide range of influences to which these philosophical processes respond. This recognition is not sufficient as a guide to responses in particular domains and situations, but it is a necessary component of such guidance. It is of assistance as a preventative of narrowness in both promoting and resisting change. By expanding the ways in which effects are produced in governance it alters these ways; but it does not carry with it any general implications of the relative desirability of either mutative or stabilizing effects.

§§21–23   The urged continuity of reflective philosophical governing processes with a wide range of other much less reflective and philosophical processes implies no depreciation of these more deliberate and refined processes, except what is entailed in a more realistic and understanding view of them. There are sobering aspects of the view with respect to the tentativeness appropriate to broad philosophical assessments and programs.

1 From time to time in the preceding chapters attention has been called to valuable insights concerning governance achieved in the Hegelian tradition that are logically separable from the idealist matrix in which these insights appeared and were for the most part developed?[1] Of

---

[1] Wrote Dewey of the 'permanent deposit' in his thinking left by this early acquaintance with Hegel:

  Hegel's idea of cultural institutions as an 'objective mind' upon which individuals were dependent in the formation of their mental life fell in with the influence of Comte and of Condorcet and Bacon. The metaphysical idea that an absolute mind is manifested in social institutions dropped out; the idea, upon an empirical basis, of the power exercised by cultural environment in shaping the ideas, beliefs, and intellectual attitudes of individuals remained.

  (*The Philosophy of John Dewey*, P. A. Schilpp, ed., p. 17.)

primary relevance to the topic of ampliative processes in philosophical governance is the breadth of the view elaborated in that philosophical tradition of the processes through which governance is effected. Together with the social aspect of governantial processes in human thought and action, the Hegelian philosophy emphasized the continuity of these human processes with others of somewhat different forms realized in other contexts, including the activities of other living creatures.

It requires no great step in expansion of the view of governance of norms advanced here to appreciate that the processes that are central to governance at the levels of self-conscious thought and action represent variations upon and extensions of processes that occur at very different levels in other contexts. In that defiant metaphysical manifesto referred to above (Chapter 7, §21) Bertrand Russell, speaking of the evolutionary origins of man, wrote, 'And from the monsters, as the play unfolded itself, Man was born, with the power of thought, the knowledge of good and evil, and the cruel thirst for worship.' The suggestion here, which is reinforced by other elements in Russell's essay, is that the power of thought appeared with Man, was exclusively resident in Man, so that with some dramatic license one might view the endowment of Man with thought as the crowning stroke in a cruel, ironic joke.

Although the rhetoric here is one of radical free-thinking, the view, for all its scientific coloration, is basically much more in keeping with the story of the creation of Man as depicted in Genesis than with the scientific story. To be sure the drama of human history is depicted as a tragedy, but it would not be the tragedy it is portrayed as being were not man in it a strong central character, who, though descendent from 'monsters,' is with his power of thought and other endowments strikingly different from other creatures who serve primarily as supernumaries in the great drama. The general view of man in relation to nature is thus, in spite of the tragic destiny foretold in his story, much more in agreement with the doctrine of 'in the image of God created He him' than with what is, in Russell's phrase, 'the world which Science presents for our belief.' In the organization of modes of response of living creatures in that world there is much more continuity between human and non-human forms of life than is provided in the Russell fable, just as there is much more continuity at the human level between those governing processes that are reflective and conscious and those that are not. With respect to human thought and action it is implicit in the thesis that an uncriticized norm is not really a norm, that the collective process of governance – of fitting norms to each other and to the circumstances in which they are followed, of generating new norms and sloughing off old ones, of revising, extending, contracting, and reconstructing norms – is not restricted to the higher levels of consciousness, to conscious reflection, inspection, inquiry and deliberation about norms. What individuals and groups do deliberately and purposefully in this regard is a continuation at a level of higher awareness of what gets done constantly and on a large scale as a by-product of activities directed primarily to other ends, but in which, as a natural consequence, the norms which guide the activity undergo a kind of implict scrutiny and criticism leading sometimes to maintenance and reinforcement, sometimes to debilitation and supersession, and sometimes to more revisionary change.

Much of the conscious generation, transmission, and maintenance of norms, and much of the criticisim carried out and composition achieved in them, involves in an absolutely indispensable way the employment of linguistic symbols and various ancillary special symbolic systems. The prominence of the linguistic means helps explain the prevalence of one way in which questions about the criticism and change of norms have been cast, namely, as questions about concepts, about conceptual change and, on the side of criticism, questions about the appraisal of possible alternative conceptual schemes. A consequence of the prominence, and of the formulation of the questions as linguistic or quasi-linguistic ones, has been the obscuration of the continuity of the general processes of governance and effecting composition of norms in human thought and action with analogous though much more rudimentary processes in non-human forms of life, especially the higher species of vertebrates. The broad metaphysical bearings of this continuity, though of great significance, are not central to the primary questions being pursued here. More central to the illumination that a sound view of governance can bring to our understanding of what we are doing when we engage in critical philosophical reflection is a recognition of the continuity of the prominent highly verbal and highly formalized processes by which criticism and change of norms is achieved, with other processes which at first view are likely to appear more radically different.

2 A concrete exemplification of the point, in the medium of group action, is that effects upon norms produced by discussion in a parliamentary body can also be produced by other means. Governance as

a product lies in the effect, not in the special means by which it is produced, and not in its own quality. The dimensions of the effect that the National Socialist party was able to produce in the norms of the German nation were astounding, as have been the effects on Chinese life and culture of the Communist revolution. On the matter of republican forms and representative government, many Hegelian writers of both the political left and right stressed that it is superficial to identify desirable political governantial effects with the products of the political processes characteristic of the nations of Western Europe and North America; and some of them even regarded this identification as a kind of thorough and sinister deception. What is being urged here is a much milder view. It is not necessary to denigrate the capacity of formal republican means to achieve desirable effects in governance in order to advance the point that these are means to ends that in some circumstances are pursued in alternative ways, and, further, that the distinctive virtues of such means cannot well be understood apart from a comparison of them with these ways.

3 Governance of norms is not restricted to the actions and speech of scientists, scholars, journalists, moralists, preachers, judges, political and other social leaders: those directly engaged in the molding of public opinion, and those who have some recognized responsibility in society for the course of public action. In all sorts of ways in the domains of social thought and of overt action, members of a community exert an influence for creation and maintenance as well as for destruction and modification of norms in that community. These ways of influencing norms vary widely among themselves with respect to their advantages and disadvantages as means of criticism as well as with respect to the changes which they are more or less consciously directed to produce. The demonstrator in the parade, the picket in front of the mayor's office, and the self-immolating priest on the street in Saigon is each, like the member of the Shaker community of several generations back, offering his action as a testimony with respect to norms. That testimony may be effective or ineffective, benign as well as malign. A movement conceived by its participants to be the vanguard of progress may achieve a step which proves to be of this kind, or one that proves to be the reverse. Or the movement may expire having achieved nothing more enduringly noteworthy than the invention of a style of furniture or such a homely convenience as a clothes pin. However undesirable in many respects they may be, however disruptive some of their effects may be to institutional practices and civilized living, the impeding

211

actions of the disaffected workman, of the saboteur, or of the terrorist must be conceived as to some extent participating in the broad process of influencing norms and institutions. We condemn such modes of procedure as a general practice, as we condemn similar ones on the part of the sulking child or the outraged parent, not because they are incapable of achieving any positive results in the way of criticism and composition, but because of some results which they are incapable of achieving and of certain consequences they have in achieving what they do. This illustrates further a conclusion drawn earlier concerning the widely honored distinction between cause and reason, and the fundamental logical distinction in which it has been subsumed and formalized, namely that between 'is' and 'ought.' One consequence of a view of reflective philosophical governance that orients it in a much broader and varied class of governing processes is the assistance such a view proivdes in dismantling the artificial wall that deductivist philosophies have helped erect between cause and reason in the study of human affairs. A breaching of this wall in theory is one of the steps needed in order to bring philosophical theory on these matters more into conformity with practice. For in various contexts of practice, as well as in some domains of theory closely associated with practice, we do recognize that this article of positivist commitment cannot be maintained. With hardly a philosophical shudder we recognize in concrete economic and political circumstances that parades, strikes, demonstrations of all sorts can be legitimate forms of persuasion, as in legal contexts we understand that the constitutional lawyer's odd expression 'symbolic speech' (badly tailored lexically as it is) must be counted to be much more than a metaphor. In recent years the term 'dialogue' has frequently been stretched to clothe in gentle linguistic dress various forms of vigorous and even violent forms of political action. It is remarkable that the great amount of obfuscation created by the indiscriminate use of this popular term has not been compensated for in any considerable degree by a philosophical understanding of the view of social development closely associated with this and cognate terms in modern times, a view which can assimilate with under-standing, and without favorable or unfavorable prejudice, effects produced in altering social institutions and practices by means other than disciplined, ratiocinative discourse.

4 Various advantages are often realized by processes of governance that are essentially linguistic or more widely symbolic: that is, processes that depend substantially for the production of their effects upon the

syntactic, semantic, and pragmatic characters of the signs employed in them. Such processes extend far beyond the commonly recognized and highly disciplined probative means of argument. They include a greatly various and numerous class of forms, some of which are treated by Ch. Perelman and L. Olbrechts-Tyteca in their *The New Rhetoric: a Treatise in Argument*.[2] A comparative investigation of all these semiotic means of governance is a project far beyond the objective and limits of the present exploration of the ampliative aspects of philosophical governance. But important for the exploration is an understanding that the view taken here of norms of thought and action, and of criticism and change of these norms, does provide for a wide variety of procedure of very various degrees of efficacy, of advantage and disadvantage. Change in norms can be produced by groups in a community acting in very clumsy ways, and sometimes in very costly ways, which again sometimes may in the circumstances constitute the only recourse available. The sulky or obstreperous child, to employ a very simple analogy, may achieve changes in the arrangements of family life at a cost of irreparable estrangement from other members in the family – irreparable damage which unwittingly the child is wreaking upon the entire fabric of family life. On the other hand, there are times when a sharp show of independence on the part of a long-suffering member of a family may be the event chiefly needed to bring into a state of healthier composition a group of norms of behavior which had slowly, but more and more seriously, been drifting or been propelled out of adjustment. One general advantage of semiotic processes of governance that has often been extolled is their capacity to substitute for more violent means of advancing criticism and producing change. One has to say 'a general advantage' because it is not always the case that incoherences in the arrangements of society, to borrow Oakeshott's language, can press convincingly for and achieve remedy without some recourse to violent means. Another advantage of these means of effecting criticism and change of norms, and one not so often remarked, is the special resources they provide for the design and acceptance of creative, novel, and liberating compositions. Two areas of great importance for the philosophy of knowledge that abound with examples of this form of criticism and change of norms are the development of great explanatory theories in science and the crafting of decisions and supporting opinions in the resolution of large-scale issues

[2] French edition, 1958; English, 1969.

213

of constitutional law. The preoccupation of philosophers with deductive models of governance has left greatly neglected the potential for illumination residing in models of ampliative governance in the latter field. In recent years the emphasis upon the revolutionary aspects of great new theories, and a large-scale respect for a distinction between the procedures of discovery and those of justification, created in the philosophy of science a climate of opinion not favorable for the appreciation of the more ordinary, less obtrusive processes of governance in this area. Some explorations in the past and some more recent ones in the history of science indicate the richness of the lode of precious ore waiting to be mined for this purpose.

5 From a historical point of view one of the most striking aspects of the deductivist view of reflective philosophical governance has been its employment in the cause of intellectual and social reform. It will be recalled that what Oakeshott identified and referred to as 'rationalism' in politics coincides substantially with the deductivist view in its application to that particular domain of thought and action. According to rationalism, Oakeshott wrote:

> Each generation, indeed, each administration, should see unrolled before it the blank sheet of infinite possibility. And if by chance this *tabula rasa* has been defaced by the irrational scribblings of tradition-ridden ancestors, then the first task of the Rationalist must be to scrub it clear; as Voltaire remarked, the only way to have good laws is to burn all existing laws and to start afresh.[3]

The deductivist, individualist view of philosophical governance was, broadly speaking, the view accepted and put into practice in the Enlightenment in Western Europe, the British Isles, and North America, in the politics of which Descartes had many progeny whom he would himself been pained to own. It was the view adhered to by Hobbes (Descartes's opponent in metaphysics), by Locke, and by the first wave of English liberals, the Philosophical Radicals. On the other hand a non-deductivist and more social view of governance developed in the Hegelian tradition in philosophy where, with the exception of the Marxist strain in this tradition, it was employed mostly for

---

[3] *Rationalism in Politics*, p. 5. A footnote here reads: 'Cf. Plato, *Republic* 501A. The idea that you can get rid of a law by burning it is characteristic of the Rationalist, who can think of a law only as something written down.'

conservative purposes, in opposition to the liberalism of the Enlightenment and the political revolution in France with which that liberalism was closely associated. All this, and the reference to Oakeshott himself, suggest the question whether the inclusion of ampliative processes as a major component of the repertory of philosophical governance processes does not carry with it a general commitment to conservatism in philosophical thought and philosophically guided action. The combined reference to Marx and Hegel suggests also that the question is not a simple one.

6 In one of its common uses the term 'conservative' signifies little more than a general attitude of resistance to change, of preference for things as they are. Enough has been said about the character of governance of norms to make clear that ampliative processes are by no means exclusively maintaining and stabilizing ones. The inclusions of ampliative processes in the repertory of governing philosophical processes does explicitly open these processes to a wide – sometimes an extremely wide – range of influence and considerations. The effects of these may be either stabilizing or destabilizing. Typically they are a mixture of both, and a good part of the governance, in which deductive processes play an essential if not sufficient role, is that of weighing and taking into account influences on both sides.

7 A philosophical opinion or judgment rendered in governance of norms in response to the wider influences to which ampliative processes are liable may also be in some respects revolutionary or radical. It is, for example, in accordance with common usage to regard as radical a change in norms or arrangements in any domain which marks a sharp deviation from accepted norms, practices, arrangements in that domain. But what is radical in one respect, in relation to one domain, may be very much in accordance with norms, practices, arrangements in one or more other domains. And domains of course impinge upon one another. The result is that often what is a radical change in science, morals, economics, law or politics when regarded solely from the point of view of one of these domains, is, regarded from a wider philosophical point of view, not radical, and may even be a basically conserving one.

8 The impression that a view of philosophical governance emphasizing ampliative processes must, in application, lead always to conservative, minimal, ameliorative results derives some deceptive plausibility from a misreading of this situation. It by no means follows that because a philosophical ampliative judgment reflects a large body of

stable components of norms, that changes favored by such judgments will be minor in relation to the particular scientific, moral, legal, political, economic, or religious norms that are its immediate objects. Mistakes of perspective on matters of change are easily made by both those advocating and those restricting change. It is easy for the romantic idealist to preach doctrines deeply imbedded in a tradition which he presumes to flout, to advertise a neglected nugget of received wisdom as if it were a new gift just made apparent to pure souls such as he. And it is easy for the uneasy conservative to mistake minor ripples of change for mighty waves, and to suppose that what are only adjustments of accepted norms or arrangements made to preserve them are rather steps to effect their complete abandonment. Throughout the 1930s in the United States of America, for example, there were many who characteristically mistook measures that seemed necessary to preserve certain fundamental features of a free-enterprise economic system as capitulations to socialism.

9 The difference between conservatives and their opponents in social matters is not that the former are, while the latter are not, altogether respectful of accepted norms. It is rather in the difference of judgment by each side of what that respect entails in situations in which governance is called for. It is a function of a sound theory of governance to illuminate how proposals for change in norms and in arrangements which issue from them reflect dispositions to change that, like dispositions also toward stability, are endemic in established bodies of norms. What well-executed governance will call for in the way of magnitude of change, and with what degree of necessity, the theory does not by itself determine once for all cases, and in advance of an acquaintance with the complex conditions prevailing in these cases. In one case sound application of the theory may lead one to advocate what in some domains of thought and action is radical and striking change; in another case the changes sanctioned may be very moderate or even minimal; in another what may be called for primarily is a conservative resuscitation and refurbishing of once well-established but presently neglected norms and practices, primarily a recovery of ways of proceeding rather than the generation of new ones. There are extended periods of history during which one or other of these, or of still other varied attitudes toward the norms and arrangements of life, will have the sanction of balanced philosophical judgment. It was Gibbon's judgment that what he called 'The Golden Age of Antonines,' the period between the death of Comitian and the accession of Commodus,

was of all periods of history the one in which the human race was most happy and prosperous.[4] If he was right, the attitude of a philosophically judicious citizen of the Roman Empire alert to his condition would naturally have been one directed to preserving the conditions of this felicity. A markedly different attitude was surely recommended to a similarly alert subject of Louis XVI of France or of Nicholas II of Russia.

10 Marx was a writer in the fields of economics and politics whose credentials as a radical are beyond challenge. Yet, what was very radical in his criticism of the capitalist arrangement for determining wages and prices, which he took to be set forth in his labor theory of value, and which in one respect was extremely antithetical to the individualist liberalism of the early and middle years of the nineteenth century, was in another and in some respects more fundamental way in agreement with that liberalism. Marx in effect accepted the fundamental moral professions of liberalism, stemming from a moral, religious, and intellectual tradition with a long history in Europe, and criticized both capitalism and its liberal defenders for their failure to adhere in practice and in theory to these professions. Thus as Sabine observed in his comment upon the 'surplus value' view of capitalist profit which Marx erected upon the labor theory of value,

> In spite of Marx's disclaimer of any moral presuppositions, his argument is more powerful when it is regarded as ethical than when it is taken as purely economic. It really sought to accomplish two purposes: first, to bring to light the ethical bias implied in the bourgeois defense of a competitive economy and to show that this bias is incompatible with the moral professions of individualist liberalism, and second, to pose the question of the nature of social justice in a highly organized society where individualism has ceased to be a tenable moral position.[5]

One does not need to dispute the sincerity of Marx's professions concerning his design in order to appreciate the wide significance and effect of his project. One has the support of multitudes of advocates of social democracy and of Christian socialism in finding some grounds upon which public rather than private ownership of the means of production and distribution may be advanced in moral, social, and

---

[4] *The Decline and Fall of the Roman Empire*, Chapter 3.
[5] *A History of Political Theory*, 2nd rev. ed., p. 789.

religious traditions which were deeply entrenched centuries, even millennia, before the term 'socialism' made its appearance in the early nineteenth century.

11 A number of writers in the philosophy of science have recently devoted great efforts to showing, by means of a thorough exploration of historical examples, the capacity of reflective thought to lead, through a progression of plausible, understandable steps, to the development and establishment of strikingly novel explanatory scientific theories. Among the more noteworthy of these writers have been, early on, N.R. Hanson, and in the later burst of investigation stimulated by the revolutionary dynamics of science portrayed by Kuhn, Dudley Shapere.[6] In the philosophy of society, of politics, of law, and the rest, a major concern has been with the capacity of broad philosophical thought to discern the need for and assist in the production of changes in norm. Here, too, most valuable illumination is provided by a historical understanding of episodes of change in social arrangements, as the above reference to Marx's views concerning price and profit were designed to show. This illumination helps one to see, what the blinders of general, unrealistic preconceptions about rules, norms, principles of action may easily obscure, namely, how the dissonance of norms of thought and action, experienced in a life informed by these norms, may lead to radical as well as moderate criticism of particular norms in particular areas, and to radical as well as moderate change in those areas. Among the many ready examples of the more striking changes that can issue from a wider reservoir of deeply entrenched norms are two important changes in federal constitutional law. The first of these was alluded to at the beginning of Chapter 7 (§4) in the discussion of the way in which criticism effected by its relations with other norms contributes to, is indeed necessary for, the definition of any norm. Struck by the deviation of *Brown v. Board of Education* (1954) from the doctrine of separate but equal facilities affirmed over half a century before in *Plessy v. Ferguson* (1896), one may neglect the massive body of moral, political and legal doctrine, particularly that encoded by that time in the equal protection clause of the Fourteenth Amendment, which was needed as logical support for this juridical reversal. For if this was to be judgment of law, of what

---

[6]Hanson, *Patterns of Discovery* (1961); Shapere, 'The Structure of Scientific Revolutions,' *The Philosophical Review*, vol. LXXIII (1964), pp. 383–94, and 'The Paradigm Concept,' *Science*, vol. 172 (14 May 1971), pp. 706–9.

constitutional law had come to be rather than simply what Justice Warren, his eight distinguished legal brethren, and other good people considered that it ought to be, it had to be grounded in norms generally accepted, not necessarily universally or in full consciousness, by the federal community of which the Supreme Court is an organ. It had to be, though not yet an explicit part of constitutional law, a part that needed to be made explicit, a legal idea whose time had come because there was a sufficient matrix in already explicit legal and other than legal norms to provide a mandate for it. Otherwise there would have been no basis for reflective judgment on the matter. And if the judgment rendered was less sound than it should have been, and as various critics have charged, it was chiefly because the Court was insufficiently scrupulous and industrious in marshalling in support of the decision its distinctive legal grounds, substituting for normative legal considerations at certain crucial points prudential considerations derived from psychological and sociological studies which, even if sound, were, in relation to the juridical conclusion, much less binding.[7]

12 The second example was discussed briefly in the immediately preceding chapter (§14) in the effort to confer more definiteness, concreteness and plausibility upon the aspect of political activity referred to by Oakeshott under the title of 'intimations.' The action of the Supreme Court in the 1930s in reversing a tradition of interpretation of the Commerce Clause that emphasized the distinction between manufacture and commerce exemplifies more prominently the employment of norms in wider areas that impinge upon the law to produce within the law striking and radical change. What was striking and radical from the point of view of this tradition in constitutional law was much less striking and radical from the point of view of other traditions in the law, and still less so in relation to more and more deeply entrenched norms concerning the responsibility of government, which in this case had to be the federal government, for certain aspects of the economic life of the country. As Levi said of certain similar developments in laws affecting commerce which had already taken place before the historic decisions just referred to,

The growth . . . [was] a reflection of the period in which increasing

---

[7]Freund, Paul, A., 'The Judicial Process in Civil Liberties Cases,' *The University of Illinois Law Forum*, vol. 1975, no. 4, pp. 493–502; and Bickel, A., *The Morality of Consent*, pp. 120–3.

government control and responsibility for the individual were thought to be proper. No one economic or social theory was responsible, although as changes came about in the manner of living, the social theory moved ahead to explain and persuade. The social theory then became useful in explaining connections. The point of view of the society changed.[8]

13 The discussion of philosophical governance opened in Chapter 1 with a consideration of the effect of the work of Hume and Kuhn in discrediting deductivist views of the development of scientific knowledge. Separated by centuries, these two writers, in very different ways, disclosed what to many readers appeared to be irreparable inadequacies in such views. One way in which inadequacy manifested itself was the incompetence of the sources depended upon to provide certain fundamental norms that in these views are quite indispensable to the processes of philosophical governance, namely, those that in the broad expanse of governance perform the function of ungoverned governors. Hence in philosophical governance we are fated to employ fundamental norms, norms of very broad and deep significance that govern us while we are incapable of reciprocally governing them. In governance we are necessarily the prisoners of large-scale pervasive norms such as those that we depend upon when, for example, we set out to defend attribution of our illness to the effect of bacteria rather than to the position in the heavens of the planet Mercury, or account for the descent of the projectile by reference to general gravitational attraction rather than that of a disposition of bodies toward natural fall.

14 In terms of Oakeshott's *tabula rasa* metaphor, what deductivist philosophy faced at this point was the impossibility of philosophical governance beginning with a smoothed tablet from which all norms had been erased. And it was this impossibility of anyone making an utter break in the governing process that was in good part responsible for the supposed threat that already accepted norms – necessarily employed and relied upon in governance – seemed to pose for the ambition and need that governance be genuinely critical and fundamental. The tablet in question was one that, once completely smoothed, was incapable of receiving inscriptions. Governance therefore had to begin with an already inscribed tablet, and, being the

---

[8] *An Introduction to Legal Reasoning*, pp. 102–3.

kind of step-by-step Cartesian procedure it was, it was thenceforward burdened with and limited by these given inscriptions. Further, since the kind of inscriptions that were necessary to perform the basic function of given inscriptions in this theory of governance were very fundamental and thorough in their effect on the whole message inscribed, the whole message had to be in serious ways determined in ways that could not be made subject to revision and changes in philosophical governance, however diligent and persistent that process is conceived to be.

15 The critical power of philosophical governance, on the deductivist-applicative view, all derives from the first inscriptions. Confidence that there are independent sources capable of yielding such inscriptions in a way that established their sovereignty over all succeeding ones, and the conception of this sovereignty passing to succeeding ones exclusively through the application of anterior ones, yielded confidence in a procedure seemingly capable of governing all norms susceptible of governance.

The discrediting of the notion of the *tabula rasa* and first inscriptions consequently left governance, as thus conceived, incapacitated. Having invested the capacity of philosophical governance to be critical in any fundamental way in this single component, the deductive view of such governance, when deprived of this component, was severely restricted and weakened. Left to it was the capacity to explore subsumptive relations among norms. Its assignment was reduced to exploring and maintaining these lines of transmission of sovereignty among norms, in the face of strong grounds indicating that the generating source from which that sovereignty was supposed to flow had been logically destroyed. To those committed to a deductivist view of governance the dissipation of the promise it had seemed to offer for more substantial governance left them with a process of philosophical governance the capacity of which with respect to accepted norms was greatly reduced, extending no further than the thoroughly conservative activities of exploring, refining, coordinating the relations among these norms and making what corrections in them the execution of these activities entailed.

16 If this analysis of the situation is substantially sound, the threat of overpowering conservatism that seemed to many to be implicit in the destruction of the *tabula rasa* myth lay not simply in the destruction of the myth but in the retention of the narrow, exclusively applicative view of governance after the adjunct myth, essential to its

support, had been destroyed. The 'first inscriptions' story was indeed important for preserving the critical capacity of philosophical governance conceived as proceeding exclusively by applicative procedure. But the rejection of that story by itself did not entail the denial of governing capacity generally. Rather it left open and suggested, as an alternative, a recasting of the view of governance to which the myth is essential.

17 Such a view is one that takes into account the ways in which, in processes of thinking and acting in accordance with norms, effects are produced in the norms themselves. The ampliative effect upon themselves of norms employed in the governing process is all of a piece with the reactive effect of the application of norms to 'instances' discussed earlier (Chapter 6, §§7–15). Just as rules are affected by their direct application to instances, so they are affected by their more indirect correlation with conditions of application through the mediation of other norms. And just as in the subsumptive process rules are sometimes changed, and sometimes confirmed and reinforced against change, so in the general governing process the effects upon accepted norms are sometimes destabilizing and sometimes stabilizing. The reciprocal effect of norms upon each other that is entailed in the processes of governance is much more easily appreciated when one thinks of what is undergoing criticism and what are the direct causes or grounds of criticism as features of life, rather than as such abstract, quasi-independent objects as those commonly substituted for them in contemporary philosophical discussions. Whatever difficulties there are in appreciating that in ampliative processes norms used as grounds for change in other norms are not immune to effects of these changes, however minute these effects in some cases may be, are magnified enormously when in place of norms one inserts as agents and patients in the supposed changes 'premises' and 'conclusions,' themselves now construed as independent linguistic or quasi-linguistic components of a deductive system. Thus construed, the consequence just emphasized concerning the reciprocal determination of components of ampliative processes is extrapolated to apply to the components of deductive processes as well. The effect of the extrapolation is not to illumine these processes, but rather, by assimilating them to ampliative ones, to expunge the genuine and valuable distinction between the deductive, applicative and the ampliative, generative employment of norms. That in ampliative processes of governance changes occur, not only in norms that are primarily the objects of governance, but also those that are

primarily means of governance, is an important consideration in meeting one possible objection to which any view of governing processes may seem liable that recognizes and insists that in governance of any norms other accepted norms are employed as means. The objection is that if an essential basis of the governance of particular norms lies in other norms that are not themselves the primary objects of the process, these latter norms, in any instance of such governance, stand as fixed limits upon the reach of the criticism and the extent of the change that the process can support.

Problems about norms, difficulties with them, governance of them and programs to change them, arise out of deficiencies in these norms, in their direct application in thought and action and in their position in the complex polities of norms of which they are features. Solutions of the problems, resolutions of the difficulties and the generation of change entail corresponding effects in some degree, great or small, in these polities. Liberalizing possibilities reside in the circumstance that in the broad process of governance and change the moved norms may also in important ways be movers, and the movers themselves moved.

When one looks upon the consequences of the rejection of the foundationist myth through the lens of a wider conception of governance, one is enabled to appreciate that the necessary employment of norms in governance does not entail imprisonment to any. Norms employed as means of criticism in a process of governance with ampliative dimensions are not thereby rendered immune to criticism in that process, since these dimensions extend the possibilities of criticism beyond limits of exclusively deductive, accumulative processes.

18 An important feature of the view of philosophical governance adopted here is its assimilation of this process into a much broader and varied class of processes constantly proceeding in the lives of both individuals and groups and also in other living creatures. This orientation leads one to attend to a wide range of determining influences to which philosophical governing processes, like other governing processes, respond, however sequestered from ampliative influence the philosophical ones may strive to be. Recognizing this wide range of influence is by no means sufficient in any particular case for discerning what responses are more desirable; but it is necessary. Necessary to a sound view of how individuals and groups respond well to certain influences is a recognition that in governance they do – and necessarily do – respond to them.

19 But a general view of philosophical governance that is sound in this regard, will not by itself take one far in guiding governance in particular situations, in particular domains. In science, morals, law, politics, and the rest, particular knowledge of the domain and detailed knowledge of the circumstances in which governance is called for will usually be required for an informed judgment about the possible ways in which governance may better proceed. General illumination of philosophical governing processes derived from their assimilation to other forms may nevertheless be helpful in preventing some of the flagrant instances of misgovernance that arise when those engaged in this activity and therefore necessarily liable to wider, ampliative influence, respond to such influences unknowingly and thus less sensitively than they otherwise may. Some understanding of the governing processes may help to reduce the shock, horror and even convulsion that the mutative effects of governance upon norms sometimes provoke among unreserved partisans of features of *les anciennes régimes* in common sense, mathematics, science, morals and other areas of life and thought. And an appreciation of the necessary function that accepted norms play in governance may reduce the number of occasions when, chastened by the excesses of Jacobin programs of governance, we are forced to learn through costly experience the lesson about governance that in Arthur Koestler's *Darkness at Noon* Rubashov is portrayed as pondering a few hours before his execution.

> Rubashov stared through the bars of the window at the patch of blue above the machine gun tower. Looking back over his past, it seemed to him now that for forty years he had been running amuck – the running amuck of pure reason. Perhaps it did not suit man to be completely freed from the old bonds ... What had he once written in his diary? 'We have thrown overboard all conventions, our sole guiding principle is that of consequent logic; we are sailing without ethical ballast.'[9]

20 While the expansion of the range of philosophical governing processes entails, in principle, the neglect of neither the mutative nor the stabilizing effects of these processes in philosophical reflection, it does alter, by greatly expanding them, the ways in which either of these contrasting effects may be produced. Both deductivist governing

[9] Penguin Signet ed., 1948, pp. 183–4.

activity, and activity incorporating ampliative processes as well, have been employed to advance both these kinds of effect. In deductive activity the differential capacity of the procedure in this regard is determined by the norms chosen to serve as the ultimate philosophical bases for the proceeding. In wider governance the weight of determination shifts to the norms under governance themselves, including the application of these norms in concrete situations, their relations, subsumptive and otherwise with other norms, and the role all these play in the individual and communal lives of which they are components.

21 A view of governing processes that maintains the basic identity of activities intentionally directed to governance with others in which this intent is much less recognized or is even altogether unrecognized by those engaged in them may seem somehow to depreciate philosophical governance and its results. Depreciation it is, surely, from the point of view of a theory that discounts on principle any governing activities or results that resist assimilation to the grand paradigm of strict applicative procedures disclosing conformities and disconformities between given norms and their consequences. Depreciation it is in the way in which in general the theory of organic evolution, when applied to man, was depreciatory, calling attention to what Darwin referred to as the 'lowly origins' of man, both with respect to his physical structures and his intellectual and moral faculties. Depreciation it is also in the way that the action of Moses was with respect to the golden calf for which the people under the leadership of Aaron, according to the Biblical story, had mistakenly conceived a marked attachment.

If the ampliative aspects of the employment of norms are as central to the governance of them as has been argued here, the philosophical procedures of adjudication, judgment, decision on norms are widely different from the procrustean models which have commonly been employed for their conception. Philosophical governance cannot be conceived, for example, on the simple model of a rain gauge collecting and recording the incidence of droplets of sensation or gratification. Neither cognitive nor moral norms – Hume seems to have been unanswerably right on this – can be developed simply from the inspection of such hypothetical gauges, no matter how protracted that inspection is conceived to be. Nor can this procedure be conceived on the model of computation according to rules expressing norms, since what is to be illuminated is not how we use norms when the conditions

225

of their application are clear and are satisfied, but how we can proceed when clear norms, clear rules, clear applications are wanting. The processes of thought in which we deliberately adjudicate among norms, in which we render judgment upon them, seem to lie at the opposite end of the spectrum from those in which our intention is not so much to fit norms to the material as, confident that fit is possible, to determine the results of their presumed fit employment. If this is the case, a model of judgment well-suited for the latter type of case may be ill-suited for the former, and a theory of governance exclusively following the latter may be incapable as theory either of enlightening in thought or of guiding in practice the procedures about which we want most to know. Incapacity of this kind has been characteristic of theories of governance devoted to ensuring in the broad fields of philosophical criticism the hegemony of the kind of computative processes developed in the well-established and well-organized branches of mathematics.

22 To one who seeks to understand the procedures and judgments of governance on the model of computation, the view elaborated here will seem far wide of the mark. On the other hand, should the development and criticism of norms be in actual practice fundamentally the way they have been described here, those features of the theory which upon that opposed view make it seem immediately and thoroughly wrong, will attest rather to its superior realism. To be sure, if the governance of norms in wide and deep philosophical reflection, like the formation of a will, or the building of a character, is a highly unregularized activity, there is little that can be done to formulate a methodology for it. Programs for the development of decision-procedures in philosophy perennially have been more distinguished for their promethean aspirations than for the support for these aspirations they draw from the now millennial-long career of philosophical practice.

The conception of deliberative, self-conscious governance as one variety of a process that has a much wider compass than this and takes a variety of forms encourages realism also in its bearing on the question of relative importance in the development of norms of the deliberative, self-conscious processes in comparison with the others. The incorporation of the deliberative, self-conscious governing processes of individuals into a vaster domain or continent of processes, many of which represent social and historical forces subject only to minor or even minute influence by any individual human being, does call for some re-examination of what can be accomplished by individual ratiocination, reflection, deliberation in this regard. This will lead to the assignment of limitations to these processes that, in contrast to our original assessments and hopes, may be somewhat unflattering and deflationary. This is no certain objection to the view. Effects of this sort, it may be observed again, are a variety of a general metaphysical reassessment of man and his place in nature that accompanied the acceptance of the theory of organic evolution. In that case, however disagreeable and disappointing it may have been for men to conceive their close family relationships with other living species, the unpleasantness and disappointment were a small price to pay for the genetic, taxonomic, and general biological, psychological, and social enlightenment that the theory was able to provide. The recognition of the long evolutionary history of our intellectual powers may have some sobering effect upon those with intellectual and moral capital invested in a theory of minds as substances endowed with an intuitive natural light, or as wax tablets blank except for those characters which experience inscribes upon them. A theory of powers with an evolutionary history may indeed have consequences that limit in important ways certain things previously conceived possible in the cultivation of such powers. And the same may be said of a theory of governance which emphasizes the social character of the norms of thought and action, and the ampliative processes that are integral to governance. Such a theory may, though sobering and restrictive in one way, be ultimately liberating in its effect, to the extent that it frees us from the compulsion to expend efforts to do what we cannot do in the cultivation of governing processes, and enables us, in the economy of our energy, to expend less upon what we cannot do and more upon what we can.

23 As norms are aspects of life, so the primary agents in the generation and control of norms are the individuals and groups engaged in that life. This is a lesson that autocrats and oligarchs, in spite of the spectacular successes they at times achieve, are repeatedly, if not permanently, taught. By no means all autocrats and oligarchs are political ones; not all who seek to dominate others make their efforts through the media of physical, political, or military force. In any case, anticipating life to any great distance, like anticipating nature, is an extremely venturesome business in which the failure rate is notoriously high. There is a lesson here for those with an appetite for large-scale governance. When there are very basic and strongly controverted divisions of opinion over warranted changes or opposition to change – for example, at the present time, concerning abortion, sexual practices,

and family life – judgments on the merits of contending alternatives and on a proper resolution of the controversy, before the event, before the slow moving, grinding body of norms of thought and action has come to 'intimate' some disposition, can be rendered by individuals only with great tentativeness.[10] The attitude appropriate to individuals employing the 'human understanding' to develop preachments concerning change of norms is, then, not that of seers reporting the deliverances of apocalyptic visions, nor the zealous vendors of dubious wisdom lampooned by Rousseau ('each hawking his wares in the market place'[11]), but rather that endorsed by Hume in his own study of the understanding, namely, one of modesty and reserve, aware that 'in general, there is a degree of doubt, and caution, and modesty, which, in all kinds of scrutiny and decision, ought for ever to accompany a just reasoner.'[12] Various writers on jurisprudence in recent years have drawn the same conclusion concerning the disposition of some members of the judicial branch of the government to deliver in controversial cases broad categorical determinations of law that exceed the limits of what can reasonably be construed as the will of the body politic, formed, refined, and articulated by its various institutions. Thus, writing of decisions on constitutional matters by the United States Supreme Court, Philip B. Kurland has deplored the sometime disposition of the court to favor expansive judgments exemplifying 'prophylactic' juridical action, to invoke 'absolutes of constitutional meaning' and neglect 'the possibility of any legitimate competing values.'[13] And A. M. Bickel, in his last and posthumous book, argued that the court's first obligation in these matters:

> 'is to move cautiously, straining for decisions in small compass, more hesitant to deny principles held by some segments of the society than ready to affirm comprehensive ones for all ... and always anxious first to invent compromises and accommodations before declaring firm and unambiguous principles.[14]

[10]Associated Press Dispatch, St. Paul, Minnesota, 5 February 1974: 'U.S. Justice Harry A. Blackman says the abortion decision he wrote one year ago will be regarded as one of the worst mistakes in the Court's history or one of its great decisions, a turning point.'
[11]*Discourse on the Arts and Sciences*, edited, with an introduction by George R. Havens, p. 154.
[12]*Enquiry Concerning Human Understanding*, Section XII, Part III.
[13]'Justice Robert H. Jackson – Impact on Civil Rights and Civil Liberties,' *University of Illinois Law Forum*, 1977, no. 2, pp. 551–2, 557.
[14]*The Morality of Consent*, p. 26.

Urging similar restraint upon moral philosophers in trying to impose items of particular moral 'legislation' upon their own constituencies, Murphy wrote in *The Theory of Practical Reason*:

> Universal wisdom is not available to us in our professional capacity as philosophers – there is simply too much that we do not know, or whose practical import we lack the experience to measure in our classrooms. But if we are true to the example of Socrates, and we know what it is like to *seek* wisdom here, and why it is important practically to be wise – if we communicate some grasp of what *being* reasonable thus requires – it may be that we can explain this reasoning at least far enough to make others sensitive to its claim upon us. For reasonableness in this sense is not the privileged possession of a cultural elite, it is the daily bread that nourishes our common life where in fact we live together in our aims and purposes, and not in mere angry physical proximity.[15]

---

[15] Pp. 364–5. Italics in original.

10
Governance Observed

prominent way utilitarian. Shapere's account.

§§14   The exemplifications of ampliative processes and the resources of governance associated with them are helpful in rebutting the enervating skeptical conclusions to which some have been led by the exposure of the poverty of deductivism.

Ampliative phases, like the deductivist phases, are integral components of the total processes of governance. Furthermore, the processes of governance in general are a much wider class than the particular species that is carried on in philosophical reflection. The question about ampliative processes is not whether they shall or shall not proceed. It is about the extent to which they can valuably be carried on with the aid of a philosophically critical consciousness. In science, as in other areas, ampliative processes, ampliative reasoning, ampliative governance are continuous with other processes through which thought and action are carried on. Ampliative emergents in positivist philosophy of science: Reichenbach and Carnap.

§§15–17   Finding ampliative reflections 'ugly.' The predicament of trying to do by deductive means something for which, in that specific situation, deduction in principle will not suffice, for which ampliative processes are necessary. Rorty and the 'bad' arguments Descartes employed in the reconstruction of mind as the mirror of nature. Most of the work of reconstruction done 'under the table' by a kind of 'unconscious sleight-of-hand.'

§§18–19   The primary issue raised by this way of viewing ampliative processes: Granted the discreditation of the deductivist-foundationist view of philosophical governance, what remains? Is there still discriminable a governing role for philosophical reflection with respect to the broad norms of thought and action with which philosophy has traditionally been concerned? Or, having given up deductivism, is governance the responsibility exclusively of science, history, and common sense? Is there no discernible, indispensable task of 'rational reconstruction' that is

continuous with inquiry? Philosophical issues arising
from and internally related to practice. Moral and
political theory in the ancient city state and in the
modern democratic state; in Aristotle and in Spinoza.
Current issues in philosophy of law posed by H. L. A.
Hart and R. Dworkin. Philosophical aspects of the
Lysenko attack upon Mendelian genetics. The
inevitably of governance.

1 On several occasions it has been emphasized that an integral part
of a norm is a kind of rudimentary governance of the mode of thought
or action it represents in relation to other modes and to the
circumstances in which this mode is evoked. Thus when in our more
reflective activities, including our philosophical ones, we engage in the
explicit criticism and reformation of norms we are not embarking upon
activity of an entirely new kind, invented, as Locke might have
satirically put it, by Socrates, Plato, or Aristotle. Rather what we are
engaging in is a continuation in greatly expanded and more self-
conscious form of a kind of activity that we have engaged in already in
some degree in following norms, because it is an aspect of norms
themselves, because learning to follow norms always entails in some
degree the capacity to expand and modify as well as to exemplify and
confirm the routine aspects of them.

In this sense the more we master norms, in the normal course of
affairs, the more we become masters *of* them, whether we understand
well what we have become or not. It was a failure somehow in this
regard, in the mastery or in the recognition of it, that led the student at
the end of his three years of study in the college of law to inquire of the
Dean why it was that in all the wealth of courses offered by the college
there was none designed to instruct the student in justice. It is success in
this regard that one regularly sees in the gradual shift from the close
following of set routines of action to a more liberal, less rigid
employment of them and a disposition to violate, expand, and adapt
them to the needs of the occasion that characterizes the norm-guided
activity of the practitioner of any art or discipline as he progresses from
apprenticeship, through competence, to expertise. Because of this we
are right in supposing, when there is need for some fundamental
reformation in the practices embodied in any art or discipline, that a
major resource for determining how the reformation shall proceed is
the informed judgment of those who are masters of the norms of that

art or discipline. Because of the functions that these arts and disciplines perform in the larger community we do not suppose that mastery of these is by itself a sufficient preparation for a curator or governor of these practices. Socrates was surely right in arguing that there is a kind of skill in the practices of the arts and sciences that does not convey in any great degree the broad understanding of them in their social context that is necessary for wise governance of them. But he did not suggest, but rather taught otherwise in a variety of contexts, that understanding of this kind is a natural extension of these skills, which are to be built upon rather than dispensed with in the educational preparation of those specially responsible for the care and cultivation of social institutions and their practices.

2 Something analogous to what Kant said about precepts and concepts applies in the philosophical governance of norms. Without intimate knowledge of the norms in the domains concerned, governance tends to be vacuous; without a broad appreciation of the wider aspects of the norms, crafts, disciplines, institutions, and pursuits of the domains, governance tends to be narrow, partial, and uninformed. Of course most governance of norms in both everyday life and in particular domains is not both reflective and philosophical; and much of it is collective rather than individual. Much either occurs below the level of consciousness or is primarily directed to the production of other than governing effects. And the overwhelming preponderance is directed to norms so minor in their effects upon the broad character of life and thought of those who follow them that their governance is unsuitable, and so is relatively immune to, reflective philosophical judgment. One does not need to be much in sympathy with the great themes of Hegel's philosophy to sympathize with his satiric comments on Plato's willingness to offer advice to parents and nurses about the rocking of infants, and on Fichte's willingness to extend *Rechtsphilosophie* to cover details of proper passport regulations.[1]

3 If one thinks of philosophical reflection always on the grand scale in which Hegel typically conceived it, one will naturally be led to adopt an attitude of great diffidence toward the capacity of this reflection to effect governance in any appreciable degree. If what counts as success in the endeavor is nothing but the apprehension of one's own time in

[1] Hegel's *Philosophy of Right*, T. M. Knox, trans. (1952), Preface, p. 11.
[2] *Ibid.*, pp. 12–13.

thoughts, and if one's own time is conceived in the epochal way of Hegel's *Philosophy of History*, then, as Hegel said in the memorable Preface to the *Philosophy of Right*, philosophy will always come on the scene too late for its apprehending thoughts to provide guidance in dealing with affairs of its time.[2] But what is suggested here is an altogether unreal choice for philosophical governance. The lone alternative to advice on the carriage of babies, or on passport regulations, is not the apprehension in thought of a whole epoch in everyday life, commerce, science, morals, law, politics, religion, art – these all together or singly. It is in some degree embarrassing to be obliged to emphasize and argue for so obvious a truth as that broad and deep understanding of the wider aspects of norms of thought and action, and the practices and institutions in which these naturally cohere, can be and is a valuable resource for the philosophical criticism of thought and action. For, among other reasons, the apprehension of one's time in thought need not always be, and is not always usefully carried on upon the global scale that Hegel had in mind in those comments. Nor indeed was it always carried on in this manner in his own thought, as is illustrated in the political philosophy set forth in such writings as the *Philosophy of Right* itself and the earlier *Constitution of Germany*. Writing some years ago, when Hegel's dialectic was a notion as much misunderstood as anathematized in American philosophy, Murphy observed that the object of this conception in Hegel was 'the process by which philosophical half-truths are set in their proper perspective from the standpoint of a wider truth that both includes and corrects them,' and that this process is indispensable to the pursuit of philosophical understanding, even if it cannot be projected by an ambitious idealism into the heart of Being.[3]

4 To be sure, the pursuit of philosophical understanding changes as life and thought change, as the concerns that precipitate and nourish the pursuit change. In the almost century and a half between Hegel and Murphy, Western philosophy had already moved further along the route from that of handmaiden of, then replacement for, systematic theology, to a greater emphasis upon modes of thinking and acting. The kind of partial truths that philosophical reflection was called upon to criticize, refine, and absorb in wider truths in the mid-twentieth century reflected in their changed character the great changes undergone in life and institutions in the West that form the complex matrix for

[3] *The Uses of Reason* (1943), p. 301.

philosophical activity. The decline of great epistemological-metaphysical-ethical systems is rendered more understandable by reference to this matrix. The institutions of higher learning in which philosophical reflection was primarily carried on continued to diverge more and more sharply from their ancestors, the religious communities of the Middle Ages. The natural sciences, followed by the social ones, increasingly entered the curricula of these institutions and through these routes and others exerted a wider influence. The interests of the various large communities of the Western world became more secular, and after the troubled period of the Protestant Reformation and the Counter-Reformation there was increased diversity of religious creed and practice throughout this world. The rising new institutions generated new problems and imparted a new cast to old ones. Issues emerged about sovereignty in a nation-state, about democracy and the rights of individuals in such a state, about proper economic arrangements, including property and the distribution of wealth, about the institutions concerned with international relations and about war, about family life, the relation of the sexes, and sexual morality. All these and many other topics stimulated reflection widely in societies in which learning was more and more widely diffused, and among individuals for whom in a less and less degree the larger questions that life posed for them were answered by the doctrine that their chief end was to know God, glorify Him, and enjoy Him forever.

5 One of the emphases of American pragmatism, especially the variety of this philosophy that was represented most notably by Dewey, was upon the particularization or localization of philosophical investigation and of whatever governance of norms of thought and action it is plausible to expect to issue from such investigation. No doubt the diminution of the influence of traditional theology was partially responsible for a shift of emphasis from the task of grasping one's time in thoughts to the less totalitarian one of grasping the wider significance of problems, issues, and controversies encountered in the conduct of life and thought according to accepted norms, and the governance in the treatment of these problems, issues and controversies that a grasp of their wider significance suggests. One effect of this particularization was to make more manifest a point that has just been urged concerning the need on the part of those engaging in reflection upon and governance of norms in any area of life, of intimate knowledge of the norms and areas involved. Even for those well prepared with this intimate knowledge and with a grasp of the wider

aspects of the norms, institutions, etc., with which they are concerned, truth remains in Hegel's counsel about the advantages of retrospective over prospective judgment on such matters. At a time like the present, when there is considerable controversy about the very possibility of philosophical governance, and about its character if it is possible, reference to the processes and results of past governance, philosophical and otherwise, is perhaps the greatest single source of illumination available on these questions. Of the various great historical exhibitions of such governance, some of which have already been utilized in the preceding chapters, one of the best known is that associated with the rise of modern physical science.

6 The end of this short treatise on ampliative philosophical processes is no place to attempt a sketch of the great period in the sixteenth and seventeenth centuries in Western thought when natural philosophy, to use the evocative terms of Leibniz, made the passage from 'Aristotle' to 'Democritus.' We now know much, and shall surely know more, of the course of scientific thought about the natural world from the time of Copernicus's *De Revolutionibus* (1543) to Newton's *Principia* (1687). And of the great body of detail now known about this period there are a few aspects of the governance that actually took place that may help fill out the picture of ampliative governance presented here. The topic, be it noted, is not just what *reflective* philosophical governance took place. It is, rather, that of some notable items of ampliative governance that occurred in the philosophical regions of natural science as that study moved from the Ptolemaic astronomy and Aristotelian physics that preceded Copernicus to the terrestrial and celestial mechanics that became established at the time of Newton. Taking advantage of the superiority of philosophical hindsight that Hegel stressed, can one learn from experience in this way? With the superior clarity of historical perspective, can one without anachronism display the relevance of these items to the ongoing developments and hence the possibilities that they represented to the participants in these developments, however well or ill they recognized them, for reflective philosophical appraisal, and possibly even some control?

7 Kuhn relates that in setting out some years ago to study this period of scientific development and the relations of the mechanics of Galileo and Newton with that of their Aristotelian predecessors, he was struck both with the incongruity of these two sets of views and, looking at the Aristotelian doctrines from the point of view of

Newtonian and post-Newtonian mechanics, with the initial implausibility, even absurdity, of some of the Aristotelian contentions about motion. It was puzzling to him that so accomplished an observer and theorist as Aristotle was in many fields could have committed such blatant errors on the topic of motion and have been followed in these errors by many in succeeding generations. This puzzlement was relieved for him later by a realization that what Aristotle was investigating under the title of 'motion' was in marked ways different from what came to be referred to by that name in Galilean and Newtonian mechanics. 'Aristotle's subjects was change-of-quality in general, including both the fall of a stone and the growth of a child to adulthood.' This difference of conception was connected with the fact that, in contrast with the more modern mechanics, the permanent ingredients of Aristotle's universe, its ontologically primary and indestructible elements, were not material bodies but rather the qualities which, when imposed on some portion of omnipresent neutral matter, constituted an individual material body or substance. Position itself was a quality in Aristotle's physics, and a body that changed its position therefore remained the same body only in the problematic sense that the child is the individual it becomes. In a universe where qualities were primary, motion was necessarily a change-of-state rather than a state.[4]

8 All the wide considerations that bear upon the question whether the 'ontologically primary and indestructible elements' in physical theory ought to be qualities, or the 'solid, massy, hard impenetrable particles' of Newton, or Leibnizian monads, or whatever – all these considerations are possible resources for the philosophical governance of the norms of thought and action that compose these and similar rival physical theories. And so, from time to time, and with various degrees of understanding and skill, they have been employed, and continue to be employed in the present day. Does elementary particle physics at the present, as Heisenberg has argued, exhibit undue influence of the project inherited from Democritus of finding the ultimate units of matter?[5] Or is it perhaps that in this area of investigation the inertia of habits of speech and thought lead us unwittingly to frame questions that we cannot well understand, just as we once asked innocently of events on distant stars whether they were

---

[4] *The Essential Tension* (1977), Preface, p. xii.
[5] 'Tradition in Science,' *Science and Public Affairs*, vol. XXIX (1973), pp. 4–10.

simultaneous, only to learn with difficulty that progress in research at this point required not only information about the stars but information about our questions and ways in which we needed to recraft them in order that we might intelligently conceive and utilize the temporal relations of such events. Many scientifically trained positivist philosophers of an earlier generation who found the ontological pronouncements of traditional philosophers objectionally undisciplined and often uninformed judged these offenses sufficiently serious to justify the wholesale prohibition of ontological considerations from the philosophical study of the natural sciences. Like many other puritanic movements this one proved to be extreme and, in the end, intellectually stifling. Just as the question of what were the ontologically primary elements was not an idle one, either for Aristotelian or for Galilean science, so, in our own day part of the reflective understanding that is inescapably involved in the conduct of physical science is an appreciation of the discriminations that may and need to be drawn between such features of physical theory and practice as entity terms, abstractions, idealizations, hypothesized objects and states, and existential suppositions.[6]

In his book on scientific revolutions Kuhn contrasted the view taken by the Aristotelians of a 'heavy body swinging back and forth on a string or chain until it finally comes to rest' with the view taken by Galileo of the same object. What the Aristotelian saw as an object moved by its own nature to seek a natural state of rest, he remarked, Galileo saw as a pendulum.[7] So, we may remark, some ancient Greeks looking at those sharp flashes across the sky saw as bolts hurled by the hand of Zeus what we see as discharges of static electricity. Reflecting upon these contrasts we are struck by the number, variety, and complexity of the influences that have led to the supplanting illustrated in them of one wide view of things by another. To suppose that these changes in metaphysics were effected exclusively, or even largely, by philosophical reflection, is of course absurd. It is equally absurd to suppose that at no place in the transition were issues confronted which philosophical reflection either did or could illuminate and thereby

---

[6] The existential implications of some aspects of the language and methods of physics are discussed and an illuminating contrast drawn between the 'Logic of Idealization' and the 'Logic of Existence Assertions' in physics by Shapere in 'Notes toward a Post-positivistic Interpretation of Science,' in P. Achinstein and S.F. Barker, eds, *The Legacy of Logical Positivism* (1969), pp. 115–60.

[7] *Structure*, p. 118.

contribute to their successful resolution. In view of the number, variety, and complexity of the influences that must have had their effects in both facilitating and impeding these changes of world view, it is perhaps not remarkable that the opinion should have become widespread that the possibility of illumination of and contribution to such changes by philosophical reflection depends upon the accessibility to that reflection of some special instrument, some *naturae speculum*. The effect of philosophical reflection was seen to be secured, not by means of an examination, understanding, appreciation, criticism, and differential endorsement of such influences, not through them but altogether round them. The effect of the dissipation of belief in such a special instrument upon those attached to this conception of philosophical governance was naturally a negative, skeptical one.

9 The experience of many modern minds at first exposure to the Aristotelian and Thomistic arguments from motion and causation to the existence of God must be similar to Kuhn's experience with Aristotle on motion generally. Brought by Aquinas perhaps to reject the alternative of an unending chain of efficient causes, and accepting with that the existence of uncaused causes, or perhaps just one of these, one is still some distance from conceiving under that phrase something resembling the God that is the object of Christian worship. What, one wonders like Hume, makes an uncaused cause of all this world a supreme embodiment of goodness; why not as good as the world is and also as bad as the world is too? And if told by Aquinas that the effect cannot be more perfect than the cause, why not also no more imperfect?

One learns fairly promptly, if one pursues the matter, that whatever may be the merits of these arguments, the questions betray substantial misunderstanding of them. The term 'cause' is historically and in many other contextual ways extremely protean, assuming different senses in accordance with the different kinds of 'why' questions we set out to answer about actions, states, events, characteristics, and so on. Thus the 'whys' of the new mechanical philosophy that began to spread in Western Europe in the sixteenth century were in many ways very different from those of the Aristotelian natural philosophy which it was to a considerable extent to replace. The kind of cause that in the eighteenth century Hume sought to analyse under the title of necessary connection was, as a part of the intellectual furniture of his century, very different from that with which Aristotle and later Aquinas were concerned. Aristotle, as F. M. Cornford observed, did not treat an eclipse of the moon as an event to be explained by connections with other events that could be formulated in what we conceive of as laws of nature.[8] It is not that he rejected such laws, which were later to be central in Kepler's discovery of the laws of planetary motion. It was, rather, that he was thinking in different ways, interested in different things. He thought of the eclipse as an attribute of the moon, a contingent character that the moon exhibits at certain times, and of the question why the moon at these times has this attribute as one to be answered by what we should call a real definition explicating the essential nature of the attribute. The question, 'Why is there an eclipse?' and the question, 'What is an eclipse?' thus coincide, and the answer to both is that an eclipse occurs when, and because, the moon is deprived of light by the interposition of the earth. 'It is clear,' as Cornford quotes Aristotle as saying in offering this account, 'that the nature of the thing and the reason of the fact are identical.'[9] If a modern reader of Aristotle on this matter finds something essential missing, what is missing is not reference to the privation of light and the interposition of the earth. These, to Aristotle, are part of the definition of an affection suffered occasionally by the moon. What is missing is answers to different sorts of 'why' questions that we now ask naturally and easily in a social and scientific milieu created for us by hosts of natural philosophers and other inquirers of whom Copernicus, Galileo, Kepler, and Newton are but a few of the better known contributors.

10 In various writings E. A. Burtt, author of the pioneering work, *The Metaphysical Foundations of Modern Physical Science* (1924) has confirmed and greatly extended some of the themes concerning the philosophical aspects of modern science that were just extracted from Cornford's discussion of the contrasting features of ancient Greek natural philosophy and modern Western science.[10] Writing of this contrast Burtt observed elsewhere that the variation of meaning undergone in the long period of Western thought by such terms as 'cause' and 'effect' has been radical.[11] The kind of order exemplified by such terms in the thought of Plato and Aristotle he categorized as

[8] 'Greek Natural Philosophy and Modern Science,' in J. Needham and W. Pagel, eds, *Background to Modern Science* (1940), p. 12.
[9] *Ibid.*, p. 14.
[10] 'The Value Presuppositions of Science,' *Bulletin of the Atomic Scientists*, vol. XIII (1957), pp. 99–106.
[11] *Ibid.*, p. 100.

essentially aesthetic, meaning by that they sought to understand nature, and man with it, as forming some kind of harmonious panorama. At the apex of this panorama was some kind of supreme good that serves as an end to which the detailed objects and events aspire and with reference to which their character is ultimately to be explained. This view of things lent itself to the increasingly religious construction that became dominant in the later Greek period and, later still, in the Middle Ages. Thus the conception of causation employed by Aquinas in seeking to discover the indirect agency of God in mundane efficient causation was one that, if successful in leading to an ultimate cause, leads to one that by being ultimate is supremely good and hence worthy of worship.

11 The Aristotelian account of the eclipse and the theological argument of Aquinas both illustrate, though in different ways, how different was the order in nature and man that our ancestors sought to investigate, how different the view of 'all the choir of heaven and furniture of the earth' out of which over the centuries our own view has developed. The divergence of view about causes between Aristotelian and Galilean physics illustrates a facet of philosophical reflection that has been neglected in much recent philosophical theory and practice and an appreciation of which is indispensable for understanding the kind of ampliative governantial function that this kind of reflection performs. Divergence about causes is integrally connected with many other divergences. It is, as F. H. Bradley said in discussing freedom and responsibility, a question of the kind of 'because' we are employing.[12] The kind of 'because' reflects the kind of 'whys' that our questions express. These in turn are reflections of the kind of activities the questioners are engaged in, the kind of individuals and communities they form, and the kinds of institutions in the communities they represent when they engage in this questioning investigation. Reflected also, of course, is the character of the subject-matter to which the questions are addressed, as that subject-matter has revealed itself in its responsiveness to this and other forms of investigation and also to the norm-forming, norm-governing influences that are alive in all areas of practical life. In their discussions of these matters both Burtt and Cornford emphasize among other differences the determinative influence upon the character assumed by the inquiry of differing ulterior ends of inquiry in these two scientific eras. Among the Greeks,

---

[12] *Ethical Studies*, second ed. (1876), pp. 55–7.

Burtt observed in still another writing, interest in technological achievements was small, while modern scientists and philosophers of science have been drawn from men moved by a concern for 'power to predict what is going to happen in the future and to control it, so far as possible, to satisfy human needs.'[13] Cornford, noting the coincidence between 'the era of modern science with its mechanistic view of Nature ... and the era of mechanical invention,' offered the judgment that the motive of achieving useful mundane results lay at the root of the other differences he found between Greek natural philosophy and modern science.[14] This was an aspect of the difference that was emphasized in an extreme degree at the beginning of the seventeenth century by the man whom Macaulay celebrated as an apostle of modern scientific progress. Francis Bacon was no doubt guilty of over-emphasizing the practical ends which, among others, the scientific institution that was developing in his day could serve. But considering the prevailing views of his time, and the deeply entrenched Aristotelianism against which he was striving, it can be argued that his views on his matter represent an exaggeration rather than a fundamental misconception.

12 The aspect of modern scientific development which is being stressed here is much broader than the pragmatic, utilitarian one and may be maintained even if, for the purposes of argument, the pragmatic, utilitarian motives of modern science are excluded from consideration. The pragmatic, utilitarian aspects of modern scientific inquiry are one species of the wider aspects of that inquiry. They represent influences that have their effect upon the conduct of inquiry, whether that effect is included in the scope of philosophical reflection on the inquiry or not. The case for ampliative reflective philosophical governance, in science, morals, politics, religion, and elsewhere, is in short that ampliative governance of these wider aspects of our pursuits and institutions is going to proceed, as it always has, whether we attend to it or not. It will go on. What is open for our determination is not whether it will, but how. And in particular, as it goes on, what is open to our influence is the extent to which it has the benefit on the part of those engaged in these pursuits and institutions of an understanding of

[13] 'Value Presuppositions,' p. 101. Cf. *Types of Religious Philosophy*, rev. ed. (1951), pp. 171-6.
[14] 'Greek Natural Philosophy,' p. 22. Two chapters of J. Bronowsi's *The Ascent of Man* (1973), entitled 'The Majestic Clockwork' and 'The Drive for Power,' give a brief, charming glimpse of some of the connections between physical science and technology in the eighteenth century.

the wider aspects of their engagements and of the pursuits and institutions themselves.

13 That part of the rise of modern science commonly referred to as the Copernican Revolution richly illustrates the effects upon the development of scientific theory and practice of wide influences that are not in a direct or prominent way utilitarian or practical. Among the influences that have been much studied are, of course, the Ptolemaic institution that Copernicus and his contemporaries inherited, also Aristotelian physics, and Neoplatonism with its Pythagorean combination of religious mysticism and mathematical metaphysics. One of the aspects of the Revolution that is illuminated by an appreciation of the complex synergistic effects of these influences is the rapidity and decisiveness with which among natural philosophers of the time the Copernican heliocentric astronomy supplanted the Ptolemaic geocentric one.

It did so in spite of the fact that there were no crucial experiments to dictate the decision between the two theories, and in spite of the fact that, Kepler's ellipses having not yet been discovered, there remained in the Copernican view a large number of insuppressible epicycles. The Copernican theory was, as it is commonly said, a simpler theory than its older rival. More precisely, as Shapere has put the matter, although it had no distinct advantage over sophisticated versions of the Ptolemaic theory with respect to observational adequacy, predictive accuracy, or number of epicycles, 'it did, in its details, provide a far more unified account of solar system astronomy.'[15] Among the characteristic disunities of the Ptolemaic theories cited by Shapere that the Copernican theory removed were: the basic dichotomy between the account of inferior and superior planets; the arbitrary dependence of deferential or epicyclic motion, and of the orientation of epicycles, on the (mean) sun; and the lack of a definite criterion for positioning Mercury and Venus in order out from the earth, or for determining the relative sizes of the planetary orbits in general. Items that on the Ptolemaic view were arbitrary assumptions or mere coincidences followed naturally from the Copernican theory.

Yet, as Shapere emphasizes, these items of disunity were not *problems* recognized as existing for the Ptolemaic theories. So long as 'astronomical theories were considered [as in much of the tradition they

---

[15] 'Copernicism as a Scientific Revolution,' in A. Beer and K. Aa. Strand, *Copernicus* (*Vistas in Astronomy*, vol. 17), pp. 97–104.

had been] as mere collections of devices, to be applied to different cases in different ways according to need for the sake of prediction, ... as mere predictive devices, constructed to 'save the phenomena,' the items cited were not and certainly did not need to be recognized as problems. However, these items did become problems when each of the rival astronomical theories was taken, as Copernicus seems to have taken his theory, as not merely an instrument of calculation or prediction, but 'as a realistic representation of the structure of the solar system.' It was indeed largely because of the high degree of unity achieved with respect to these items by the Copernican theory that it became easier at this time to view astronomical theory as realistic and representational, rather than merely a predictive, fictional device. But when the Copernican theory itself was so viewed, it came into conflict with certain portions of Aristotelian physics, so that the acceptance of this theory, realistically interpreted, was in turn a beginning, important step in the transition to the new physics that culminated in the next century in the work of Newton.

One begins to appreciate some of the logical momentum at work in this rich and fascinating episode of theory change in astronomy when one begins to look upon the rival theories in question, not as sentences to be parsed, or logical propositions to be analysed, but more importantly, as rival programs for the governance of the norms or practices of this particular intellectual institution; when one thinks of what sort of institution astronomy had been in the centuries preceding Copernicus, and of what sort of institution, according to certain tendencies in it, it might become. If astronomy, hitherto primarily an institution for celestial calculation, was in the process of giving increased emphasis to another mission, that of developing an acceptable cosmology, and was therefore in the process achieving a new identity among the cognitive and other institutions of the time, then there was strong logical impetus to the change, rooted in the inner dynamics of the governance of the norms or practices of these institutions. 'Simplicity,' then, suggesting as it does, a somewhat subjective quality discriminated by a kind of refined logical taste, appears to be a questionable, pale misnomer for the kind of strong dynamic that is not peculiar to this case, but rather is characteristic of any large-scale scientific change. Commenting upon the synthetic unity that is easier to recognize in the Copernican theory than to analyse, Shapere observes that 'nothing is to be gained in illumination, and much is lost because of highly misleading associations, by referring to such considerations as "aesthetic".' Yet such was the kind of extremity to which the philosophy of science was driven when it set out to understand this particular episode of scientific change, after having first resolutely blinded itself to some of the aspects of these considerations that are most important for their illumination.

14 This book began with an observation on the coincidence of a lesson to be learned from Hume with one emerging from Kuhn's influential work on scientific revolutions: the lesson of the poverty of deductivism. It has been a hard lesson for contemporary philosophers to absorb; hard in being difficult to absorb, and hard also in that when once absorbed it has seemed in the minds of many to lead us to disturbing conclusions about the limits of governance carried on by philosophical reflection. That there is at any time a large and very important segment of our norms of thought and action – the 'first principles' of thought and action in science and, by extension, in other domains – that are not tractable to *deductive* governance has seemed to many to lead to the less restricted conclusion that they are hence not tractable to philosophical governance in general. In a variety of ways, appealing to a variety of grounds, the attempt has been made in this book to reveal that this broad and philosophically enervating conclusion is, in relation to the premise from which it has been drawn, a *non sequitur* of large dimension. This is not because the premise about the capacity of deductive governance is in some subtle way flawed or misunderstood. The revealed incapacity of deductive governance will not be restored by the appeal to some new recherché form of that kind of governance: not by transcendental deductions, not by formalization *à outrance*, or by the elaboration of new calculi (of inductive probability, of social utility, of systematic simplicity, and the rest). The exposed limitations of deductive procedures as instruments of the philosophical governance of norms are limitations in principle. They signify a need, not for increased diligence in the exploitation of the highly deductive phases of governance, but for a greater balance in the theory and practice between the deductive and the ampliative phases.

The ampliative phases of governance, like the deductive ones, are components of a total complex of governing processes. Neither phase needs to be invented by or for philosophy. They antedate philosophy, though as components of philosophical governance they reflect in their character the distinctive ends that this kind of governance serves. They do not require recognition by philosophically conscious individuals to proceed, but, unless recognized by such, may be expected to proceed in a less philosophically understanding way. In particular, with respect to ampliative governance, the effects of the wider influences that have been stressed in the preceding comments on the development of modern science but which are abundant in other areas of life and thought will exert their influence in a less knowing way.

Not all scientific thought is philosophical, but some is; not all moral or religious thought is philosophical, but again, some is. The wider aspects of norms of thought and action in science, morals, and elsewhere are much more manifest at the social, institutional level than at the individual one. There have been many fine, indeed great scientists, who have been little concerned with the larger aspects and effects of their work; even some, like Darwin, who in their work were contributing mightily to a profound revolution in their own field. Among others, like Galileo early, and Einstein, Bohr, and Heisenberg in this century, the deductive and ampliative strands of their thought are woven into a seamless fabric. In the thought of such philosophically conscious individuals one sees exemplified the large truth about science as a great social institution, that the deductive and ampliative aspects of the governance of it are dependent upon, as they are continous with each other. This illustrates concretely the close relations emphasized earlier in more abstract contexts between the routine and the problematic, and the applicative and the defining aspects of our employment of norms of thought and action. On this view philosophical reflection is a natural and sometimes necessary form that the governance, which is a natural outcome of these close relations, assumes. As there is more to the law of a given community than the accepted, manifest legal practices in it, and more than a codification of these, so there is more to the normative content of any particular science at any given time than a codification of the accepted, manifest, recognized norms of that time. That this is so in the case of science was early recognized in that extremely naturalistic philosophy of science, logical positivism, that flourished widely though briefly in Western philosophy in the middle of this century. The severely operationist character of the philosophy was early mitigated, for example, in Reichenbach's project of giving a 'rational reconstruction' of the methodological aspects of science, and in Carnap's similar project of giving an 'explication,' incorporating a 'rectification,' of inductive probability. Minor as was the element of reconstruction and rectification in these two projects respectively, to the extent that wider considerations had to be appealed to in the choice of reconstructing, rectifying frameworks (e.g., in the choice of basic functions in Carnap's probability theory), these represented the thin edge of the wedge of ampliative governance entering into philosophical views that were in inception and intention fundamentally deductive.

These two closely related themes, of the continuity of philosophical reflection in science with other forms of governance in this field, and the consequent naturalization of the philosophical governance of norms, may easily and surely be extrapolated from science to such other great domains of disciplined life and thought as morals, law, politics and religion. There is implicit in all this a recognition that philosophical reflection neither is nor can be, in these and other areas, the sole form that legitimating governance of norms takes. How effective reflection can be as a means of governance seems to vary from case to case and to depend upon a great variety of conditions. There are surely some contexts sometimes, in some areas, in which we may have to conclude as Locke in a famous phrase concluded about the possibility of our attaining knowledge of the connection of the powers of physical substances, that here the capacity of legitimating philosophical governance 'extends but a very little way.'

15 The familiar Andersen story tells about people who mistake a young swan for a duckling, and appraising its appearance by duckling standards, are naturally led to regard it as ugly. Very like this are many individuals who, appraising ampliative processes exhibited in philosophical reflection by deductive standards, judge them, as Levi was led to judge the ampliative processes he found to be indispensable components of legal reasoning, to be 'imperfect.' In his *Philosophy and the Mirror of Nature* (1979) Richard Rorty persuasively exposed a great many of 'ugly,' in-principle-imperfect deductions born of epistemology-dominated philosophy during the past four hundred years. The language in which we reflect upon our affairs, as well as conduct them, is constantly liable to revision, a cardinal fact that many philosophers constantly miss or deny. Seeing in their own time some need for revision, they respond by endeavoring to construct a language that will fill the need in such a way that it will not arise again. Yet at the outset, in fixing upon the basic characteristic of the language they offer, they take as deductive procedure (Rorty's corresponding term is 'normal discourse') what is highly ampliative, revisive, and reconstructive. Regarding any philosophical governance and change of norms that is not reducible to deductive forms of these as in principle

preventable, they have been led, in rationalizing various needed items of change in science, morals, politics, and elsewhere, to endeavor to derive them by deductive means. Where these items of change are fundamental ones, requiring alteration in the resources of deductive governance itself, these philosophers are put in the impossible position of attempting to derive deductively what is deductively underivable. The analogy here with questions of intraparadigmatic resources and the processes of interparadigmatic change, as conceived by Kuhn, is close. The predicament of those engaged in philosophical reflection in this way is that of needing to provide by the means of normal science results that can be provided only by science when it transcends normality and takes on a revolutionary character. Or, in the predominantly linguistic terminology employed by Rorty, these philosophers are trapped in the impossible project of achieving by means of normal discourse results that can only be achieved by the aid of discourse that is hermeneutic and abnormal. The results can be achieved only in this way because they entail fundamental changes in the normal resources themselves; or put negatively, they cannot be achieved by argument alone, because the resources of argument coincide with the resources of normal discourse. 'The problem for the edifying philosopher [devoted to the facilitation of change of discourse] is that qua philosopher he is in the business of offering arguments, whereas he would like simply to offer another set of terms ...' (370).[16] Bound by traditional compulsions to present arguments, which is to say deductions, for the inarguable or non-deducible, he is a fertile source of arguments that are bad.

16 Another name for the 'mirror of nature' mentioned in Rorty's title is 'mind,' as that is conceived in the very influential mind-body dualism to which Descartes, as natural philosopher and metaphysician, made such enormous contributions. The arguments of Descartes in support of the particular conception of the mind that is a component of this dualism, are among the clearest examples Rorty gives of the essential inconsistency of a project directed to achieving what in the language of the present book would be termed ampliative results by strictly deductive means.

Nothing important hinges here upon the coincidence between the term 'deduction' and the *deductio* emphasized by Descartes in the *Rules* as one of the two sole methods of obtaining knowledge by the use of

---

[16] Hereafter page references to *Philosophy and the Mirror of Nature* will be given in the above manner.

our natural capacities in contrast with what is available through the avenues of divine revelation. For one thing, Descartes was no formalist, as he explicitly indicates in his remarks on the syllogism; and what he himself conceived and engaged in under the rubric of 'deduction' was a procedure far less analytically stringent than what is now covered by this term in accepted philosophical usage. And, for another thing, as this crucial term has been employed in the present book, it diverges in its own way from this accepted usage. This too must be kept in mind in construing the claim that the Cartesian arguments concerning the mind are deductively deficient.

It is furthermore not necessary for present purposes to cite the details of the deficiencies in these arguments claimed by Rorty. The broad grounds for the detailed deficiences lie in a predicament different from the one usually associated with Descartes's name. For his broad philosophical purposes Descartes needed a view of mind that was fundamentally different from that embodied in the Platonic, Aristotelian, and Thomistic tradition, in a word, different from that embodied in the 'normal' philosophical discourse of his day. The urge to argue for this different conception had to be self-defeating, since argument entailed completing the job exclusively with the resources of 'normal' discourse, whereas these resources could be exclusively normal only if the difference in the conception rendered it logically foreign to them, the weakness of the argument thus representing a form of rejection symptom to a seriously invasive, unassimilable foreign body.

17 In the Preface to *Appearance and Reality* F. H. Bradley reports finding in his *Notebook*, among other epigrams, the comment that 'Metaphysics is the finding of bad reasons for what we believe upon instinct,' and there is surely more than cynicism here. Rorty employs part of this epigram in his comments upon the point in Descartes's construction of the mind, where in an unusual step Descartes assimilates as 'indubitable,' and hence mental, two very different sorts of thing: mathematical truths and momentary states of consciousness. What plays the role of 'instinct' in this case is, of course, Descartes's desire to draw a line of demarcation which, like the line drawn by Pope Alexander VI in the western hemisphere, would identify the rightful territories of two competing parties, the new mechanical philosophy and the more traditional human studies. Presumably if the Pope had professed to *find* that line rather than draw it, professed to find on land and sea characteristics showing that Nature, or Nature's god, had intended them to be on the one side Spanish and on the other

Portugese, his diplomatic stroke would have begun to assume some of the reason-in-the-service-of-instinct character that can be discerned in Descartes.

The original Line of Demarcation was drawn through distant uncharted seas and unexplored lands populated by savages who could not be expected to make trouble over the difference, as assigned sovereign political lords over them, between the Kings of Spain and Portugal. Compared to this, the task of Descartes was like drawing the boundary of a proposed independent Protestant nation in Northern Ireland, or an independent Jewish state in Palestine. The construction of the Cartesian *mens* out of the antecedent *nous*, *ratio*, or *intellectus* required a forcible abstraction of pains and sensations from the body and a concomitant forced marriage of these with such traditional components of mind as apprehended universals and mathematical truths embodying them. All this entailed a radical reconstruction of conception and view, in consequence of which, as Rorty puts it, Descartes was committed to 'trying to hold on to standard Platonic and scholastic distinctions with one hand while deconstructing them with the other' (58). It must have been something like the sailors of Neurath's ship trying to change the masts and rigging in the midst of a hurricane.

As one would expect, the results were muddled and imperfect, forming, with similar reconstructions on the part of the other great philosophers the basis for a whole academic industry devoted to the analysis and exposure in exquisite detail of obscurities, shifts of meaning, and non sequiturs of great philosophers who, because they were great were bound to perform in ways that judged by the standards of deduction, of normal discourse, must be counted as intellectual errors, but who could not themselves have earned the assessment of great had they not performed in these (deductively) erroneous ways.

With his Gallic subtlety and style Descartes, as Rorty reconstructs him, avoided much of the erroneous procedure he would have had to engage in in advancing explicit arguments for his radically altered view of mind, by avoiding explicit argument itself. Rather, 'he allowed ... most of the work of changing the notion of "mind" to be done under the table, not by any explicit arguments but simply by verbal maneuvers which reshuffled the deck slightly, and slightly differently, at each passage in which the mind-body distinction came to the fore.' Rorty's further explanatory comment on the limitations of argument as an instrument of intellectual revolution is similarly provocative in tone.

'Such unconscious sleight-of-hand,' he writes,

> when practiced by men of Descartes's boldness of imagination
> [*caveat timidus?*], is an occasion for gratitude rather than censure.
> No great philosopher has avoided it, and no intellectual revolution
> could succeed without it. In 'Kuhnian' terminology, no revolution
> can succeed which employs a vocabulary commensurable with the
> old, and thus none can succeed by employing argument which
> make unequivocal use of terms shared with the traditional
> wisdom. So bad arguments for brilliant hunches must necessarily
> precede the normalization of a new vocabulary which incorporates
> the hunch. Given that new vocabulary, better arguments become
> possible, although these will always be found question-begging by
> the revolution's victims (58n).

18 Beyond possible questions of accuracy of historical interpretation
there is an issue of substance here concerning ampliative processes in
philosophical thought. The outlines of the position on this issue that is
called for by the general doctrine of the present book should now be
clear. So eager has Rorty been – and he surely has had much
provocation – to discredit one kind of would-be philosophical
governance, that the momentum of his vigorous campaign has carried
him far beyond what needs to be said, and may justly be said, about
philosophical governance in general. The primary campaign is directed
against what in the preceding discussions has been characterized as
deductivist, foundational governance; and it is an impressive campaign,
effective at various points in discrediting the claims of a philosophical
discipline that, proceeding from data not accessible to ordinary men
and scientists, by methods of a quite special and independent kind –
from this position of splendid isolation and sovereignty – aspires to
'adjudicate the claims of science and religion, mathematics and poetry,
reason and sentiment, allocating an appropriate place to each.'(212)
The delusory idol to be broken is that of a discipline 'which will pick
out a given set of scientific or moral views as more "rational" than the
alternatives by appeal to something which forms a permanent neutral
matrix for all inquiry and all history' (179. Also 269, 271–3, 315,
392).

If one supposes this idol exposed and thereby discredited, how far
does this exposure and discreditation extend to philosophical
governance in general? In the main, Rorty's position appears to be that
the iconoclasm has carried away with it the general credibility of claims

made on the part of philosophical reflection to effect acceptable governance. The specific question about governance addressed here is not to be identified with other related questions, about the role of a special group of people in the intellectual community identified as 'philosophers,' or about philosophy as a special discipline and subject of research and teaching in institutions of higher learning. It is a question about the capacity of a certain kind of reflection on the norms of thought and action to contribute to judgment concerning and governance of these norms, and with that to the ends that these norms serve in thought, action, and human life in general. Ampliative reflective processes transcend the limits of Rorty's category of normal discourse, and Rorty is extremely hesitant, in spite of what he has said about Descartes and other great philosophers in this regard, to give approval to any concerted, disciplined activity directed to such procedures and such results. He recognizes that there is a valuable residual task that reflection upon discourse can perform. Since discourse is bound to change in various ways at various times, a kind of service to be performed by a hermeneutic offspring of philosophy, if not by philosophy itself, lies in facilitating changes by promoting understanding of emerging alterations, and preserving normal discourse at any given time from becoming so ossified that needed changes are rendered unduly difficult or impossible. Reflective thought thus has a role to play in the 'conversation of mankind,' but it is a role, for all of its importance, that is not to be conflated with any of the inquiries, carried on through normal discourse, to which it may and does contribute. Philosophy, he writes, has 'no more to offer than common sense (supplemented by biology, history, etc.) about knowledge and truth,' 'conversation is not implicit inquiry' (176, 318). Hermeneutics is not 'another way of knowing,' but an activity or pursuit better seen as another way of coping (356). Edifying philosophers, those participating in the constant hermeneutic service, 'have to decry the very notion of having a view, while avoiding having a view about having views' (371).

19 There is at this point an important difference between the task assigned to philosophical reflection by Rorty and that urged in the present book. According to the view of this book, Rorty's disclaimers are more relevant to the deductivist, foundational epistemology against which he directs his heaviest attack, than against the kind of ampliative reflection upon the wider aspects of our pursuits that has been illustrated in a number of ways throughout this book, and in the

present chapter by reference to some early episodes in development of modern science. His sharp criticisms are more applicable to those who, in carrying out their reflection on accepted norms of thought and action, first attempt a withdrawal from the pursuits of which the norms are constitutive and regulative features, and, in that withdrawal, with some special esoteric methods and materials, presume to issue rules for the direction of the mind, hand, and heart: presume, in this intentional ignorance of the way the world is, to give instruction, as Hegel saracastically put it, as to 'what the world ought to be.'

It is not this kind of would-be deductive, epistemological, foundational, and in the end dispensable governance that the present book has sought to illuminate. The kind of ampliative philosophical governance that has been the object here, a form of the general ampliative governance of norms, is, like the wide genus to which it belongs, a form of activity that in certain circumstances in our thought and action in accordance with norms is quite indispensable. Whether it is advantageous to call it philosophical reflection, rather than conversation, hermeneutics, or abnormal discourse is less important than recognizing this composite aspect of it: that it may not be dispensed with, and that in its own way it is all of a piece with other reflection, conversation, interpretation, and discourse. More generally, as Emile Meyerson said of *ontology* and science,[17] philosophical governance of norms in any wide area of human thought and action is all of a piece with the other less governantial aspects of the employment of norms in any such area, be that area morals, law, history, politics, religion, or any of the developed fine or practical arts, say, poetry, painting, or architecture. The wider and deeper exploration of the virtuous life, both individual and communal, was a natural and in the end inescapable aspect of life in the city-state of Athens in Plato's time, just as the wider and deeper exploration of the related claims of liberty and equality in a modern democratic capitalist state is a natural and inescapable aspect of life in our own. Similarly the two monumental moral theories of Aristotle in ancient times and Spinoza later can be well understood as each representing a critical reflection and rational reconstruction of moral beliefs and practices of the time in which each was developed. And as is especially clear in the case of Spinoza, the criticism and reconstruction advanced by each of these moral theories

---

[17]*Identity and Reality*, K. Loewenberg, trans. (1930). Dover edition, N.Y., 1962, p. 384.

reflected cultural philosophical determinants of a very extended kind (for example, in Spinoza, epistemic and ontological determinants issuing from the philosophy of seventeenth-century science).[18] The wider and deeper exploration of the nature of law that is attempted by such current rival theories as the general positivist 'rules' theory of H. L. A. Hart and the more Kantian 'rights' theory of R. Dworkin is a natural, and, in the end, inescapable aspect of life in a modern society in which a most important determinant of the character of the constantly changing life we lead is the character of the laws by which we are governed, including the kinds of governance of these laws carried out by the legislative, administrative, and judicial institutions devised for the purpose. Philosophical reflection upon the aims, methods, results, and consequences of some branch of science, upon the broader character of the activities carried out in this institution, and upon the relation of this institution with others in the community – philosophical reflection upon all these and other broad aspects of the pursuit is in its own way as much a part of scientific thought as any other. And the same may be said of the judgments on these matters to which such reflection leads. It is a matter of no great importance whether these reflections and judgments be called 'scientific' or 'philosophical' except as the choice of rubric makes some difference in our understanding of what we are doing when we engage in them. The term 'conversation' performs well in stressing the difference between the deductive, normal aspects of our activities and the ampliative, abnormal ones. But it does obscure in a serious way the governing functions of ampliative reflection, as that is illustrated in the wide philosophical reflections of such men as Galileo, Descartes, Hobbes, Locke, and Leibniz concerning the mathematical, the mechanical, the 'primary' as distinguished from the 'secondary' qualities of material objects.[19]

For a broadly and deeply informed understanding of modern physical science it is a matter of great importance how these aspects of it are recognized, how they are placed and understood in a wide view of human activity and institutions. On occasion Rorty does express some recognition of what, in the pattern of Burtt, we may speak of as the

---

[18]For some expansion on this point see Stuart Hampshire, *Two Theories of Morality* (1977), and Burtt, 'The Religion of Science,' in *Types of Religious Philosophy*.

[19]The choice of the term 'conversation' fairly reflects Rorty's view of the capacity of philosophical reflection to contribute to the resolution of the issues he recognizes as posed in these topics. (*Mirror*, pp. 57, 62, 131, 210, 264.)

metaphysical and epistemological 'foundations' of modern physical science. But in the main the view he offers of the processes of reflective thought devoted to such foundations is deprecatory, as the term 'conversation' adopted for these processes itself suggests. Looking at and working in the natural philosophy of his day, Descartes wanted to understand, as Rorty says, 'the superiority of the New Science to Aristotle, the relation between this science and mathematics, common sense, theology, and morality,' and all this at a time that the very notion of what it is to be scientific, in the now accepted sense of this term, was being formed by Galileo and others in a protracted process of which Galileo's confrontation with Cardinal Bellarmine was one episode (210). From our vantage point several centuries later we can see that Galileo has carried the day. The complex web of norms of thought and action covered by the term 'scientific values' is now a common and splendid inheritance of us all. But the question of whether Galileo and others were 'rational' in forging this complex web Rorty firmly rejects as 'out of place.' 'What could show that the Bellarmine-Galileo issue "differs in kind" from the issue between, say, Kerensky and Lenin, or that between the Royal Academy (*circa* 1910) and Bloomsbury [or that between the stances toward the inheritance of acquired characteristics taken by Julian Huxley and by Trofim Lysenko?]' (330–1)?

Reference to these highly diverse issues, and to governance with respect to them, serves as a useful reminder that ampliative processes of governance are no more infallible than deductive ones. While deductivist programs seem surely destined to fail, more liberal programs drawing ampliatively upon wide cultural resources by no means surely succeed. One of the distinguishing characteristics of the governantial program in genetics associated a few decades ago with the name of Lysenko was its extreme misuse of some of the wide relations connecting this crude theory about the inheritance of acquired characteristics with a social program designed by Communist authorities to appeal to 'prisoners of starvation' throughout the world who might be misled by 'reactionary' Mendelean genetics to suppose that there is some correspondence between their genetic make-up and the social prisons within which they are immured. The history of holistic programs of both the extreme right and the left, and both ecclesiastic and secular, richly testifies that, though ampliative processes are generally indispensable to philosophical governance, they are in themselves no sufficient condition of success, or even of benign results. Where governance of an ampliative kind is called for, it makes a great difference to the results of it how it is performed.

If the term 'rational' injected into the questions about governance here is an obstacle, let it be expunged. There remains an issue about philosophical reflection. From time to time in the conduct of affairs and in reflection upon them the need arises for the critical appraisal, revision, reconstruction, and reconstitution of the norms of thought and action through which we carry on these activities. Can philosophical reflection, in the form of ampliative processes of thought contribute directly to these criticizing, appraising, governing activities? If so, in general, what resources are at its disposal and how may it properly employ them? The contrast between the view advocated in this book and the similar but diverging one just examined may be of assistance to some in achieving a more perspicuous, and, in the end, more humanly helpful view of this aspect of philosophical thought.

Index

Allport, G. W., 133

Ampliative governance (effects), ix–x; exemplifications in legal thought and action, 190–4, mathematics, 194, modern physical science, 218, 236–47, political thought and action, 186–90, 193–4, 217–18, social science, 194–5; inevitability of, 147–52, 245–6; stabilizing and destabilizing, 214–19, 222–5

Ampliative processes: Part 3 *passim*; compared with deductive processes, ix–x, 3–6, 10–11, 33–4; close conjunction and interdependence with deductive processes, 39–40, 119–20, 135–9, 245–6; characteristics emphasized by: B. Blanshard, 92, B. Bosanquet, 91–2, J. E. Creighton, 90–1, J. Dewey, 92, C. I. Lewis, 92, L. Wittgenstein, 92–3; reasoned character of, 180–3; in the sancta of deductivism, 121–2; and intuition, 179–80; and skepticism, 182

Anscombe, G. E. M., 167n

Bickel, A. M., 219n, 228

Black, M., on Claude Bernard, 167n

Bode, B. H., on habit and intelligence, 132–3

Bradley, F. H., *Ethical Studies*, 241n; *Appearance and Reality*, 166, 249

Bronowski, J., *The Ascent of Man*, 242n

Burtt, E. A.: on the contrast between

Greek natural philosophy and modern science, 240–2

Cause, versus reason, 164, 212

Chesterton, G. H., 169

Coherence, deceptiveness of this term, 94–5, 186–7; compared with "concept", 26–8

Composition of norms, 139, 147–51, 156–7, 163

Concepts: disadvantages of the term, 26–8; institutional aspects of, 27–8

Concrete universal, 125–30; and identity-in-difference, 128–30; and open-texture, 126–7; and the Principle of Identity, 129

Conscience; the notion expanded, 89; communal roots of, 87–90

Copernican Revolution: as exemplifying ampliative governance, 242–4

Cornford, F. M.: on Aristotle's explanation of eclipses of the moon, 239–40

Creighton, J. E.: on the social aspects of thinking, 90–1

Criticism and doubt: hyperbolic forms of, 202–4

Deduction: and philosophical "foundations", 18–19; as applicative, 4–5; as not requiring necessity of certainty of result, 32, 59

Deductive and ampliative processes, 24; four contrasting aspects of, 32–5, 181–3; close relations and

257